Date Due

May 6 '64			
Mar 2 '66			
Nov 2 66			
Jun 8 70			
Oct 11 72			
	PRINTED	IN U. S. A.	

THE EARLY CHURCH

THE
EARLY CHURCH

Studies in Early Christian History and Theology

by

OSCAR CULLMANN

Edited by

A. J. B. HIGGINS

THE WESTMINSTER PRESS
PHILADELPHIA

Published simultaneously in Great Britain and
the United States of America by the S C M Press Ltd, London
and The Westminster Press, Philadelphia

First published MCMLVI

Nos. I, II, IV, VII, VIII and IX translated by A. J. B. Higgins
Nos. III, V, VI and X translated by S. Godman

Library of Congress Catalog Card No.: 56-5476

PRINTED IN THE UNITED STATES OF AMERICA

Contents

ABBREVIATIONS

J.B.L.   *Journal of Biblical Literature*

R.B.   *Revue Biblique*

R.H.P.R.   *Revue d'histoire et de philosophie religieuses*

T.W.N.T.   *Theologisches Wörterbuch zum Neuen Testament*

Z.N.T.W.   *Zeitschrift für die neutestamentliche Wissenschaft*

Foreword

PROFESSOR CULLMANN is well known from the English versions of his two major works, *Christ and Time* (1951) and *Peter: Disciple–Apostle–Martyr* (1953). His smaller works, *The Earliest Christian Confessions* (1949), *Baptism in the New Testament* (1950) and *Early Christian Worship* (1953), have also been widely read. The present collection of some of his shorter writings and articles will, it is hoped, be equally welcome, especially to those who would not have easy access to them as originally published. The material has been chosen with great care and with the object of presenting outstanding examples of Professor Cullmann's contributions to varied aspects of early Church history and theology. The first article, on Higher Criticism, obviously serves as a useful beginning to a volume of this kind; the study of the origins of Christmas is one of the standard discussions of the subject, and its position near the beginning of the book seemed appropriate. The interesting study of the plurality of the Gospels (number 3) is followed naturally by the long discussion of the problem of Tradition, which is a work of quite outstanding importance. The next three studies have a certain mutual relationship. Numbers 8 and 9 are short studies based on specific New Testament passages, and the last essay, on the attitude to the outside world adopted by the early Church, an ever relevant issue, forms a suitable conclusion.

I wish to acknowledge the help and courtesy of Professor Cullmann in making suggestions, in answering questions, and in readily sending me such of his publications as were not easily accessible, and to thank him for his co-operation in the sometimes difficult decision as to what ought or ought not to be included in this volume. I wish also to thank the Rev. R. Gregor Smith, the Editor of the S.C.M. Press, for all that he has done in helping this book to fruition, and especially for his original invitation to me to undertake the editing of a collection of Professor Cullmann's writings, a task which I regard as a high privilege and honour. Other duties made it impossible for me to undertake all the translating myself, as well as the task of editor, without delaying publication unduly. I am therefore happy to acknowledge the work of Mr. Stanley Godman, who translated numbers 3, 5, 6 and 10. For all the other translations I am responsible. For the convenience of English readers I have substituted references to the English translations of certain books for those originally given.

Grateful acknowledgement is made to the editor of *The Student World* and the World's Student Christian Federation for permission to reproduce the first paper in this volume; and to the following for permission to make and publish here English translations of the other papers as indicated by their numbers in the table of contents: to the Heinrich Majer Verlag, Basel (number 2); to the editors of the *Theologische Zeitschrift* and the Faculty of Theology of the University of Basel (number 3); to Delachaux et Niestlé S. A., Neuchâtel (numbers 4, 6, 7 and 10, and the footnotes in number 2, which do not appear in the original German edition); to the Evangelischer Verlag A. G., Zollikon-Zürich (number 5); to Messrs. C. W. K. Gleerup, Lund and the *Seminarium Neotestamenticum Upsaliense* (number 8); and to the editor and publishers of the *Annuaire 1953–1954, École Pratique des Hautes Études* (number 9). I should like to make special reference to *The Tradition*. Professor Cullmann in his Foreword to this study explains that it is an expansion of two articles. These were published in the *Scottish Journal of Theology* in 1950, p. 180–97 ('*Kyrios* as Designation for the Oral Tradition concerning Jesus (*Paradosis* and *Kyrios*)') and in 1953, p. 113–35 ('Scripture and Tradition'). As the translator I have consulted and, in places, made considerable use of these articles where the material happens to correspond, and I am grateful to the editors for acceding to this. At the same time, even where the material corresponds, I have used my own judgment in every sentence, so that it is fair to claim, I think, that the total result is an individual rendering of what, with its numerous changes and additions and much fuller documentation, is virtually a new work.

A. J. B. HIGGINS

Dedicated to

DR FLOYD V. FILSON
Dean of McCormick Theological Seminary, Chicago

in gratitude and friendship

AUTHOR'S PREFACE

It may seem presumptuous of me to have accepted the kind invitation of the S.C.M. Press to publish already a collection of some of my essays which have appeared in recent years in German or French theological journals and series. Such collections are usually published posthumously, or at least at the end of a scholar's career. I hope, however, to be able to continue for many more years my work on the beginnings of Christianity and on the theological understanding of the New Testament, and I believe I am still capable of the possible and necessary development and even correction of my thought.

My main reason for agreeing nevertheless to the publication of the present volume is that the studies collected here make clearer the critical-theological position which informs my larger and better-known writings.

In the coming years I hope to complete further larger works on which I have long been working. My *Christology of the New Testament* will appear in a few months' time. I think it is important, also in view of these forthcoming publications, that my critical-theological position should be made quite clear—especially since I have not committed myself to any of the current theological trends.

Above all I trust that two facts will emerge clearly from these papers. The first is that I adhere unreservedly to the historical-philological method as the foundation of all interpretation of the oldest Christian documents. The second is that just as resolutely I reject the theological preconceptions of a modernizing interpretation which are commonly associated with the historical-philological method—preconceptions which, in the interest of some philosophical theory or other, seek either to strip off as a mere external garment or forcedly to reinterpret the very thing which is *central* to the faith of the first Christians. These methods, much favoured at present, I reject precisely for scientific reasons.

Critical study ought to have in common with the Christian faith above all *the obedient willingness simply to listen to what the authors of the New Testament have to say to us*, without too quickly, from the very beginning, confusing the issue by introducing the other question whether we can reconcile their faith with modern philosophical theories. Such a mixture of two different questions can only obscure correct exegesis of the texts.

I also hope that the essays in this volume will show that from different angles I always come again to the same conclusion, namely, that the real centre of early Christian faith and thought is *redemptive history (Heilsgeschichte)*, especially in its consistent application to the post-resurrection age in which we live—to the time of the Church and of the already now realized, though invisible, kingship of Christ who reigns at the right hand of God. Formerly the idea of *Heilsgeschichte* was used only in dogmatic works. My aim is to bring it to the forefront in interpreting the New Testament itself.

To my friend Dr. A. J. B. Higgins, Lecturer in the New Testament in the University of Leeds, I express my sincere thanks for all his help in editing and supervising the translation of the present collection of essays.

This volume is dedicated to Dr. Floyd V. Filson, Dean of McCormick Theological Seminary, Chicago, who has contributed so much to the fact that my writings have been made available to the English-speaking theological world. It is my hope that the publication of this volume in English will stimulate further that discussion with British and American scholars which I have found so fruitful.

Basel—Paris   OSCAR CULLMANN
September 1955

I

The
Necessity and Function of
Higher Criticism

First published in *The Student World*,
vol. XLII, no. 2, second quarter, 1949,
p. 117–33, Geneva

The Necessity and Function of
Higher Criticism

THE CONTROVERSY about exegesis raised a storm of excitement after the publication by Karl Barth of his commentary on the epistle to the Romans, particularly between 1920–30.[1] Since then there has been a certain silence on the subject. However, at last, and fortunately so, it has begun to come up again.

The writer of these lines himself took part in the first debate by publishing an article in 1928 in the *Revue d'Histoire et de Philosophie religieuses*.[2] It was at that time above all things necessary to support Karl Barth in his defence of the legitimate scientific nature of 'theological exegesis'—a term, by the way, rather unfortunate—in opposition to the tendency then in vogue to consider that only philological and historical exegesis was scientific; and to show that the philological, psychological and historical interpretation of a text was only partial and that any scientific exegesis which was worthy of the name must not stop there. We made an effort to prove that, while based upon historical, psychological and philological considerations, serious exegesis must always be concerned to shed light upon the different theological ideas contained in the Bible, and it must pass beyond the circumstances in which these were expressed.

In order to achieve this aim we must not limit ourselves to establishing the relation of these ideas to the writer who formulated them, or the epoch which gave them birth; they must also be considered absolutely and by themselves. For example, if we seek to

---

[1] See the prefaces to the second edition of K. Barth's *Römerbrief*, 1921, and to the third edition, 1922. See also among others, R. Bultmann, 'Über das Problem einer Theologischen Exegese des Neuen Testaments' (*Zwischen den Zeiten*, 1925, p. 334 f.), and the controversy E. Brunner—L. Koehler in No. 27, 29, 31, 32 and 36 of the *Kirchenblatt für die Reformierte Schweiz*, 1926; E. v. Dobschütz, *Vom Auslegen des Neuen Testaments*, 1927; E. Fascher, *Vom Verstehen des Neuen Testaments*, 1930; F. Torm, *Hermeneutik des Neuen Testaments*, 1930.

[2] See 'Les Problèmes posés par la méthode exégétique de l'École de Karl Barth' in *R.H.P.R.*, 1928, p. 70 f.

understand some Pauline conception such as justification by faith, it is not enough to look for the psychological motive behind the idea in the personality of St. Paul, or in certain circumstances of his life, nor yet to determine the influence of Judaism and Hellenism upon the development of the apostle's thought. Such a process, however indispensable, cannot begin to tell us anything about the intrinsic and objective truth contained in the idea of justification by faith. A commentary on the Pauline epistles, which was limited to the study of such questions, would only shed light on the apostle himself. A genuine and complete interpretation must go much further and must try to develop *in modern language* the objective ideas expressed in the text.

Studying the truth for itself

The Pauline text aims at communicating to us an objective truth which has validity not only for the apostle, but for all men. It is essential that we should take this aim seriously and study the truth for itself; in this manner giving proof of true *scientific humility*, while also respecting the *a priori* of all historical study—that is to say, that a writer long dead and regarded as outside the historical plane has something to teach us which we did not know before. A naive 'historicism', which thinks it can 'understand' a theological text from antiquity without laying aside historical and philological preoccupations, assumes that we are endowed with previous knowledge about the *objects* of all theology—a knowledge which might be called normative and which is never modified by any additional evidence from the side of the authors who are being studied. In this way considerations which were purely archaeological, philological or psychological would suffice for the understanding of a classical text, because all we should have to do would be to establish historically what the prophets, or apostles, for example, had written, and because we were already in possession of a complete solution of the problem *in advance* which we had obtained in a lordly fashion and quite independently of the text before us.

This naive lordliness is wholly opposed to any sound scientific method whether in reference to the Bible or to any other document. In the realm of the Christian Church, which claims to base its knowledge of God on the scripture, it is most markedly obvious that such an attitude to biblical texts is impossible. Such an attitude could only be based upon an impossible *a priori* which would enable us to understand, and hence to judge, the theological ideas of the prophets and apostles, thanks to knowledge which had already come to us in another way. It would therefore be sufficient, in order to understand what these ideas were, to remain wholly confined to the domain of history.

In our 1928 article we indicated that the same is true of all studies of the past. For example, the interpreter of the *Pensées* of Pascal cannot withdraw either to a position which is exclusively historical. It is not enough for him to know the historical details of the life of Pascal, the influence of Jansenism and of the polemic against the Jesuits on the evolution of Pascal's thought, nor yet to grasp the lines of his character by a psychological study. He must attempt to penetrate to the very subject which Pascal wished to express.

The writers of the philosophy of history and of music find themselves *mutatis mutandis* faced with a similar task. The historian of music who studies the works of Bach, of Mozart, or of Beethoven is certainly doing the work of a historian, and yet it is not enough to emphasize in the work of these composers the influence of the setting in which they found themselves, or the circumstances of their life or their genius. It is not even enough for him to be familiar with the technical operations which were used in their age. He must also himself be a musician and able to reach the objective reality which these composers expressed in their work.

After the First World War, the majority of those who specialized in biblical exegesis were subject to such deterioration professionally that it became necessary to insist upon these rather elementary truths which are self-evident in other domains.

Our debt to the nineteenth century

However, it seems that the moment has now come to defend the necessity of philological and historical criticism and to underline the great value of Higher Criticism for the understanding of the Bible, thus doing justice, while using all necessary reservations, to the debt of theology to the nineteenth century.

The theological importance of the period up to 1914 is to be found precisely in the application of all forms of human knowledge to the study of the Bible. It is easy today, as we have just done, to point out the obvious errors made by the naive 'historicism' of the period which was incarnate in the person of Adolf von Harnack (a man acclaimed by popular admiration and who personified scientific passion applied to such researches).

Where should we be today in our biblical exegesis—whatever our theological leanings—without the patient textual study of Tischendorf in Germany, or Westcott and Hort in England, their many rivals and their countless successors? Where should we be now if Wellhausen had not raised the problems of the literary criticism of the Old Testament, questionable though his theories may be? Or where should we be without the systematic study devoted by H. Holtzmann to the solution of the Synoptic question? Even to the school of 'The History of Religions', which is perhaps overmuch decried today—to the work, that is to say, of Gunkel, Gressmann, Bousset, Loisy—we owe results which cannot be ignored in any sound interpretation of the Bible. In the more restricted sphere of the theology—in the real sense—of the New Testament, which is perhaps the particular inspiration of the generation which succeeded 1919, we must never forget our debt to Albert Schweitzer, however much we may have to criticize him for raising the question of eschatology.

The writer's experiences with students have convinced him that the new generation of students is often ready to pass judgment in a summary and essentially negative fashion upon all this philological and historical work. He cannot conceal his suspicion that in many cases the superficial lordliness with which some of them dismiss philology and history, which, they explain, are quite out of date as a means of unfolding the divine Word, is ultimately rooted in the law of minimum effort. They make 'theological exegesis' a pretext for passing as quickly as possible from philological study with its greater austerity, and its demands on their abnegation, to systematic studies. It would, however, be unfair to accuse all who depreciate philological and historical exegesis of laziness.

In other cases it is clear that we are meeting a pietistic suspicion of 'secular' methods. Such students are not afraid of work, but are afraid to endanger their faith in the authority of the Bible. We shall see later on that this attitude involves a false conception of the nature both of biblical revelation and of the faith.

Finally a third type of student does not try to avoid philological work, nor the problems raised by biblical criticism. But even while he recognizes in principle the usefulness, and even the necessity, of philological and historical researches, he is tempted to stress their purely 'preliminary' character; indeed he thinks that he can limit his study to delving into some commentary or some well-known dictionary in order to concentrate on the theological meditations inspired by the biblical text. He, too, is not aware of the close relation between philological interpretation and the theological interpretation of the biblical text.

We propose in the following pages to deal: first, with the theological basis which underlies a philological and historical exegesis; second, with the role of philological and historical exegesis.

(1) The Theological Basis of Higher Criticism

Anyone who underestimates the necessity and the role of philological and historical exegesis in the first place proves that he has a false theological conception of the nature of biblical revelation. In fact, the very essence of the central affirmation of the Bible has to do with history. The biblical revelation in both the Old and New Testaments is a revelation of God in history, in the history of the people of Israel which found its achievement in the incarnation of Jesus of Nazareth and worked itself out through the history of the primitive community. The central message of this revelation is found in the New Testament, every book of which states as its end this fundamental and eminently theological confession: Jesus of Nazareth is Christ the Lord. But as soon as we speak of Jesus of Nazareth, we speak of history, and the history of Jesus presupposes a relationship both with the history of Israel and with the history of the primitive Church. To be sure this history is but, as it were, a very thin stream which flows within the broad river of world history. And yet this narrow path continues through the whole course of world history and cannot be detached from its background. Seen from the angle of world history (which we call secular history), biblical history— the history of the divine revelation—is of no significance and at the most represents merely a collection of news items, or events of local importance. From the opposite angle, the history of the Bible claims to be at once a part of world history and the very norm which gives world history some direction.

The error of allegory

Thus in the theological affirmation which is at the foundation of the New Testament: 'Jesus of Nazareth is Lord', history (that is to say, Jesus of Nazareth) is itself the subject. In other words, any 'theology' in the New Testament is not only related to history, but is of the very essence of history. For this reason it is wholly impossible to pretend to give an interpretation to the New Testament which can be called 'theological', and which does not take account of history. Here lies the fundamental theological error of all allegorical interpretation, whether classical or modern, which purports to uncover the 'eternal' meaning which lies behind the historical facts quite independently of these historical facts. For allegorical exegesis history is merely a symbol, behind which it looks for something else; whereas in reality history in its temporal progression lays before us the eternal salvation of man.

When Professor R. Bultmann of Marburg in our own days seeks to rob the New Testament of its mythical character—which in other words we may call the history of salvation—(*Entmythologisierung* [3]), his method of approach to the study of the New Testament is less remote than it seems from the allegorical method. To be sure, Bultmann takes the historical and philological study of the text very seriously. Unlike the 'allegorists' he does not start off with an idea ready-made which he is determined to find at all costs in the text; on the contrary, he deliberately begins from historical study. And yet he only uses history in order to rid himself more easily of history, at least of the 'history of salvation'. His *a priori*, which he has certainly not drawn from the Bible, is that, in the New Testament message, the history of salvation is no more than a purely external shell, which could and should be removed from the New Testament writings in order to reach the very kernel.[4] In spite of all differences, this *a priori* reduces the distance between Dr. Bultmann and the allegorists. In reality biblical history is neither the symbol nor the image, nor the mythological framework of 'temporal existence'. It is the 'history of salvation' and as such stands in a double relationship to secular history; on the one hand, the latter

[3] See R. Bultmann's 'New Testament and Mythology', in *Kerygma and Myth*, E.T., 1953, p. 1 f.
[4] The historicity of this biblical kernel is recognized by Bultmann, but just not in the meaning of the biblical *oikonomia*. We are surprised and regret that Bultmann, as he says himself in his critical study of our work *Christ and Time* entitled 'Heilsgeschichte und Geschichte' (*Theologische Literaturzeitung*, 1948, col. 659 f.) has not seen the distinction which we made between world history and the history of salvation. As long as he does not see that the New Testament speaks definitely of a divine *oikonomia* which concerns a temporal succession of events—not the 'temporality of existence'—it is to be feared that our discussion will have no very satisfactory result. See further on note 8.

is its background [5] while, on the other, secular history is wholly determined and judged by the criterion of biblical history.

In this relation, is any distinction to be drawn between the historical and the didactic books of the Bible? It may be thought so, but the distinction is really only an apparent one.[6] In reality the didactic books, that is to say, the writings of the prophets in the Old Testament and of the epistles in the New Testament, are equally in the last analysis directed to the revelation of God in biblical history. On the other hand, the so-called historical books of the Bible always have as their own subject the particular history of the eternal salvation of man. Now, since in the Bible theology is a history and this history is the essence of theology, there is clearly no means of drawing a fundamental distinction between the historical and the didactic books. The theological reasons we have given and which explain why biblical exegesis, in accordance with its theological aim, cannot get on without historical interpretation, have validity in one group as in the other.

The Word became flesh

This theological necessity is seen still more clearly when, setting aside the essence of the biblical message, we come to the nature of the *transmission* of this message. The divine revelation was given form for us at a definite moment of history and by means of men who belonged to their own age, and who used a human language which was spoken in that age. This transmission—human as it is— partakes, precisely in its temporal and humanly imperfect nature, of the essence of the great biblical truth. In revealing himself to men, God became flesh. The process by which were shaped the particular books of the Bible, and later on, the canonical collections of the Old and New Testaments, was an ordinary historic process and yet is itself an element in the revelation. Indeed in its very ordinariness it is part of the divine revelation. The Word became flesh, and this truth applies equally to the compiling of the Bible. Starting from this point we realize that, if we despise the purely historical study of this process for the accidental and human character of its expression, we are in danger of falling into a heresy as old as Christianity: docetism. For the docetist the incarnation of the divine Word,

---

[5] Note the mention of the emperor Augustus, Luke 2.1, and that of the emperor Tiberius, Luke 3.1.

[6] We laid too much stress upon this distinction in our article of 1928.

which is the subject of the Bible, is not real, but only apparent since it would be unworthy of God that he should take a material form.

The witness of the apostles has not reached us in a form, the divine nature of which would strike our senses as miraculous. If it were so, faith in the divine Word would not be the faith of which the New Testament speaks. Real faith inevitably presupposes the 'scandal of the cross'. This is faith in Christ. 'Can any good thing come out of Nazareth?' (John 1.46). 'Shall the Christ come out of Galilee?' (John 7.41). This is faith in the Church, the body of Christ, which from the very first hour was made up of sinners. The human way, with all the element of 'scandal', in which the books of the New Testament were written and the canon constituted, is the necessary 'rock of offence' which God desired, and on which alone true faith and the divine inspiration of the Bible could be founded. Within this process, containing as it did all human defects and every kind of secular influence, the Holy Spirit was at work, so that the Word of God might be revealed to humanity. This is faith in the 'inspiration' of the Bible, so long as the 'scandal' is not removed. Let us think of this 'scandal': that we have four different narratives of the life of Jesus, two of which at least do not even come directly from the group of the Twelve and which do not agree with each other. Let us think of another 'scandal': that for the whole New Testament we have different manuscripts of which the texts do not harmonize and which sometimes, as in Galatians 2.5, teach two precisely opposite lessons! From the beginning efforts have been made to hide that particular scandal just as they have been made to hide the scandal of the humanity of Christ and of the imperfection of the members of the Church. We have shown elsewhere [7] how the Gnostics tried to set on one side the scandal of the plurality of the Gospels by substituting one alone. The theories of the *verbal* inspiration of the Bible in the strict sense of the word show the same preoccupation.

If God designed the human form in which the Holy Spirit transmitted the divine Word, and if this transmission is itself an element in the history of salvation, we must, if we would hear the Word of God in the Bible, understand this form both in its process of evolution and in its fixed characteristics; must, in other words, pass through historical and philological study.

[7] 'The Plurality of the Gospels as a Theological Problem in Antiquity', no. 3 in this volume.

(2) The Role of Higher Criticism

If we say that philological and historical exegesis consists 'in applying a preliminary study' to the theological understanding of the text, we have not precisely defined its task. Its role is in reality a triple one. In the first instance, since biblical theology is seen as essentially a 'history of salvation', the theological exposition of texts should bring out in many cases a historic linking together of the facts of the past, the present and the eschatological future. In the second place, historical and philological exegesis should define and describe the human and accidental *setting* within which the biblical revelation has had to show itself at a given moment of history and in the world situation where the writers found themselves. In the third place—and we would chiefly insist upon this point—the aim of historical and philological exegesis is to control the numerous ideas and suggestions which a text brings us and to remove from the interpretation those which do not bear examination.

Taking history seriously

On the first point we must emphasize that we are not attempting to make use of history just in order to set it aside later on. 'Jesus the Christ', the centre of the biblical message, has to do with history, as we have said before, and must be bound up with both the history of Israel and the history of the apostles as well as of the birth of the Church of Christ. Although here we are speaking of a very *particular* history, a biblical history,[8] it is none the less *history*. If we are to take seriously its theological importance for man's salvation we

[8] When Bultmann, in his article, 'Heilsgeschichte und Geschichte' quoted above, says that he does not see how far the meaning of the word 'history' is different for us in the two phrases the 'history of salvation' and 'universal history', we can only answer that the difference has no effective bearing upon the historical character of facts which are common to the two kinds of history, nor yet upon the temporal character of the connection between the facts, but only upon the choice of these facts and the perspective in which the New Testament sees them by reason of the central place occupied there by the death of Christ. *Mutatis mutandis*, it is a case of the same relationship which exists between universal history and the choice necessarily made among the data of that history by a certain 'philosophy of history' which looks at everything from a particular angle. The comparison is an imperfect one, but it does bring out the fact that, to be a 'biblical history', that is, a very restricted history seen with a peculiar perspective, the history on which the New Testament tells us our salvation is based, is none the less a real history and one, in consequence, to which historical categories must be applied.

must also take the historic process seriously and realize that it expresses itself in both theological and historical categories. For instance, we shall not take out of the history of Israel all that really makes it a history, but we shall show how the conceptions of election and substitution, thoroughly theological as they are, are yet realized, in biblical theory, through this self-same historical evolution.

History is not in this case a sort of puzzle in which our task is to discover something different from what it really is, that is, just the history of Israel, which does not so far teach us anything about Jesus of Nazareth as a historical person, but rather leads up to the consummation of history in his person. If we seek faithfully to pursue this line of consummation we must not turn it into allegory, nor yet break up history into different isolated stories which can only find their true meaning outside the framework of the history of Israel before Jesus Christ. Rather we shall bring out the historical sequence into the light of day, so that the divine plan (what the New Testament calls *oikonomia*) may become evident not *behind* but *within* history itself.

We have pointed out elsewhere [9] that the writers of the New Testament saw all this history, which was centred in the death and resurrection of Christ, unfold according to a principle wholly different from that of modern historiography. And yet, if we are to be able to see the succession of certain facts in this plan of salvation, we must learn how to combine with theological thought a historical viewpoint which presupposes both a knowledge of the facts and the capacity to link them together in a definite perspective. In other words, if we are to see the line which leads from Israel to Christ, and from Christ to the Church, we must be both theologians and historians.

Defining the human setting

It should be an easier matter to find agreement among modern interpreters with regard to the second function of historical and philological exegesis. We have seen that the biblical revelation was transmitted in the language and ideas of the time and through the human personalities of writers whose individual characteristics influenced their work. Here we must first of all refute an attitude of mind which is dear to the upholders of the liberal view, that we

[9] *Christ and Time*, E.T., 1951, p. 19 f.

find in the Bible side by side with truths which are valid for all time others which are adapted to the ideas of the period. Now we must emphasize that biblical texts as a whole wear a dress which belongs to the time of their writers. The external aspect of the biblical message is wholly adapted to the ideas of the period. We cannot say that in one passage the Holy Spirit is speaking through the writer, while in another it is only the writer who speaks as a man of his own time.

In fact, the Holy Spirit can only speak in human language, and that language must always bear the stamp of the period and of the individuality of the biblical writer. For this reason philological investigation, historical research and any knowledge we may possess of the setting in which the writer lived, or the circumstances of his life, help to provide us with a 'transparency' through which, by an effort of theological concentration, we may see *with* the writer the truth which he saw and *with him* may attain to the revelation which came to him. We must thoroughly understand this historic 'transparency'; our vision through it must be so clear that at any moment we may become the actual contemporaries of the writer. Thus it depends upon the understanding which philological and historical methods provide that this 'transparency' of which we speak should cease to be an obstacle and should begin to be the means of approaching the theological examination of the truth.

We must not dismiss the weight of any science which is auxiliary to history: philology, archaeology, papyrology, textual history, literary criticism of sources, secular history, the general history of religions and psychology all have their value. Surely after what has been said we need not insist upon this. Let us, however, say a word about psychology. In our day by a natural reaction against certain exaggerations, or obvious abuses, psychology is eliminated, perhaps too thoroughly, from exegesis. Yet it is not wholly irrelevant to know, for example, in what circumstances of his life the apostle Paul wrote such and such an epistle. Here again we must take seriously the fact that revelation has come to us through the channel of a human personality, nor is it irrelevant for the study of the Pauline epistles that we should learn from the book of Acts the chief stages in the life of the apostle. While we are on this subject we must observe that, if the question of the authorship of a certain biblical writing is no longer of such overwhelming importance as it used to be, it is at least of value in helping us to understand the text. To take an example: if it were true, as the Roman Church insists, that the epistle to the Hebrews was written by St. Paul, then exegesis, in order to explain this, should refer to the other Pauline epistles more thoroughly than it would have done had there been nothing in the theory.

Perhaps it may be supposed that as regards the study of the language and other influences of the time upon the text to be interpreted, historical and philological exegesis is really only of a 'preliminary' nature. But in reality it is not enough for exegesis to use all this necessary knowledge merely *at the beginning* of its task in order thereafter to have a free course in its theological research. There must always be a continual interchange of results between historical study and theological penetration, so that each may enrich the other. For this reason the critic must be both historian and theologian. A division of work can only be an impediment to the *interior dialogue* which must be held continuously between historian and theologian.

Controlling theological interpretations

We shall understand this still more fully if we look at the third function of philological and historical exegesis. It would be a great mistake to believe that the ordinary believer, who has no historical knowledge, could not in some direct method grasp the thought of the biblical writer. He can often understand the revelation at the basis of the text by a direct intuition which is wholly adequate. To speak theologically, the Holy Spirit, who has been at work in the prophet of the Old Testament, and the apostle of the New, can work in the same manner in the believing reader and so reveal to him the wisdom of God by the Spirit (I Corinthians 1.18 f.). In certain cases the reader may, as it were, jump over the intermediate stages through which exegesis has necessarily to pass, in order to avoid the obstacle caused by the human setting of the revelation. Frequently the reader may, through the inner witness of the Holy Spirit, avoid the roundabout road of historical study. If this were not so, we should have serious reason to doubt the scriptural principle on which the Christian life is based.

None the less the biblical critic is called to interpret scripture through his own particular training, and is bound to follow the straight and narrow way which we have sketched out for him. This is all the more necessary because the biblical word, which we may either approach directly or else through philological or historical study, arouses many and varied ideas in the reader. The apostle's advice to 'search the spirits' must be equally applied to the interpretation, which is to say, that the interpreter must subject his own ideas to the severe control of scripture. The critic who has a real gift for the theological understanding of a text—I mean the *good* exegetical critic—is exposed, more than mediocre critics, to the danger that he may introduce into his interpretation ideas which are not in the text. Here, then, the very *greatest humility* is necessary in the commentator. The critic faces his severest trial when theological ideas spring up all around him, meet, get entangled, conflict and are combined. At the peak of his spiritual joy as an interpreter he meets his greatest temptation, the temptation of the critic.

At this point, and in all cases, philological exegesis is indispensable, both to control the theological ideas suggested by the text and to eliminate those which are shown by study to be alien to the text. Here the scholar must regard his own personal discoveries with a pitiless eye, however seductive they may be. From this point of view the critic is asked to display a higher degree of abnegation than any other scholar, for he must also resist the temptation to bring two texts into harmony when their affirmations do not agree, if he is convinced that such a synthesis is incompatible with the critical control exercised by philology and history; this he must do, however admirable the synthesis may seem to him, and however painful the biblical antinomy with regard to one point or another, once the synthesis has been rejected.

Any future historian of the theology of the twentieth century ought, we feel, to emphasize at the outset that it is the century of theological exegesis. It must be admitted that biblical critics are more conscious today of their particular task: that of explaining to the modern world as faithfully as possible the theological purpose of all biblical texts. It is not mere chance that this century has given birth to the great project of the theological dictionary of the New Testament published by G. Kittel. Karl Barth must always be remembered with gratitude for having raised implicitly in his commentary on Romans the problem of exegesis—whatever reserves some of us may have about its contents. This commentary has reorientated exegesis as a whole by calling it back to its aims. It would be wholly unjust to rebuke the writer of it for underestimating the efforts of the philologists and historians who have worked on the

Bible, or for dismissing the results of their work.[10] It is, however, the third role of historical exegesis—by which I mean its function of control—which he seems somewhat to have neglected in some of his interpretations. It is perhaps true that no critic can boast of having subjected his finest discoveries to such control, those at least which have given him most joy. But it seems to us that Barth is particularly open to this danger, not only because of the richness of his thought, but because systematically he seems to treat philological and historical explanation as too exclusively *preliminary* in character.

For this reason we have not stopped in these pages at justifying historical and philological criticism in a purely general fashion. We have tried to be more precise in emphasizing that it must never be considered as wholly a preliminary work. It must rather accompany exegesis *from its beginning to its end*.

The great and unique responsibility of biblical exegesis is to be faithful to the text in a radical manner, even if the exegetical result of this is but modest and may perhaps at first seem useless for either the dogma or the practical life of the Church.[11] Philological and historical interpretation has a high calling, to help the biblical critic to fidelity to his task, and to keep him from overstepping the precise and narrow limits which the Church with justice demands of him.

[10] We hope that the regrettable affirmations of the preface to *Kirchliche Dogmatik*, III (2), 1948, p. VII f., on the work of the exegetes, discarding as they do the sane attitude taken up in the preface to the second edition of the commentary on Romans, do not represent the writer's last word on the question, whatever disappointments the critics have caused and will still cause him.

[11] When Barth speaks, in the preface to vol. III of the *Kirchliche Dogmatik*, of 'dogmatic responsibility' of the exegete and implicitly reproaches the critics for ignoring it, accusing them of '*ahnungslos in die Landschaft hineinzureden*', he does not realize that the responsibility of the critic is simply to confine himself to his own limited task. It is only by observing this restriction that he will do a service to the dogmatist.

II

The Origin of Christmas

Translated from *Weihnachten in der alten Kirche*, 1947, Basel. The footnotes, and the last two references in the Foreword, are taken from the French edition, *Noël dans l'Église ancienne*, 1949, Neuchâtel.

Foreword

THE FOLLOWING PAGES had their origin in a scientific dissertation, read to a learned audience. But here the material has been rewritten for a wider public, and all technical discussions have been omitted. The questions to be discussed are extremely complicated; and far from being fully clarified, need a good deal more investigation. At first sight, therefore, a popular treatment seems impossible, although Arnold Meyer gave a quite successful one in his rather larger work some thirty years ago. Since then learned studies and discussions have gone on without, so far, achieving final agreement on all points. Yet scholars are agreed about the main outlines of the historical developments; and their general conclusions can and should be made available in an easily intelligible form to a wider circle of educated people. The amount of ignorance of the elementary facts of Church history and the history of dogma, even where importance is attached to general education, is amazing. The result is that catchwords and slogans are all too readily accepted. This has indeed happened in the study of the origins of Christmas, for the origin of the festival has been confused with that of customs associated with it.

The latter problem is not dealt with here. We shall confine ourselves to a quite different question, that of the origin of Christmas in the early Church, and this demands an historical sketch. Of course, the question of the *nature* of Christmas inevitably arises, and on it opinions are sharply divided. Is it pagan or Christian? This will be treated within the historical framework and in connection with the historical results. The problem of the claim of the Christmas festival to a place within the Christian Church is a theological one, upon which our method will be able to shed some light.

Those who are interested in the learned studies and more technical discussions, upon which the present work is based, may begin with H. Usener, *Das Weihnachtsfest*, 2nd edn., 1911. A different standpoint is adopted by L. Duchesne, especially in *Les origines du culte chrétien*, 5th edn., 1920. Among more recent studies of particular problems may be mentioned K. Holl, *Ursprung des Epiphanienfestes*

(*Ges. Aufsätze*, II, 1928, p. 123 f.), and B. Botte, *Les origines de la Noël et de l'Epiphanie*, 1932. Also two notes by G. Brunner (*Jahrbuch für Liturgiewissenschaft*, 1935, p. 178 f.), and K. Prümm (*Stimmen der Zeit*, 1938–39, p. 215).

The Origin of Christmas

Our Christmas festival of December 25th was unknown to the Christians of the first three centuries. Down to the beginning of the fourth century this day, subsequently to become a central date in the Christian Church, was allowed by the Christians to pass by unhonoured and unsung, without any assembling together for worship, and without Christ's birth being so much as mentioned. By contrast, we shall see that in the pagan Roman empire December 25th was dedicated, as his special festival, to the worship of the sun.

Before the birth of Christ came to be celebrated on December 25th, it was commemorated in the east, and later also in the west, on another day, January 6th. But its association with a definite day could not have been of fundamental significance for the nature of the festival, for the simple reason that, apart from individual attempts to calculate a definite date, the Church of the first three centuries accepted the fact that we are quite ignorant of the date of the birth of Jesus.

This brings us to our first enquiry.

(1) *The Date of the Birth of Jesus*

The evangelists do not tell us the day of Christ's birth, and there is no other source of information at our disposal. Luke's nativity narrative mentions the shepherds in the fields—a hint of the time of year to which Luke assigned the birth of Jesus, but that is all. This is meagre enough, especially when it is realized that in Palestine the shepherds are in the fields from March–April until November, and so spring, summer and autumn would all come into the picture. That is all that can be deduced from the Gospel accounts about the date.

In the absence of more precise information some early Christians attempted to divine the date by indulging in all sorts of speculations, which are totally devoid of historical value, and received no official recognition in the early Church. They were merely individual efforts to calculate the date, and they diverged widely from one another. I give just a few examples. In a document dating from the year 243,[1] March 28th is given as Christ's birthday.[2] Why March 28th? The writer starts from the passage in Genesis in which God at the creation separates the light from the darkness. He explains this as meaning that light and darkness formed two equal parts. Consequently, the creation of the world must have taken place on a day when day and night were of the same length. Now in the Roman calendar the vernal equinox, when day and night have the same length, was on March 25th, and so this was the first day of creation. Further, in the creation story God made the sun on the fourth day, that is, March 28th. And since for Christians, according to Malachi 4.2, the Messiah is the 'sun of righteousness', it follows that Jesus must have come into the world on March 28th.

There are other sources belonging to the first three centuries which also expressly place the birth of Christ in the spring, for example, the Clementines.[3] But they do not agree about the date. By the use of all sorts of arithmetical and imaginative ingenuity some of them assign the birthday of Jesus to April 19th, others to May 20th.[4] April 2nd is also mentioned. This preference for the spring is due both to the belief that the beginning of the world took place in the spring, and to the fact that Jesus died in the spring. His life must end, it was felt, with the completion of a natal year.

In the rarer cases, where a date in the winter was chosen, it was still the spring which was the starting-point of the calculation. The conception of Jesus was placed in the spring, and his birth then took place nine months later, in the winter. This is how December 25th may have been decided upon at one time,[5] because it corresponded to March 25th, nine months before; and so the latter was observed simultaneously as the day both of creation and of Christ's conception, and in addition as the day of his death. But in any case, down to the first half of the fourth century, no greater importance was attached to December 25th than to the many other dates we have mentioned. January 6th would have been arrived at in a similar way: it is nine months after April 6th, which would then be regarded as the day both of Christ's death and of his conception.

This unrestricted indulgence in fanciful speculations proves that

1 Wrongly attributed to Cyprian. *De Pascha computus*, ed. Hartel, III, p. 248 f. See Usener, *op. cit.*, p. 5.
2 *Op. cit.*, p. 251 f.
3 *Hom.* I, 6.
4 According to Clem. Alex., *Stromata*, I, 21, 145.6 and 146.4 (ed. Stählin, p. 90).
5 Julius Africanus in his *Chronography of the Year 221*.

the Church did not yet attach any definite dogmatic importance to the question of the date of the birthday of Jesus. Clement of Alexandria, at the end of the second century, pours ridicule upon those who claim by such methods to establish the date of Christ's birth.[6]

(2) The Festival of January 6th

We have seen that in the first three centuries great individual freedom in attempting to determine the day when Jesus was born was accompanied by official indifference to the matter on the part of the Church. The realization that the true date was unknown shows that the first impulse to celebrate Christ's appearance on earth was provided, not by a date, but by theological considerations. In the course of our enquiry we shall be faced with the problem whether this basically theological idea goes back to a pagan festival, or whether it springs from the reflections and needs of Christians, and so whether conceptions which belong to a pagan festival play only a secondary role in the Church's choice of a date.

In the earliest period the Christians not only accepted the fact that the date of the birth of Jesus is unknown; they felt besides no need to celebrate Christ's coming down to earth at all. The primitive Church was far more interested in Christ's death and resurrection than in his incarnation. Every Lord's Day (later called Sunday) was a 'day of resurrection' and, in addition, there was a single Christian festival, that of Easter, which, along with the holy days associated with it, celebrated Christ's death and resurrection. Similarly, the festivals in honour of the apostles and martyrs in early Christianity were associated not with their birthdays, but with their deaths. Writing at the beginning of the third century, Origen objected to the celebration of any birthday, as being a pagan custom. He points out that in the Bible only the heathen and the godless (Pharaoh and Herod) celebrated their birthdays.[7]

But these considerations could not apply to Christ, for he was indeed more than a martyr or an apostle; he was the redeemer of mankind! Even though the essential act of salvation was only completed in his death, still it was unavoidable that his entry into the world should come to be construed as soteriological in the highest

---

[6] *Stromata*, I, 21,145.5 (ed. Stählin, p. 90). It is true that elsewhere he himself seems to allow November 17th as the date of Christ's birth.

[7] *Commentary on Matthew XIV*, 6 (ed. Klostermann, p. 30). See also *Hom. in Levit.*, VIII, 3.

degree. That is why, as early as Matthew and Luke, special accounts were written to throw light upon the birth of Jesus; and John, too, described its supernatural quality from his own standpoint. Once faith in the crucified and exalted Lord had been taken as the starting-point of theological reflection on the question of Christ's person and work, his incarnation was bound to become more and more central in devout speculation. Eastern Christians in particular pondered the mystery of God's entry into the world in a human person. There were various possible ways of understanding this event. Some held that the divine Christ first appeared on earth in the human Jesus at the moment of baptism. This is the heretical view, according to which Christ, a divine being, could not have entered a fleshly existence completely, but was only temporarily united with the human Jesus from the baptism when the voice of God declared: 'Thou art my beloved son'. On the other hand, in what later became the orthodox view of the Church, God appeared in the very person of the historical human Jesus, and so the divine Word entered the world at the very moment of his birth. In these christo-logical ideas we see the real beginnings of the Christian festival of Christmas. We are told by Clement of Alexandria in particular that the followers of the Alexandrian Gnostic Basilides, who lived in the second century, celebrated the baptism of Christ on January 10th or 6th.[8] This is at present our earliest source for dating Christmas. Basilides and his followers represented the heretical opinion that the divine Christ first *appeared* on earth at the baptism of Jesus; and their festival of the baptism was accordingly called Epiphany, *epiphaneia* being the Greek word for 'appearing'. So, while the disciples of Basilides celebrated the mystery of Christ's entry into this world at the beginning of January, the festival still had nothing to do with the *birth* of Jesus. The latter obviously, in their view, possessed no central religious significance, since for them the real divine Epiphany coincided with the baptism of Jesus.

Why did they celebrate this festival of the baptism in the early part of January, and in particular, on January 6th? The Gospels, which do not give the date of the birth of Jesus, are equally silent about that of his baptism. It has been rightly pointed out in this connection that, in the pagan world, a feast of Dionysus, associated with the lengthening of the days, was held on January 6th; that in Alexandria itself the birth of Aeon to the maiden Koré was com-memorated on that day; and that it was probably observed as the

[8] Clem. Alex., *Stromata*, I, 21, 146.1 (ed. Stählin, p. 90).

day of Osiris. In the night before January 6th the waters of the Nile were said to possess special miraculous power. This fact explains why the disciples of Basilides chose this date for the festival of Christ's baptism: it was in order to proclaim, in distinction from the heathen, that the true divine being who had appeared upon the earth was Christ, who entered this world in the Jordan at the moment when the voice uttered the words: 'Thou art my beloved son.'

What has all this to do with Christmas? This festival of the baptism kept by the disciples of Basilides on January 6th was adopted from its heretical opponents by the orthodox eastern Church, which borrowed certain other ecclesiastical customs. Now we have seen that Christ's baptism was originally celebrated simply because it came under the same heading as his manifestation, or Epiphany, which was the dominant idea of the feast. On the other hand, the Church outside heretical circles followed the nativity narratives in the Gospels, and regarded his birth, and not his baptism, as the real appearing of Christ upon earth. Possibly, indeed, many heretical Gnostics themselves assigned both baptism and birth to January 6th. But especially when his divinity was being discussed at the beginning of the fourth century, Christ's birth was bound to be regarded as the occasion when he was manifested. In any case it is an established fact that by the first half of the fourth century the Church was observing Epiphany on January 6th, and in so doing conjoined the baptism and the birth of Christ. Not that anything was removed from the original baptism festival, but rather that the celebration of the birth was added. The festival was divided into two parts according to the order in which the two events took place. The night of January 5th–6th was devoted to the festival of Christ's birth, the day January 6th to that of his baptism. Thus, before the birth of Christ came to be celebrated on December 25th, that joyful event was commemorated on the night of January 5th–6th.

There is an Egyptian papyrus of the beginning of the fourth century which contains a kind of liturgical formula intended for a church choir, with the liturgical parts for the choir to sing in response to the reading by the priest.[9] The numerous finger-marks show that the leaf must have been much used. It is clear from another liturgical note on the reverse side that it concerns the feast of Epiphany of

[9] Published by G. Bickell in *Mittheilungen aus der Sammlung der Papyrus*, Erzherzog Rainer, 1887, II, p. 83–86. Cf. Usener, *op. cit.*, p. 196 f.

January 5th–6th, when Christ's baptism in the Jordan was commemorated. The fragment concerns that part of the festival devoted
to the birth of Christ. This interesting papyrus contains the oldest
Christmas liturgy we possess, and in it Christmas is still observed on
the night of January 5th–6th. To the reading of the biblical account
of the story of Christ's birth at Bethlehem, the flight into Egypt,
and the return to Nazareth, the choir responded by singing the
following Greek hymn:

> 'Born at Bethlehem
> Brought up at Nazareth
> Dwelt in Galilee.'

Then the priest would have read the story of the Magi from the
Gospel of Matthew, and the choir responded:

> 'We have seen a sign from heaven,
> the shining star.'

After this the Christmas story from Luke 2 was read, and the
choir responded:

> 'Shepherds in the field tending their flocks were amazed, they fell
>   on their knees, and sang: Glory to the Father.
> Halleluiah.
> Glory to the Son, and to the Holy Ghost.
> Halleluiah. Halleluiah. Halleluiah.'

Such was the way in which Christ's birthday was celebrated on
January 5th–6th at the commencement of the fourth century.

At Alexandria other additional elements were associated with the
birth and baptism of Christ in this early Christian Epiphany festival.
Besides the appearing of Jesus at his birth and his public appearance
at his baptism, his manifestation in his miracles was recalled: the
miracle of the changing of water into wine at Cana (to which the old
pagan belief in the miraculous powers of the Nile may have given
support), and the feeding of the multitude; while the star, which
the Magi from the east had seen, was always mentioned as the
first manifestation. This story of the star is the one remaining element of the many-sided Epiphany feast of January 6th as it was kept
in the early Church.

A description of this festival has also been preserved by the fourth-century Syrian Church Father Ephraem.[10] He calls the festival of January 6th the most sublime of Christian festivals. He says that on this day every house was decked with garlands (perhaps a distant ancestor of our Christmas tree). Ephraem describes the tremendous joy which reigned in the entire Church. The very walls of the church building, he declares, seem to exult on this day, and the children utter nothing but words of happiness. Then he specially describes the beautiful nocturnal festival. 'The night is here,' he cries, 'the night which has given peace to the universe! Who would sleep on this night when the whole world is awake!' Then is celebrated the birth of Christ, with the adoration of the shepherds and the appearance of the star. The following day was dedicated to the adoration of the Magi and to the baptism of Christ in the Jordan. In one of his own hymns Ephraem seeks to combine the different elements of the Epiphany festival.

> 'The whole creation proclaims,
> The Magi proclaim,
> The star proclaims:
> Behold, the king's son is here!
> The heavens are opened,
> The waters of Jordan sparkle,
> The dove appears:
> This is my beloved son!'

In this poem we see how closely at this date Christ's baptism and birth were combined and focused together in the concept of his advent.

The feast of Epiphany continued for a long time to be celebrated in Palestine with extraordinary splendour. We have the well-known account of it by the noble pilgrim Aetheria, who spent three years in Palestine.[11] She cannot find words adequate to describe the magnificence of the festival, and the beauty of the singing which resounded from the midst of the enormous multitude of people. She tells how all, along with the bishop, repair in solemn procession to Bethlehem on the night of January 5th–6th, in order to hold a service at night in the cave where Jesus was supposed to have been born. Before daybreak the whole procession moved off to Jerusalem singing hymns continually in honour of Christ who had come to

[10] Thomas J. Lamy, *Ephraemi Syri hymni et sermones*, I, 1882. Other 'De nativitate domini sermones' have been published by Petrus Mobarek (Benedictus), cf. Usener, *op. cit.*, p. 202, n. 9.

[11] Ethérie, *Journal de voyage*, 'Sources chrétiennes' 21, Paris, 1948, p. 203 f.

the world. As January 6th dawns they reach Jerusalem, and enter the Church of the Resurrection, whose interior is illuminated with incredible brightness by the light of thousands of candles. There they sing psalms and the priest offers prayers. Then all depart to rest for a few hours. Towards midday they reassemble in the Church of the Resurrection. The first part of the festival ends at midday, and in the evening the second part commences with renewed splendour.

In all three descriptions the idea of light plays a large part, and is given a symbolic meaning. The appearance of Christ in the world is already depicted in the New Testament as the entry of the light into the darkness. This may have had something to do with the special choice of January 6th, the day on which the lengthening of the days was celebrated by pagans as the birth of Aeon. But it is not at all probable that this gave the start to the Christian festival, since the idea of the light, which appeared in Christ and dispersed the darkness, is as old as Christianity itself, and can be traced throughout the whole of the New Testament.

The details of these ancient descriptions of the Epiphany festival of January 5th and 6th are included in order to show that the whole complex of Christian thought connected with our Christmas was already present in it in liturgical form. It will not do to speak of Christmas only as a feast observed on December 25th. The fact that Christmas was celebrated during the Epiphany feast of January 6th, together with a festival of the Magi, the baptism and the wedding at Cana, in no way alters the fact that all the Christian ideas connected with Christmas were expressed liturgically and symbolically in this festival, and that the separation of the nativity festival from its association with Epiphany actually imported no essentially new idea.

The question whether Christ was actually born on January 6th was entirely secondary. It would hardly have occurred to anyone to ask whether the events which were being commemorated simultaneously at this festival all took place on January 6th. The important thing was not the date, but Christ's 'appearing' for which the festival stood. So it was quite easy for the date of the celebration of his birth to be changed in the course of the fourth century. And so we come to the festival of December 25th.

(3) The Festival of December 25th

When and why was the nativity festival separated from Epiphany as it has just been described, and given a special date of its own, December 25th? There is still no complete agreement among scholars on the chronological question. The most probable assumption is that this took place in Rome between 325 and 354, after the older Epiphany festival had already come from the east to the west, perhaps even to Rome. December 25th is attested in Rome as the day of Christ's birth in the year 336,[12] and must have been observed as such even before this under Constantine the Great.[13] Possibly in Rome at first the older Epiphany festival continued to be observed in its original form for a time, after the new festival was well on the way to becoming naturalized.

Now what are the reasons which led to the separation of the festival of Christ's birth from Epiphany, and to its transference to December 25th? I should say at once that the calculation which assigned the birth to December 25th, which we come upon occasionally among many other similar calculations, can scarcely have given the initiative. The determining factor was rather the dogmatic development of christology at the beginning of the fourth century. Moreover, in the pagan world December 25th was observed as a specially important festival in honour of the sun god, and the emperor Constantine the Great pursued the deliberate policy of uniting the worship of the sun with that of Christ.

[12] According to the *Chronography of Philocalus of the year 354* (Th. Mommsen, *Über den Chronographen vom Jahre 354* (*Abh. d. sächs. Ges. d. Wiss.*, I), 1850, p. 631). The main controversy between H. Usener and L. Duchesne centres on this text. Usener uses it as the basis of his claim that December 25th was first observed in Rome as Christ's birthday in 354, since even in the previous year, according to Ambrose's account of the consecration of his sister Marcellina (*De virg.*, III, 1), the birth of Christ was still commemorated on January 6th. But in the *Bulletin critique* of 1890 (p. 41 f.) Duchesne establishes the important fact that the first edition of the *Chronography* must have been written before October 336.

[13] Professor U. Holzmeister has called attention to the suggestion of G. Brunner (*Jahrbuch für Liturgiewissenschaft*, 1935, p. 178 f.) and K. Prümm (*Stimmen der Zeit*, 1938–39, p. 215) that the festival of December 25th could date from the reign of the emperor Aurelian (270–75). They point to Sermon 202 of Augustine (Migne, *P. L.* 38, 1033) which upbraids the Donatists for not observing January 6th along with the Catholic Church. These two scholars think that it can thus be concluded that when the Donatists seceded from the Church in 311 they were already accustomed to observe December 25th, and that therefore this date was known to the Church from that time and probably much earlier, from the time of Aurelian, whose fondness for the worship of the sun is well known. Ingenious though this argument is, it contains too many doubtful hypotheses. As Usener (p. 15 f.) had already pointed out, Augustine's censure of the Donatists for failing to observe January 6th does not imply that they celebrated Christ's birthday on December 25th.

In the first place, at the famous Council of Nicaea in 325 the Church expressly condemned the doctrine that God himself did not become incarnate in Jesus at his birth. This involved the rejection of all other interpretations, including the one that Jesus was adopted by God at his baptism. In the decisions of the Council a very important part was played by the Roman Church. It is easy to understand how these debates favoured, as we have seen, the spread of a birth festival as such, quite apart from the question of date; and how, from the standpoint of dogma, the connection of a nativity festival with that of the baptism under the common theme of 'appearing' must in time have been felt to be theologically objectionable. For was not this to combine orthodoxy with heresy? The tendency, then, to dissociate the festival of the birth from the Epiphany festival is to be explained as the result of christological speculation.

But this raised the problem of finding a new date for the nativity festival. Here a very influential factor was the existence, in Mithraism which was widespread in the Roman empire, of a cult of the sun whose chief festival fell on December 25th, the winter solstice. We have seen that the symbol of light shining in darkness, which is fundamental to the New Testament, is already inherent in the festival of Christ's appearing upon earth, and that the choice of January 6th had given expression to it. Now, when it was a question of a date for the separate and independent festival of Christ's birth, the day which had the first claim to attention was one in proximity to January 6th, a day which in the pagan Roman world was the day, without any question, in honour of the light, the sun, namely, December 25th. Before the introduction of Mithraism, the Roman emperors had already built a temple to *sol invictus*, the 'unconquered sun god'; and in the third century splendid festive games were held on December 25th in honour of the conquering rising sun. Great bonfires were lit, whose purpose was to help the sun to climb above the horizon. The worship of the 'unconquered sun' assumed a more concrete form in Mithraism, which was especially popular among the Roman soldiers, and was for some time in the third century a serious rival of Christianity.

It is understandable, therefore, that the Roman Church intentionally opposed to this pagan nature cult its own festival of light, the festival of the birth of Christ, the infant Jesus, who in Simeon's song was hailed as 'the light to lighten the Gentiles'. Time and again the Church calls to mind that the words in Malachi 4.2, 'For you shall the sun of righteousness arise', are a prophecy of Christ. Ambrose, bishop of Milan, for example, says in a sermon in which he expressly contrasts the pagan and Christian festivals: 'Christ is *our* new sun!'[14] Augustine, again, alludes to the pagan festival of December 25th in his summons to Christians not to worship the sun on this day, like the pagans, but him who created the sun[15]; while Pope Leo the Great rebuked the sorry faith of those who celebrated Christmas as the birth of the sun instead of as that of Christ.[16] In any case, these utterances show that the fixing of the festival of Christ's birth on December 25th was not done in ignorance of the pagan significance of the day.

Of course, Constantine's deliberate policy of combining the worship of the sun and that of Christ certainly helped in all this. But it should now be taken as settled that Constantine was not so much a Christian as a conscious syncretist: he strove after a synthesis of Christianity and the valuable elements in paganism. Christianity was the religion he most favoured simply because its organization made it the best able to unite the empire. But Constantine may well have thought that the multifarious religions of the empire could somehow be carried on within the single framework of Christianity. We hear nothing of any deliberate attack on paganism, nor did he renounce paganism until he received baptism on his death-bed. Certainly he strove for a reform of paganism in the direction of Christianity: he abolished the pagan system of oracles, the offering of private sacrifices and certain grossly immoral temple cults. All his life, however, he promoted the worship of the sun. He allowed himself to be represented in two statues as the sun god with shining rays, and permitted the following inscription to be placed on the pedestal: 'To Constantine, who brings light like the sun'. It was certainly Constantine's intention to combine the worship of the sun with the worship of Christ; and that was possible because the sun was itself one of the Christian symbols of Christ.

It was with this end in view that, in the year 321, he introduced the Christian Lord's Day as an officially authorized weekly day of rest; for it coincided with a day dedicated to the sun god. From the middle of the second century the term 'Sunday' occurs for the former 'Lord's Day'. This means that Christian thought about the redemptive act of the resurrection of Christ (which is, of course, the

---

[14] Sermon VI, Migne, *P. L.* 17, 614.

[15] Sermo in Nat. Dom., 7, and Sermo in Nat. Joh. Bapt., Migne, *P. L.* 38, 1007 and 1302.

[16] Sermon XXVII, Migne, *P. L.* 54; see 'Sources chrétiennes' 22, p. 143 f.

Christian meaning of Sunday) had already become associated with
the symbolism of the sun. So bearing in mind Constantine's parti-
ality for sun worship, it is plain that one of his most far-reaching
Christian measures, giving the Christian Sunday a legal status, was
intended by him at the same time to bring the pagan sun worship
in a Christian form into Christianity.

The analogy of Sunday, which certainly became the official holy
day under Constantine, seems to make it probable that it was as
early as Constantine, and through his influence, that the festival of
Christ's birth was changed over to December 25th, the great festival
of the sun. Christ's birth was now linked up with the sun on December 25th in the same way as his resurrection with Sunday (the day
of the sun).

Admonitions like those of Augustine and Pope Leo had now
clearly become necessary, for this deeply-rooted pagan festival of
the 'unconquered sun god' did not, in fact, simply disappear, but
persisted in many practices which passed over into the Christian
festival. So when Christmas was separated from another Christian
festival, that of Christ's baptism, it fell under the influence of a
pagan one. At first this influence was felt in Christmas *customs*.
We learn, for instance, from a Syrian theologian that Christians
also now began the practice of lighting bonfires on this day.[17] But
the idea that Christ is the light of the world shining in the darkness
is independent of the festival of December 25th; it was already
there in the feast of January 6th. Indeed, it was in Christianity from
the very beginning, independently of any festival.

(4) *The Spread of the Festival of December 25th*

We have still to enquire how, from the second half of the fourth
century, the festival of December 25th spread from Rome throughout the whole of Christendom. Rome sought to get the Churches
of the east also to accept this Christmas festival thus separated from
Epiphany—an endeavour by no means universally easy, for many
eastern Churches firmly adhered to the practice of observing the
festival of Christ's birth in its old form as an Epiphany festival on
January 5th–6th. Opposition was particularly stubborn in Syria.
Rome tried in vain, probably for a decade from 375, to establish the
observance of December 25th at Antioch. Success was first achieved

[17] A scholiast of Bar Salibi, see Assemani, *Bibl. Orient.*, 2, 164. German translation
of the text in Usener, *op. cit.*, p. 349.

by the great preacher Chrysostom. In his well-known Christmas sermon of December 20th, 386,[18] he adjured his hearers to present themselves on the 25th, five days later, in order to celebrate Christ's birth, 'that mother of all festivals', 'which inspires in all the greatest reverence and awe'. Let everyone 'leave his home, that we may behold our Lord lying in the manger, wrapped in swaddling clothes, a wonderful and awe-inspiring sight'. A great throng obeyed his summons; and Chrysostom used the occasion of his well-known Christmas sermon to convince the members of his Church that Christ's birth must be celebrated on December 25th, because Christ was actually born on that day. As evidence, he not only appeals to supposed Roman records, but employs complicated calculations, which are as worthless as the rest. It was only because of the effort to make December 25th the universal Christmas Day that importance first began to be attached to the question of the historical date of the birth of Jesus. Hitherto this had played a secondary role. Eloquently Chrysostom expresses his joy that Christmas, unknown at Antioch less than ten years ago, has now begun a new and vigorous life there, 'as if it were already a tradition of many years coming from the earliest days of the Church'. Chrysostom succeeded in establishing once for all the feast of December 25th in his Church.

In the meantime the festival had been introduced in 379 into Constantinople under Gregory of Nazianzus, the defender of the divinity of Christ. Egypt continued opposition for a longer time, and did not finally submit until the year 431. But it was especially at Jerusalem that there was the greatest reluctance to countenance the idea that the old Epiphany festival of January 6th should surrender its main content to a new festival. In vain did Jerome expend his eloquence; the Christians of Jerusalem considered that, as they lived in the Holy Land, they had a better knowledge of tradition than those who dwelt in the distant west. In the course of this conflict more and more attention was paid to the insoluble problem of the date, about which the Church of an earlier period had maintained a healthy reserve, even though it celebrated Christ's birth with special pomp. The situation was now quite different; one side endeavoured to prove that Jesus was born on January 6th, the other on December 25th! Probably not till the middle of the sixth century did the Palestinian Church abandon its opposition to December 25th. Only one Church, that of the Armenians, whose attitude earned them the reproach of being 'men with hardened heads and stiff

18 Migne, *P. G.* 49, 351 f.

necks',[19] has continued down to the present day to commemorate Christ's birth not on December 25th, but on January 6th.

(5) Historical and Theological Conclusions

Finally, what conclusions are to be drawn from the history of the origin of the Christmas festival which has been sketched above?

(a) Christians have never kept Christmas on a historically accurate date, whether on December 25th or on January 6th. The earliest observances of Christmas did not commemorate a date at all, but a fact whose supreme importance for the Christian Church is not confined to a particular day—namely, the appearance of Christ upon earth.

(b) The impulse to celebrate Christ's birth did not come from outside, but was a consequence of theological reflection on the fact of our redemption, the fact that God became man in Jesus Christ, and condescended to our estate.

At this point, of course, Christians were faced with the question whether there was New Testament authority for devoting a special festival to the incarnation of Christ, or whether those early Christians were right who altogether rejected such a festival as un-Christian. And it must be said that *over-estimation* of this festival, in particular giving it any precedence over Good Friday and Easter, is certainly at variance both with Christian practice, which originally included only the latter, and with the theology of the primitive Church. In the New Testament the central events in the story of Christ are his death and resurrection. His incarnation must be viewed in the light of these events, and not *vice versa*. From this standpoint the Christian year should begin not with Advent, but with the round of celebrations at Easter.

Nevertheless, granted this subordination, it is entirely in accordance with the faith of the New Testament to make the birth of Christ the object of a special Church festival. The evangelists Matthew, Luke and John dwell on this event, seeking each in his own way to shed light on it; and in doing so they are only spokesmen of the community which handed down their traditions. In this connection we must make a special note of the hymn, quoted by Paul in Philippians 2.6 ff. It mentions the incarnation of Christ, but it is purely and simply because it deals with his crucifixion and exaltation as Lord that it makes any mention of his becoming a

[19] Jacob Bar Salibi, see Assemani, *Bibl. Orient.*, 2, 164.

servant. This hymn can appropriately be called a Christmas hymn.

Moreover, the liturgical form of the oldest festival of Christ's birth, as seen when we were discussing the vivid descriptions of the Epiphany feast, betrays specifically Christian features. The central idea expressed in liturgical form, that Christ, the light of the world, enters into the darkness, is certainly not derived from the festival of Mithras, the 'unconquered sun god'. This latter was observed on December 25th, whereas the former, as we have proved, was neither more nor less than part of celebrations of Epiphany held on January 6th. Moreover, as found in Epiphany, it is scarcely probable that the idea is derived primarily from a pagan solstice festival observed on January 6th; rather, it is one of those early Christian, New Testament conceptions, which may be accepted as certain. Where the New Testament indulges in theological reflection on the meaning of Christ's incarnation, there we find, in the prologue of the Gospel of John, this thought coming to expression: 'The light shines in the darkness'.

(c) On the other hand, the choice of the dates themselves, both January 6th and December 25th, was determined by the fact that both these days were pagan festivals whose meaning provided a starting-point for the specifically Christian conceptions of Christmas. Constantine's attempt to combine the worship of the sun with that of Christ has certainly to be repudiated from the New Testament point of view, like all Gnostic attempts to merge Christianity in a general religious syncretism, with the resulting loss of its central features. Yet the theologian has to ask whether, in terms of the New Testament, there is not a theological significance in the developments we have described, at the end of which the date of the birthday of Jesus, which dating we know to be without a historical basis, was fixed and observed on a day dedicated to a cosmic natural phenomenon. The New Testament suggests that this was more than mere symbolism; it is a pointer to a theological belief held by the early Church, that Christ is at one and the same time the redeemer of mankind and the redeemer of the whole creation; that the salvation linked with his name applies to the whole universe, just as the fall of man involved the whole creation in the curse. Since mankind and the rest of creation thus form a solidarity, the redemption of man involves the redemption of the whole creation. The view expressed everywhere in the New Testament is that Christ, the redeemer of men, also participated as an agent in the creation of the world. The solidarity of creation and redemption is shown most clearly in the great central event, the atoning death of Christ. That is the meaning of Matthew's narrative of the darkness and the earthquake (Matt. 27.45, 51) which accompany the death of the redeemer; while Paul, in the epistle to the Colossians (1.20), describes in his own way the supernatural work done on Good Friday, declaring that God through the blood of Christ made peace, not only with men, but with all things in heaven and on earth.

The festival of Christ's birth must be regarded in the light of Good Friday. And so it is entirely in line with the New Testament that, like the latter, Christmas should also be symbolically associated with a phenomenon of nature. The same association, from a different angle, finds expression in Matthew's nativity story, when he tells about the star at Bethlehem.

Christmas, then, centres our attention on the christocentric character of the New Testament revelation, in which everything, the whole creation, is made to refer to Christ, because it looks for its redemption in him (Rom. 8.19 f.). And again, the fact that the 'unconquered sun god' was conquered in the end, and yet that his birthday was not so much suppressed as made subordinate to that of our Saviour Jesus Christ, reminds us that in the New Testament every revelation of God in nature is secondary to his revelation in the sacrifice made by Christ.

In conclusion I quote from the Christmas sermon of Ambrose, which I have already mentioned, a passage which seeks to express these ideas. 'Well do Christian people call this holy day, on which our Lord was born, the day of the new sun; and they assert it so insistently that even Jews and pagans agree with them in using that name for it. We are happy to accept and maintain this view, because with the dayspring of the Saviour, not only is the salvation of mankind renewed, but also the splendour of the sun. . . . For if the sun withdrew its light when Christ suffered, it must shine at his birth with greater splendour than ever before.' [20]

[20] Ambrose, Sermon VI, Migne, P. L. 17, 614.

III

The Plurality
of the Gospels as a
Theological Problem
in Antiquity

A Study in the History of Dogma

Translated from 'Die Pluralität der
Evangelien als theologisches Problem
im Altertum', *Theologische Zeitschrift*,
i, 1945, p. 23–42, Basel

The Plurality of the Gospels as a Theological Problem in Antiquity

IT IS NOT our purpose to deal here with the problem of the origin of the fourfold canon of the Gospel. That would have to be dealt with on its own in a treatise on the history of the canon. In any case it is a question that can only be answered in very general outlines since the extant sources make it impossible to ascertain the various historical stages which led to the Church taking several Gospels as the norm and not just one, four Gospels, that is, from a much greater number of accounts of the life of Jesus that were already available in the second century. As far as the detailed history of the fourfold canon is concerned we are therefore very largely dependent on conclusions *a posteriori*. I should like to mention the latest of the theories to be propounded, that of Walter Bauer in his book *Rechtgläubigkeit und Ketzerei im ältesten Christentum*, which appeared in 1934. It is related to his main thesis, according to which the Christian world of the time, split by many different conceptions of the Gospel, was first compelled to face the problem of orthodoxy by the ecclesio-political aspirations of the Roman Church. According to Bauer, in the Roman Church and the Churches within its sphere of influence, only the Gospels of Matthew and Mark were recognized for a long time, whilst the Gospel of Luke, which was discredited by its exploitation at the hand of heretics, was only accepted after some hesitation, and direct resistance to the Gospel of John was only given up about the year 200, at a time when the reasons which had at first placed the fourth Gospel in a dubious light had lost some of their weight. Bauer's argument includes some assertions worth consideration, bold and intentionally hypothetical though they are. He maintains that Papias only recognized Mark and Matthew; that Justin did not regard the Gospel of John as authoritative, and that Ignatius of Antioch used the Gospel of Matthew, not the Gospel of John.[1]

---

[1] In spite of important points of contact in certain details, this conception of W. Bauer's differs from earlier views as expounded, for example, by A. v. Harnack

Other scholars regard particular aspects of the development differently. As soon as an attempt is made to achieve some precision in the matter it becomes impossible to avoid interpretations which inevitably differ from one another.

In the present study we shall take into account the more or less assured explanations of the origins of the canon only in so far as they serve to illuminate another question which is to be the subject of our enquiry: how far was the fact of a plurality of authoritative evangelists felt to be a theological problem in the ancient Church? The answer to this question will no doubt shed an indirect light on the problem of the historical origins of the canon.

(1) *The Problem*

The fact that the Church takes the fourfold canon of the Gospels for granted makes it difficult for us to see how the matter ever became a problem at all. The idea that in reality the four Gospels are all based on one and the same εὐαγγέλιον represents the solution of the theological problem that has finally won the day, and which is adequately expressed in the headings of our Gospels: εὐαγγέλιον κατὰ Μαθθαῖον, Μάρκον, Λουκᾶν, Ἰωάννην. This conception may have existed implicitly before but it was not taken for granted everywhere, and A. Jülicher is wrong when he writes in his *Introduction to the New Testament*[2]: 'There was no need to be any more offended by four Gospels than by ten or thirteen epistles of Paul, or by the numerous parallel accounts of parts of the Old Testament story (Kings, Chron., Isa. 36–39).' We shall see that it was indeed a problem for many Christians, and that apart from the answer implied in the headings to the Gospels it was also solved in a number of heretical ways.

in 'Die Entstehung des Neuen Testaments' (*Beiträge zur Einleitung in das N.T.*, VI), 1914. The latter also regards the establishment of the fourfold Gospel canon as a compromise which took place under the influence of the Gospel of John. According to Harnack the admission of this Gospel played an all-important part in the establishment of a plurality of canonical Gospels. The champions of the Gospel of John had finally enforced their will against its opponents in Asia Minor, the Alogi, but the other Gospels which had already been adopted were not given up, so that it was in Asia Minor that the basic problem of a plurality of Gospels had first arisen.

[2] 7th edn. (revised in conjunction with E. Fascher), 1931, p. 502. A. Jülicher therefore considers a 'striving after Gospel harmonies' very unlikely. A. v. Harnack, *op. cit.*, p. 59, has already refuted this.

In the period when there was still no established canon it was by no means universally considered natural that different and, to some extent, divergent accounts of the life of Jesus should be regarded as equally authoritative. When the need to possess a New Testament canon alongside that of the Old Testament gradually emerged and apostolic authorship was required as the criterion for canonicity, it was inevitable that the combination of our four Gospels should give offence. This is obvious from the various attempts which were made to remove the cause of the offence. If it is necessary to have not one but several accounts of the one life of Jesus which must be the foundation of all Christian belief, it is as good as admitting that none of them is perfect. It was only too easy for the combining of several accounts of the life to be interpreted as a depreciation and disparagement of the individual Gospel. The comparison which Jülicher draws between the Gospels and the Pauline epistles, of which a number were included in the New Testament, is beside the point, since, whereas it was easy to grasp the fact that Paul had written to a number of Churches, it might well seem strange that the fundamental and unique events of the life of Jesus had to be described by several different authors.[3] Jülicher's reference to the parallel accounts in the books of the Kings and the Chronicles in the Old Testament is more an argument on the other side, for it is a well-known fact that the two books of the Chronicles originally formed the first part of a history which included the books of Ezra and Nehemiah, but in the Hebrew canon the Chronicles come *after* Ezra and Nehemiah. The reason for this unchronological arrangement is that, to begin with, only the second part of the whole work, namely Ezra and Nehemiah, was canonized, whereas the first part, the later books of the Chronicles, was not accepted. Doubts were felt about accepting them into the canon just because their contents run parallel to those of the earlier historical books of the Old Testament.

The only other canonical books that can be quoted for comparison are the five books of Moses. The Gospels have been felt to form exact parallels to them, not least because one of them opens with

---

[3] Disregarding that obvious fact, the Muratorian canon deemed it necessary to point out that Paul wrote to *seven* Churches. It attempted to prove that the number of epistles is not accidental but based on the number of the seven Churches, the symbol of the unity of the Church. This argument is based on just as false a presupposition as Irenaeus's contention with regard to the plurality of the Gospels.

the same words, ἐν ἀρχῇ, as the book of Genesis. The Gospels provide the basic account of the main events of the New Covenant, just as the books of Moses open the story of the Old Covenant. In fact, however, this obvious parallel between the Pentateuch and the Gospels merely aggravated the offence caused by the plurality of the Gospels. It is true that the Pentateuch contains parallel accounts of the same facts, which modern research attributes to different authors. But this variety of authorship meant nothing to the ancient world, since the five books were regarded as the work of the one prophet inspired by God: ἡ κατὰ τὸν Μωυσέα πεντάτευχος.[4] In contrast to the basic unity of the Pentateuch the New Testament contained not merely two but several parallel accounts by different writers. And even when the plurality was reluctantly accepted it was still not easy to see why these particular Gospels and not others should be adopted. From the standpoint of apostolic status Matthew did not appear to be particularly representative, and of the four Gospels later included in the canon only two of the writers, Matthew and John, were apostles at all. The two other Gospels, Mark and Luke, were only attributed to followers of apostles. The fact that the Church fathers laid special emphasis on the relation of Mark to Peter and Luke to Paul shows that scruples did exist which it was thought necessary to dispel. Being the follower of an apostle was not considered quite equivalent to being an actual apostle. One can see that from Tertullian's treatise against Marcion. In order to refute the great heretic's one-sided preference for the Gospel of Luke he emphasizes the fact that Luke was only the follower of an apostle and that his Gospel could therefore never be adequate on its own.[5]

In any case the plurality of the four Gospels aroused a widespread feeling of arbitrariness and chance which seem incompatible with the requirements of canonicity. This is shown by the efforts to explain the fourfold Gospel and also to do away with it.

(2) The Dual Tendency to Multiplicity and Reduction

The problem, and also the attempts to solve it, really appeared as far back as the time when the oldest Gospels were being written, long before the separation of the fourfold canon. In fact, most of the Gospels arose in the first place from an awareness of the problem

[4] Epiphanius, Haer., 8.4, 5.
[5] Adv. Marcionem, 4.2: 'Porro Lucas non apostolus, sed apostolicus: non magister, sed discipulus'.

of plurality, and each Gospel represented an attempt to solve it anew. But we must not forget that in the early period the idea that their writings might be used canonically was far from the authors' own minds. Each evangelist desired, in all probability, to proclaim the all-important facts of the life of Jesus better than his predecessors had done, 'better' meaning in this case not more accurately, more in accordance with the standards of modern scholarship, but more in keeping with the 'cause' which makes this life the centre of all history for the Church of the risen Lord. From this theological, or rather, christological angle, to which prime importance is attached, and quite rightly so, in works on the history of the form of the Gospels, it was supremely important to make an adequate record of the Church's traditional knowledge of the life of Jesus, particularly in its christological aspect, by collecting and sifting the scattered fragments of the oral tradition. If one of the accounts had proved itself entirely satisfactory in the early Church 'many' others would not have 'undertaken' (Luke 1.1) [6] to write a Gospel. The fact that Matthew and Luke incorporated some of their predecessors' work shows that they did not reject the previous Gospels, but, on the other hand, it was clearly not their idea that the earlier Gospels should be set alongside their own and form a kind of unity: it was more their intention that their work should be self-sufficient and an improvement on that of their forerunners.

The question, which has often been raised, whether in the earliest times a new Gospel was intended to 'supplant' or to 'supplement' the previous ones is irrelevant as far as the older Gospels is concerned, that is, those written before the formation of the canon. For it presupposes that the idea of the canon already existed. It certainly was not the intention of the writers of the Gospels of Matthew and Luke to 'supplant', say, the Gospel of Mark, since it could only have been 'supplanted' if it had already been regarded as canonical. On the other hand, the later writers did not intend to 'supplement' it in the sense of wanting to set their own Gospel alongside the previous one. For in this case there would have been no point in admitting certain of Mark's narratives into their own work. They simply wanted to write a new and independent Gospel, one

6 Origen, *Hom. I on Luke* (IX, 4 f.), endeavours to relate this ἐπεχείρησαν merely to apocryphal Gospels, the Gospel of the Egyptians and the Gospel of the Twelve Apostles. See also Eusebius, *H.E.*, 3.24. Origen was mistaken in thinking that the third evangelist intended severe criticism of his predecessors in using this word; the prologue simply means that his Gospel was designed to give a better picture.

which would do the greatest possible justice to the Church's understanding of Christ.

The same applies to the Gospel of John. Here, too, the question raised by Hans Windisch in the title of his book (published in 1926), which may be translated as [7] *John and the Synoptics: did the fourth evangelist intend to supplement or replace the earlier Gospels?* is not quite in accord with the facts, inasmuch as the evangelist did not intend either to 'supplement' or to 'replace' the Synoptists. Windisch himself rejects the supplementing theory and we heartily agree with him, for even if it can be shown that some of John's narratives presuppose events which we only know from the Synoptists, it must not be inferred that the writer did not record them simply because he thought his readers could look them up in the Synoptic Gospels. Even in the Johannine narratives which have no parallel at all in the Synoptic Gospels many purely historical details are omitted that one might well have expected in a really vivid report. On the other hand, the evangelist does write in 20.30 that there are 'many other signs' not recorded in this book, and that he had only written his Gospel 'that you may believe that Jesus is the Christ, the Son of God'. This surely does not mean that he wanted to refer his reader to other Gospels. He wanted rather to offer a self-sufficient Gospel describing the fact of Christ in accordance with the fundamental revelation which it contains. It should be noted, however, that this intention was not bound up with any polemical animus against his predecessors.[8]

This striving of each Gospel writer to do better than his predecessors, not attacking their works, however, but partly incorporating them in their own, could not but be of supreme service to the 'cause' in apostolic times. Admittedly, one result was a multiplicity of Gospels from the very outset. This plurality was based on the very real feeling that none of the previous attempts to describe the human life of Jesus could be considered entirely successful. The trend towards a multiplicity of Gospels existed from the very beginning. But it was accompanied by an opposite tendency to

[7] My addition. The German title given by Professor Cullmann is *Johannes und die Synoptiker: wollte der vierte Evangelist die ältern Evangelien ergänzen oder ersetzen?* [Ed.]

[8] In *Das Johannes-Evangelium* (ed. by C. A. Bernoulli, 1914, p. 481 f.) F. Overbeck advocated the 'supplanting' theory in its most extreme form. He relied on 21.20 f. to support the theory that the evangelist himself justified the canonizing of his Gospel, thereby indirectly occasioning the canonizing of the four Gospels.

reduce them all to a single Gospel. Every evangelist wanted to present the 'pure' Gospel, making use, though, of his predecessors' achievements. Thus the Gospels of Matthew and Luke can already be called Gospel harmonies. If the two-source theory, meaning two written sources, were beyond all doubt,[9] one could call the Gospels of Matthew and Luke a '*Diadyoin*', on the analogy of the Diatessaron written by Tatian; but on B. H. Streeter's hypothesis [10] more than two writings were combined.

The dual trend towards a multiplicity of Gospels and towards the reduction to a single Gospel underlies the whole of the subsequent development: on the one hand, Gospels are produced in vast numbers; on the other, a process of reduction or rejection becomes inevitable. But the difference from the apostolic age is that the increase in the number of Gospels is no longer conditioned primarily by the legitimate endeavour to pass on the testimony of the incarnate Lord more perfectly than before, but by all kinds of purely secular interests in legendary details, such as had already existed on the periphery of the earlier development of the Gospel tradition, but which now became predominant; and as the connection with the apostolic traditions weakens with the passing of time, so the results of the new trend become more and more questionable.[11] Therefore the tendency to reduce the number of Gospels is intensified and comes increasingly to the forefront as the idea of the canonical validity of Christian writings assumes more definite shape.

A logical reduction would have consisted in an outright return to one particular Gospel. And, in fact, only one Gospel was in use in some Churches long before the canon was finally settled. There is reason to believe that only the Gospel of Matthew was at all widely read in Palestine, that there were Churches in Asia Minor which only used the Gospel of John from the very outset, that in Egypt only the Gospel of the Egyptians was accepted as valid among the Gentile Christians.[12]

[9] The form-historical enquiries into the oral tradition have admittedly made it very doubtful whether the *logia* source is really a written source.

[10] B. H. Streeter, *The Four Gospels*, 1930.

[11] See Karl Ludwig Schmidt, *Kanonische und apokryphe Evangelien und Apostelgeschichten (Abhandlungen zur Theologie des A.u.N.T.,* 5), 1944.

[12] Clem. Alex., *Stromata*, I, 9, 63; III, 13, 93; Origen, *Hom. I. on Luke* (IX, 5). The Hebrew Gospel mentioned by Clem. Alex., *Stromata*, II, 9, 45 and V, 14, 96, and Origen, *Comm. on John* 2, 12.87 (IV, 67) was probably the only Gospel used by the Jewish Christians in Alexandria, as is also assumed by W. Bauer, *op. cit.*, p. 56.

It should now be easier to understand why the establishment of four canonical Gospels became such a problem. Why did the logical solution of reducing them to a single Gospel not prevail? From the historical point of view it should be noted that the mutual *rapprochement* of the various Churches, some of which took one Gospel as the norm, some another, contributed to the reduction not being carried out consistently but stopping as it were halfway at four Gospels.

The main theological explanation of this development, however, is the legitimate concern that we have seen to be the principal reason for the tendency to multiply the Gospels in the early period: the conviction that none of the Gospels had recorded the whole wealth of Christ as revealed in the incarnate Lord. The original tendency to a multiplicity of Gospels worked against the tendency to unity, so that some reduction took place but not a reduction to a single Gospel.

There is the additional factor that apostolicity was required as the criterion of authenticity. The example of Bishop Serapion of Antioch shows how in the last resort not only the name of the author but the actual content determined whether a Gospel was to be considered apostolic or not.[13] Purely legendary growths and Gnostic speculations formed the main tendency of most of the Gospels written between 150 and 200. This inevitably strengthened the desire to accept into the canon the few Gospels which displayed a really apostolic outlook and could be guaranteed to go back to the apostolic age. Thus it came about that the Gospels of Mark and Luke, which were only indirectly apostolic, were included in the canon as well as Matthew and John. It should be stated at once that this assessment of the Gospels of Mark and Luke was theologically correct, however accidental the grouping together of the four Gospels inevitably appeared. That the grouping of several Gospels in the canon was the theologically correct solution will be even more apparent when we have seen how false was the basic approach from which the attempt was made to replace this plurality of canonical Gospels by a single Gospel. On the other hand, we shall also see the falsity of the attitude which Irenaeus adopted to defend the fourfold Gospel.

[13] Eusebius, *H.E.*, 6.12. Confiding in the apostolic name, the Bishop had first allowed the reading of the Gospel of Peter. On closer investigation, however, he ascertained that the contents were of a Gnostic character and forbade its use.

(3) *The Various Attempts to replace the Four Gospels by a single one*

One way to eliminate the multiple Gospel was the one indicated by the evangelists of the apostolic age: to create a new Gospel. But the spiritual justification for such an undertaking which still existed in the apostolic age was lacking later on. In the post-apostolic age one of the purposes behind these endeavours was to supplant other Gospels. Thus we hear of a εὐαγγέλιον κατὰ Βασιλίδην.[14] It is not clear, however, if this was a harmony produced intentionally by Basilides or whether he claimed to have written an independent Gospel in the manner of the old evangelists, making a critical use of his predecessors' work. The fact that he maintained that he was in the direct succession of the apostles, through Glaucias, Peter's interpreter,[15] suggests the probability of the second hypothesis. In contrast to the old Gospels, however, this was very likely an early example of deliberate resistance to the plurality of the Gospels.

The same is true of the Gospel of Peter which was written in Syria probably about the middle of the second century. The fact that it was attributed to Peter is typical of the intention that lay behind it. We have seen that the four old Gospels—with the exception of the Gospel of John—were not ascribed to any particularly outstanding apostle. A Gospel that went out under the name of Peter, the spokesman of the apostles, would be likely to supplant all the others from the very outset and achieve such a degree of canonical authority that the other Gospels might well seem quite unnecessary.

In the same way we find the criterion of apostolicity combined with the tendency to unity in the title 'Gospel of the Twelve' which, according to Origen,[16] contains an apocryphal Jewish-Christian Gospel.[17] All twelve apostles were claimed to be responsible for the one Gospel. It is a document which claims to be independent, though in fact it keeps quite close to the Gospel of Matthew. Thus it was possible for one of the well-known old Gospels to take the place of the fourfold Gospel which was already becoming established. The fact that, as we have seen, a single Gospel had been used

[14] Origen, *Hom. I on Luke* (IX, 5).

[15] Clem. Alex., *Stromata*, VII, 106.4.

[16] *Hom. I on Luke* (IX, 5). The fact that Origen uses the genitive and not κατά is probably not intended to weaken his assertion regarding the authorship, as has sometimes been thought.

[17] See H. Waitz, *Z.N.T.W.*, 1912, p. 388 f.; A. Schmidtke, *Neue Fragmente und Untersuchungen zu den judenchristlichen Evangelien*, 1911; Waitz, *Z.N.T.W.*, 1937, p. 60 f.

from the very beginning in some areas made this all the easier. But whereas previously this use of a single Gospel had not been connected with any polemical intention, the exclusive preference for one of the four signified a deliberate rejection of the other three. In the same way the Gospel of John was played off against the Synoptics. Overbeck[18] and Harnack [19] have pointed out that by its very nature this Gospel 'tolerated no other gods beside it'.[20] The Muratorian canon reproduces a legend about the origin of the Gospel of John which could only have been originally intended to commend the fourth Gospel as *the* Gospel. According to the legend, John invited the other apostles to fast with him for three days. They were to tell one another what was revealed to them during this fasting. In the same night Andrew dreamt that John was to write down everything in their name and all the other disciples were to check what he wrote. Obviously the idea of the legend was to endow the Gospel of John with the combined authority of the twelve apostles and so make all other Gospels unnecessary. We learn from Irenaeus [21] that in Docetic circles—we do not know which—only the Gospel of Mark was recognized and among the Ebionites only the Gospel of Matthew.[22] The best known of all the attempts to confer exclusive authority on one of the four Gospels is that of Marcion. He singled out the Gospel of Luke as the one exclusively valid Gospel.[23] On the other hand, according to Tertullian,[24] he did so 'in order to smash it to pieces'. In fact, he was convinced that by his 'purifying of the text' he had restored the one original Gospel which Paul had received from Christ.[25]

What is particularly important for us, however, is that he gave classical expression to the principle that there could be only one Gospel. As chief witness he quotes the apostle Paul, who speaks of the Gospel in the singular in Romans 2.16, thereby clearly indicating that anything apart from the one Gospel must be a forgery.[26]

18 *Op. cit.*, p. 481 f.

19 *Op. cit.*, p. 49.

20 Irenaeus, *Adv. Haer.*, III, 11.7 says the Valentinians favoured the Gospel of John. On the other hand, Irenaeus writes (*ibid.*, III, 11.9) that they had a Gospel of their own, which they called '*evangelium veritatis*'.

21 *Adv. Haer.*, III, 11.17.

22 *Ibid.*

23 Irenaeus, *ibid.*, and Tertullian, *Adv. Marcionem*, 4.2.

24 Tertullian, *ibid.* Marcion also considered the connection of this Gospel with the name of Luke a falsification.

25 See Harnack, *Das Evangelium vom fremden Gott*, 2nd edn., 1924, p. 39 f.

26 Origen, *Comm. on John*, 5.7 (IV, 104 f.).

Origen was quite right to refute this exegesis, which was also adopted by Celsus.[27] But it shows that the sagacious Marcion clearly saw a widely-felt problem, though he solved it heretically by applying the all-too-consistent logic which was so typical of him.

In his Gospel harmony, the so-called Diatessaron, Tatian took quite a different line, though it had already been traced out to some extent in the old Gospels of the apostolic period. In this case the single Gospel was attained not by creating a new Gospel or by singling out one of the old Gospels, but by blending the four undisputed Gospels into one. This amalgamation was not brought about by a mere juxtaposition of our Gospels—a method that was considered inappropriate—but by harmonizing them. We have seen that, strictly speaking, the Gospels of Matthew and Luke are themselves Gospel harmonies. The new factor in Tatian's attempt is that he concentrates quite deliberately on harmonizing the four Gospels, and evidently intends to supplant the four canonical Gospels. It is still not quite clear if his secondary purpose was to work into the harmony other traditions to which he had access or even a fifth Gospel, or whether the deviations of certain of his narratives from our four Gospels are due to his use of a text different from ours. Many other problems of literary criticism arising from the Diatessaron still await solution.[28] This is not the place to deal with them, however.

That we are right to regard the plurality of the Gospels as one of the problems of the early Church is proved not so much by Tatian's experiment in itself as by its great success. The old Arabic translation as well as the Dutch translation discovered in 1923 [29] suggest that the Diatessaron must have circulated far beyond the confines of the Syriac Church. The authoritarian action which Theodoret was forced to take in the fifth century (confiscation of all copies of the Diatessaron) in order to replace the Diatessaron by the four separate Gospels [30] also shows that the fourfold Gospel was not yet taken for granted.

Tatian's attempt to produce a Gospel harmony was not the only

[27] *Contra Cels.*, 2.27. According to him the Christians had treated the Gospel 'like drunkards' by 'recoining it three and four and many times'.

[28] The Greek fragment from Dura discovered in 1935 has raised anew the question whether the original language was Greek or Syriac. See C. H. Kraeling, *A Greek Fragment of Tatian's Diatessaron from Dura*, 1935.

[29] It is based on an old Latin translation. See D. Plooij, *The Liège Diatessaron*, 1929.

[30] Theodoret, *Haer. fab. comp.* I. 20. See F. C. Burkitt, *Evangelion da-Mepharreshe*, 1904.

one. We hear that Bishop Theophilus of Antioch also combined the four Gospels in a harmony.[31] Unfortunately not a trace of this has been found. As already mentioned, it is impossible to know for certain how far Basilides's Gospel represents an intentional harmony, like Tatian's, or, as seems more probable, claimed, like the older Gospels, to be based on traditions and special knowledge of its own.[32]

(4) *The Basic Error of the Forcible Attempts to reduce the Number of the Gospels*

In the last resort all the various attempts to replace the four Gospels by a single Gospel originated in a basically Docetic tendency which overlooked the fact that the Gospel had to be recorded by several writers in the apostolic period, since it was impossible for this revelation, which claims to be more than mere biography, to be reproduced by one person in all its fullness. Gospels are intended not simply to state historical facts, but to proclaim a revealed religious truth based on historical facts. The revelation took place, however, on the human level. It is, therefore, Docetism to be scandalized by the fact that there is apparently no deeper reason why the oldest Gospels to come down to us were written by these four particular men. The plurality of the Gospels, the fact that there are four Gospels, is simply an expression of the human way in which the Gospels originated. That the revelation is clothed in this completely human garb; that the unity, the one divine εὐαγγέλιον of Christ resides within the human multiplicity of the four Gospels: this is just what the New Testament means by faith. It is the same faith that confesses that the man Jesus of Nazareth is Christ, that the Church which consists of sinners represents the body of Christ.

It is no mere accident that the men who were responsible for the various attempts to replace the four Gospels by a single Gospel upheld a conception of Christian teaching differing from the New Testament, and were therefore heretics: Basilides, the Valentinians, the author of the Gospel of Peter, Marcion, Tatian. They were all Gnostics, that is, more or less Docetists, and it is also no accident that Irenaeus mentions that the 'Docetists' only recognized one Gospel, that of Mark. We shall see, however, that even the oldest

31 Jerome, *Ep.*, 121, 6.15.
32 But it might be permissible, from a purely historical point of view, to regard the liberal 'Lives of Jesus', examined and rejected by Albert Schweitzer, *mutatis mutandis*, as attempts undertaken with the modern resources of scholarship to create a scientifically valid Gospel harmony.

justification of the fourfold Gospel, which derives from Irenaeus, is based on the same fundamental error as the Gnostics' arguments against it.

(5) *The False Reasons for the Fourfold Gospel propounded by Irenaeus*

The pains which Irenaeus took in this matter [33] demonstrate once again how necessary it was to defend the fourfold Gospel in the early Church—obviously it was still widely felt that the number had been chosen quite arbitrarily. But the way Irenaeus solved the problem was precisely the way it ought not to have been solved. He tried to show that the fourfold Gospel was in no way based simply on the historical situation of the Apostolic Church, but that the number four was a divinely ordained number essential to salvation. The fourfold Gospel tallied with the significance of the number four in all the divine institutions of creation and redemption. The world was governed by the number four: there were four points of the compass, four main winds. Thus the Church, which was dispersed throughout the world, must rest on four pillars, in other words, the four Gospels. The whole scheme of salvation was based on the divine number of four. God had bestowed four covenants on man: the covenants with Noah, Abraham, Moses and Christ. Irenaeus dwells, however, with special affection on the four living creatures of Ezekiel (1.10) and the Revelation of John (4.7) in which he sees a representation of the four Gospels—an idea, by the way, which was to influence Christian art, though later on the parts of the four beasts were distributed differently among the evangelists.[34] By means of an exegesis which is quite subtle in parts, the Gospel of John, which begins with the glorious story of how Christ was begotten from the Father, is connected with the 'royal' beast, the lion; the Gospel of Luke, which has a priestly character (Zechariah!, the fatted calf of Luke 15.23!) is connected with the young bull; the Gospel of Matthew, which begins with the genealogical tree of the human race, is associated with the beast that had a man's look; and the 'short and swiftly moving' Gospel of Mark is likened to the eagle. And so Irenaeus concludes: 'The beasts are fourfold; the Gospel is fourfold; the divine scheme of salvation is fourfold.' 'Since God made all things to number, so the Gospel had to be written thus and had to be based on a certain number.'

[33] *Adv. Haer.*, III, 11.8.
[34] See T. Zahn, *Forschungen zur Geschichte des neutestamentlichen Kanons*, II, p. 257 f.

Irenaeus, therefore, represents the fourfold Gospel as a miracle. He tries to show that it is not based on a purely human situation at all. But this line of argument leads him into dangerous waters. For it means that at bottom he admits that purely human circumstances were left out of account when the Gospels were formed into a group. He fails to appreciate the fact on which the plurality of the Gospels was based even in the apostolic age: the fact that the immeasurable fulness of the truth about the Christ who appeared in the flesh cannot be exhausted by the evangelists, because they are only humanly imperfect instruments of the divine revelation, and that it was absolutely necessary for all the available records of the life of Jesus, deriving from apostolic times, to be collected. Irenaeus failed to see that this stumbling-block of the humanly inadequate communication of divine revelation must be accepted, since, according to the New Testament, it is the beginning and end of the Christian faith that God became man in Jesus, and his Church on earth is made up of imperfect human beings involved in a process determined by historical circumstances.

(6) *The Theologically Correct Reasons for the Fourfold Gospel*

The problem under discussion cannot be solved by the artificial theory of a miraculous origin of the Gospel canon exempt from human agency. In the face of these false solutions one is bound to admire the astonishing historical and theological assurance with which the Church proceeded when it settled on the fourfold canon. It abstained from seeking for uniformity in the writings of the evangelists. It simply held fast to all the Gospels from the apostolic age to which it had access, and without any hesitation it put two more or less representative apostles alongside two less-well-known figures from the apostolic age. It accepted this lack of uniformity and the risk of arousing the impression that the whole procedure was based on mere chance. It did not merely rely on the authors' names but, as we learn from the story of Bishop Serapion [35] and indirectly by comparing our four canonical Gospels with the apocryphal Gospels, it examined the contents of the various lives, thereby interpreting the postulate of apostolicity correctly. The efforts to establish the formal apostolicity of the four Gospels which soon began in the Church may be regarded as an attempt to confirm the rightness of the original judgment.

[35] See above, n. 13.

Besides his theologically valueless speculation on the fourfold Gospel Irenaeus provides a valuable hint regarding the correct theological argument for the fourfold canon, which consists in seeking the uniformity of the Gospel in the material itself, that is to say, in the one Gospel which the individual evangelist sees, from a different angle. Irenaeus writes that 'the fourfold Gospel is sustained by the *one* Spirit: ἐνὶ πνεύματι συνεχόμενον.[36] There is also a reference to this fundamental uniformity in the Muratorian Canon which is much nearer the mark than the legend about the origin of the Gospel of John which is preserved in the same document: 'Even though different beginnings are recorded in the Gospels, this need not have the slightest effect on the beliefs of the faithful, since everything is explained by the one Spirit that informs all of them.' In the same vein Origen replies to Marcion's assertion, which was adopted by Celsus, that there could only be one written Gospel, apart from which all others must be forgeries,[37] by saying that 'it is one Lord who is preached by all'.[38]

The description of the Gospels as εὐαγγέλιον κατὰ Μαθθαῖον, κατὰ Μάρκον, κατὰ Λουκᾶν, κατὰ 'Ιωάννην,[39] which had probably become current by the middle of the second century, best does justice both to the true unity of the four Gospels and the necessity of having a number of different authors. It is a question of combining different witnesses to the one Gospel.

This argument in favour of a plurality of Gospels is in accord with the results of modern research into the historical origins of the Gospel tradition which we owe to form-criticism. According to this, the early evangelists were merely collectors of a tradition created by the Church and its needs. These needs of the early Church were the basis of the true unity of the oral tradition. This does not necessarily cut out the literary individuality of the various evangelists. But that individuality must not be measured by the criteria of secular writing. The ecclesiastical argument for the fourfold Gospel, as expressed in the headings to the Gospels with their reference to the common subject-matter, is only intelligible if it is realized that our Gospels are not biographies, not 'memoirs of the apostles', as

[36] *Adv. Haer.*, III, 11.8.
[37] See above, n. 26.
[38] *Comm. on John*, 5.7 (IV, 104 f.). On Origen's attitude to the Gospels see the fundamental work by Einar Molland, *The Conception of the Gospel in the Alexandrian Theology*, 1938.
[39] It is generally assumed now that κατά signifies direct and not merely indirect authorship.

Justin wrongly calls them, but just testimonies to the faith, all of which originated in one and the same oral tradition of the early Church seen from different points of view.[40]

Four *biographies* of the same life could not be set alongside one another as of equal value, but would have to be harmonized and reduced to a single biography in some way or other.[41] Four Gospels, that is, four books dealing with the content of a faith, cannot be harmonized, but require by their very nature to be set alongside one another. And in any case the faith cries out for manifold witness.

[40] In this connection Karl Ludwig Schmidt also refers to the headings of the Gospels in *Le problème du christianisme primitif*, 1938, p. 23.

[41] On the difficulty which was felt with regard to the books of the Chronicles owing to their parallelism to the books of the Kings, when the Hebrew canon was being settled, see above, p. 41.

IV

The Tradition

The Exegetical, Historical and Theological Problem

> And beginning with Moses and all the prophets, he interpreted to them in all the scriptures the things concerning himself. And their eyes were opened and they knew him. They said to each other, Did not our hearts burn within us . . . while he opened to us the scriptures?
>
> LUKE 24.27, 31, 32.

Translated from *La Tradition*, 1953, Neuchâtel

Foreword

THE VERY HIGH LEVEL and the objectivity of almost all Catholic reactions to my book on St. Peter [1] encourage me to continue the ecumenical debate in the same spirit of candour and honesty. Later I hope to take up again the main themes of the discussion arising out of that book. But here, as a preliminary to that, my aim is to present the results of my study of the problem of the tradition. This question, as Père Daniélou has rightly observed,[2] is closely connected with the subject of my book on St. Peter. Thus these two works are complementary one to the other: that on St. Peter raises the problem of the tradition, that on the tradition the problem of St. Peter.

In September 1949 I read a paper entitled '*Kyrios* as Designation for the Oral Tradition concerning Jesus (*Paradosis* and *Kyrios*)' to the *Studiorum Novi Testamenti Societas* at Oxford.[3] Since this was a strictly exegetical study, I made hardly any reference to the dogmatic problem of 'scripture and tradition'. But in June 1952 a group of Catholic and Protestant friends invited me to address them on this very question. The paper read on that occasion has been published,[4] and Père Daniélou has written a reply to it,[5] in which, while strongly opposing my arguments, he preserves throughout an admirable spirit of scientific objectivity. Although his arguments do not all seem to me to have the same force, most of his objections are interesting and instructive and, in my opinion, are a contribution to progress in the debate.

In this reply, as in most of the Catholic reviews of my book on St. Peter, one argument especially is brought forward: scripture, a collection of books, is not sufficient to actualize for us the divine revelation granted to the apostles. I believe the answer to this is to

[1] *Peter: Disciple—Apostle—Martyr*, E.T., 1953.
[2] *Dieu vivant*, no. 24, p. 115.
[3] Published in *Scottish Journal of Theology*, 1950, p. 180 f., and in *R.H.P.R.*, 1950, p. 12 f.
[4] In *Dieu vivant*, no. 23, p. 47 f. (and, as 'Scripture and Tradition', in *Scottish Journal of Theology*, 1953, p. 113 f. [Ed.])
[5] 'Réponse à Oscar Cullmann', *Dieu vivant*, no. 24, p. 107 f.

be found in the former of my two articles mentioned above. For this reason I have adapted it to fit the plan of the present work of which it now forms the first section and, so to speak, the foundation. The second and third sections reproduce the substance of my article 'Scripture and Tradition', but on almost every page account is taken of criticisms of the article in its original form made by Catholic scholars and especially by Père Daniélou in *Dieu vivant*.[6] Thus the present synthesis of my earlier writings on the tradition represents a new orientation, but the main theses remain unchanged.

I should like, in conclusion, to repeat the wish expressed in the preface of my book on St. Peter, which I have seen to a considerable extent already realized. This is that the present discussion, without arousing false hopes or illusions, should really bring us together by our common effort to seek the truth in obedience to Christ, and by the sincere desire to understand one another better, without reserve, but also without forgetting that, on whichever side we stand, we call upon the same Lord.

[6] Henceforth abbreviated as Daniélou, 'Rép'.

The Tradition

The Problem

On the old problem of 'scripture and tradition' everything possible would seem to have been said. In taking it up here my purpose is to turn the debate in a particular direction. I wish to show that the New Testament speaks very positively of a tradition, namely, the tradition of the apostles, while it resolutely rejects the so-called explanatory tradition which the rabbis placed alongside and even above the Old Testament scriptures. In other words, I wish to apply the problem of scripture and tradition to the apostolic and post-apostolic tradition. I use the term 'apostolic' in its strict historical sense, and not in the extended sense often given to it by Catholic scholars who identify apostolic and ecclesiastical tradition.[7]

Firstly, I shall try to prove that the New Testament regards the Lord exalted to the right hand of God as the direct author of the tradition of the apostles, because he himself is at work in the apostolic transmission of his words and deeds. Secondly, by examining the conception of the apostolate, I shall attempt to determine the connection between the apostolic tradition and the post-apostolic tradition and the difference between them. Thirdly, I shall enquire whether this distinction is confirmed by the history of the early Church, and whether, in creating the canon, the Church itself deliberately separated apostolic from ecclesiastical tradition, so as to make the former the norm of the latter.

(1) *The Apostolic Tradition and the Lord exalted to the right hand of God (Paradosis and Kyrios)*

The work of the form-critics on the Gospels has directed our attention more than ever before to the development of the oral

[7] See J. N. Bakhuizen van der Brink, *Traditio in de Reformatie en het Katholicisme in de 16e euw. (Medelingen der Kon. ned. Ak. van Wetenschappen, afd. Letterkunde*, N. R. XV, 1952), p. 28. This important work on the sixteenth-century controversy points out other distinctions to be made in the use of the word 'tradition' or 'traditions', especially that between *traditio activa*, which is a function of the Church, and *traditiones passivae*, i.e. the formulae themselves. The writer thinks agreement is possible on the former, which, in the view of the Reformers, is confirmed by scripture.

tradition which preceded the fixing of our Gospels in writing. Whether the Gospel material was, at least partially, already written down in smaller collections of single or several words of Jesus or of narratives about him, or whether, as with the oldest Jewish traditions, it was only transmitted orally, is not a question of primary importance here. Besides, it would be impossible to determine with any exactness the contents of such collections. That is also true, as M. Dibelius has rightly stressed, of the much-quoted Q source.[8] Accordingly, the whole stream of tradition, whether oral or written, in so far as it is not yet channelled in our Gospels, is to be handled as a unit.

When we speak of the traditions in the early Church, we must constantly bear in mind the parallel in the Jewish tradition of the rabbis. We shall see that the apostle Paul used exactly the same Greek word, παράδοσις, which was familiar to him from his Jewish past as the pupil of Rabbi Gamaliel. But Jesus rejected in a radical manner the *paradosis* of the Jews. How, then, could Paul without more ado apply this apparently discredited notion to the moral precepts and doctrines which the early Church regarded as normative?

The problem is still further complicated by the fact that, instead of 'tradition', Paul sometimes says 'the Lord' (*Kyrios*), as, for example, in quoting words of Jesus (I Thess. 4.15; I Cor. 7.10, 25; 9.14).

In I Corinthians 11.23 he joins these two expressions when he writes: 'I received (the tradition) from the Lord'. There follows the account of the institution of the Lord's Supper: 'The Lord Jesus in the night in which he was betrayed . . .' 'Εγὼ παρέλαβον ἀπὸ τοῦ κυρίου. Why 'from *Kyrios*'? Why not 'from the Church'?

This passage is usually, but wrongly, treated in isolation, and has given rise to two different interpretations. The one maintains that the passage is not concerned with tradition in the usual Jewish sense, which would necessitate the presupposition of a chain of successive human intermediaries, from whom Paul received the account, but that it is a question of a direct, immediate revelation from the Lord. This came to Paul in a vision, just as in Galatians 1.12 he asserts that he has not received the Gospel from men, but by a direct revelation, an *apokalypsis*—an obvious reference to Christ's appearing on the road to Damascus. This interpretation was given by Lefèvre d'Étaples, followed by Bengel in his *Gnomon*. More recently it has

[8] *From Tradition to Gospel*, E.T., 1934, p. 233 f.

been taken up with special emphasis by F. Godet,[9] by A. Loisy,[10] who wrongly regards this whole passage as an interpolation, and by W. Heitmüller.[11] The French deniers of the historical existence of Jesus, P. L. Couchoud [12] and P. Alfaric [13] have used the same explanation in support of their theories. They believe that they can find in this passage a sort of classic example of the one source of stories about Jesus: Paul had a vision, and made its content into history.

If this interpretation of I Corinthians 11.23 is right, that is, if the words 'I received from the Lord' mean 'I received the account of the institution of the Lord's Supper directly in a vision from the Lord', then this passage will have nothing to do with the problem of 'the tradition' which we are discussing. It will not deal at all with transmission of tradition in the Church.

However, the great majority of scholars of all shades of opinion agree that this interpretation is not accurate, and that the words: 'I received from the Lord' do not exclude the normal transmission of tradition in the Church. I mention here H. Lietzmann,[14] J. Weiss,[15] E. B. Allo,[16] J. Héring,[17] R. Bultmann.[18] Also M. Goguel has shown, against the deniers of the historical existence of Jesus already mentioned, that in reality these words presuppose a historical transmission of the facts.[19]

There is, then, agreement among many scholars of different schools and even confessions. But if this interpretation is correct, why does Paul use the surprising expression 'from the Lord' in referring to a tradition he has received from the Church? Here, though differing a little in detail, the various interpretations more or less agree that with the preposition ἀπό Paul points to the

9 *Commentaire sur la première Épître aux Corinthiens*, ii (1887), p. 160 f.
10 'Les origines de la Cène eucharistique' (*Congrès d'histoire du christianisme* i, p. 77 f.).
11 'Zum Problem Paulus und Jesus', *Z.N.T.W.*, 1912, p. 321.
12 *Le mystère de Jésus*, 1924, p. 141.
13 'Le Jésus de Paul', *R.H.P.R.*, 1927, p. 276 f.
14 *An die Korinther I–II (Handbuch zum N.T.)*, 4th edn. by W. G. Kümmel, 1949, p. 57, and see Kümmel's note, p. 185.
15 *Der erste Korintherbrief (Krit. exeg. Kommentar zum N.T.)*, 1910, p. 283.
16 *Première Épître aux Corinthiens*, 2nd edn., 1934.
17 *La première Épître de saint Paul aux Corinthiens (Commentaire du N.T.)*, 1949, p. 100.
18 *Theology of the New Testament*, E.T., vol. i, 1952, p. 150.
19 'La relation du dernier repas de Jésus dans I Cor. 11 et la tradition historique chez l'apôtre Paul', *R.H.P.R.*, 1930, p. 61 f.

chronological origin of the whole presupposed chain of tradition, and the words 'I received it *from the Lord*' mean 'I received it through a chain of tradition which *begins* with the Lord'.

This solution of the difficulty will have to be tested, but first it must be pointed out that this is a hypothesis and that we are bound to use a hypothesis in the attempt to answer this question why the words ἀπὸ τοῦ κυρίου are used in this particular case. I wish, however, to propose a somewhat different hypothesis. I agree with the great majority of scholars that I Corinthians 11.23 does not refer to a vision, but to a tradition of the Church; but I differ as regards the words 'from the Lord', which I shall attempt to interpret within the framework of the whole problem of *paradosis* in the New Testament. I shall show that, seen in this perspective, the designation *Kyrios* can be understood as not only pointing to the historical Jesus as the chronological beginning and the first link of the chain of tradition, but to the exalted Lord as the real author of the whole tradition developing itself within the apostolic Church. This hypothesis best explains St. Paul's direct identification of the apostolic *paradosis* with *Kyrios*: the Lord himself is at work in the transmission of his words and deeds by the Church; he works through the Church.

This idea is assumed already in Chrysostom's interpretation of our passage, when he writes (*Hom.* 27.4): 'For today also it is the same one who produces and delivers everything, even as at that time'. This statement of his, however, needs qualification. The text of Paul does not justify the attribution to the Lord of all later Church tradition till 'today'. Nevertheless, as regards the *apostolic* tradition, Chrysostom seems to have defined correctly the connection in the New Testament between *paradosis* and *Kyrios*.

The course of our argument in this chapter will now be as follows. In the first section we shall undertake to show that for Paul the *paradosis*, in so far as it refers to the confession of faith and to the words and deeds of Jesus, is really Church tradition which has a parallel in the Jewish *paradosis*.[20] In the second section we shall bring out the relation of this tradition to the direct *apokalypsis* of the Lord to the apostles. In the third section we shall examine this

[20] This point seems important because J. Daniélou ('Rép.', especially p. 110 f.) is inclined to reserve the word 'tradition' for the post-apostolic tradition, and to call the apostolic tradition 'revelation'. While justifiable to a certain extent in principle, this use of the words seems to me to lack precision. The objective revelation is the person and work of the incarnate Christ.

conception of *paradosis* against the background of Pauline theology and see if it is paralleled in Johannine thought. Finally, in the fourth section, we shall discuss the relation between this tradition and the apostolic office.

(*a*) Jesus and the early Church lived in an atmosphere entirely permeated with the concept of tradition. Rabbinic interpretation of scripture had been placed more and more as a norm alongside and even above scripture. Jesus rejected this whole παράδοσις τῶν πρεσβυτέρων as the work of men which, instead of explaining scripture, set it aside (Mark 7.3 f.; Matt. 15.2). The slogan of pious Jews was 'hold fast the tradition' (κρατεῖν τὴν παράδοσιν, Mark 7.8). Jesus took it up in his ironical saying: 'You leave the commandment of God, and hold fast the tradition of men' (Mark 7.8).

But in the Pauline epistles we find the whole Jewish *paradosis* terminology, and, what is more, we find it used in a definitely positive way, as in the exhortation to the Thessalonians: 'Hold the traditions' (κρατεῖτε τὰς παραδόσεις, II Thess. 2.15). Also we find the other expressions connected with the idea of tradition used very like technical terms: the synonym for κρατεῖν: κατέχειν (I Cor. 11.2; 15.2); 'stand in the tradition' (στήκετε, I Cor. 15.1; II Thess. 2.15); and especially 'receive' and 'deliver' (παραλαμβάνειν, παραδιδόναι, I Cor. 11.2, 23; 15.3; I Thess. 2.13; II Thess. 2.15; 3.6; Rom. 6.17; Gal. 1.9, 12; Phil. 4.9; Col. 2.6, 8).[21]

It is a mistake to try to find the origin of these terms, as E. Norden[22] does, in the language of the Hellenistic mystery religions. It is quite clear that this whole terminology is Jewish in origin. παραλαμβάνειν is the translation of the Hebrew *qibbel min*, παραδιδόναι of the Hebrew *masar le*. And the exact correspondence of the two Pauline passages in I Corinthians shows that it is a matter of purely formal expressions:[23]

I Corinthians 11.23: (ἐγὼ) παρέλαβον (ἀπὸ τοῦ κυρίου) ὃ καὶ παρέδωκα ὑμῖν.

I Corinthians 15.3: παρέδωκα ὑμῖν (ἐν πρώτοις) ὃ καὶ παρέλαβον. The verbs in the principal and subordinate clauses are simply interchanged. This is because the very essence of tradition is that it forms a chain. At all events it is clear that these are Jewish formulae, by which the rabbis refer to the *halakha* and the *haggada*. In the other

---

[21] On the expression φυλάττειν παραθήκην in I Tim. 6.20; II Tim. 1.14, see C. Spicq, 'Saint Paul et la loi des dépôts', *R. B.*, 1931, p. 481 f.

[22] *Agnostos Theos*, 1913, p. 267 f.

[23] See J. Jeremias, *The Eucharistic Words of Jesus*, E.T., 1955, p. 129 f.

passages mentioned above it is sometimes Paul, sometimes the Church, which 'received'.

The word καί must also be particularly noticed, for it certainly belongs to the formula derived from the *paradosis* terminology. We find it not only in I Corinthians 11.23 and I Corinthians 15.3, but also in I Corinthians 15.1: τὸ εὐαγγέλιον . . . ὃ καὶ παρελάβετε. E. B. Allo [24] has rightly pointed out that in I Corinthians 11.23 this καί must refer to the manner of transmission: 'I received the tradition in the same way as I handed it on to you—by *mediation*'.

This throws light also on the addition, ἀπὸ τοῦ κυρίου, in I Corinthians 11.23, which then does not exclude mediation. Although this addition does not occur in I Corinthians 15.3 f., the form of expression is exactly parallel, and so a chain of tradition is presupposed there also. J. Jeremias [25] has shown that in I Corinthians 15.3 f. the content of the *paradosis*, which is introduced with this formula, is linguistically un-Pauline. This is a further indication that Paul has taken over a text already fixed before him. The same must be true of I Corinthians 11.23, even though Paul declares that he has received the account of the institution of the Lord's Supper 'from the Lord'. Moreover, M. Goguel [26] and recently also R. Bultmann [27] rightly maintain that this account could not have been written down by Paul on the basis of a vision, because it clearly represents a more developed stage of the tradition than the parallel Synoptic accounts.

But what is the *content* of the παράδοσις according to St. Paul? Firstly, moral rules which, after the fashion of the *halakha*, concern the life of the faithful (e.g. I Cor. 11.2; II Thess. 3.6; Rom. 6.17; Phil. 4.9; Col. 2.6) [28]; secondly, a summary of the Christian message expressed as a formula of faith and uniting facts of the life of Jesus and their theological interpretation (e.g. I Cor. 15.3 f.); and lastly, single narratives from the life of Jesus (e.g. I Cor. 11.23).

The primitive *paradosis* probably consisted of a summary of the *kerygma*. But by the time of Paul the tradition had gone a step further

[24] *Op. cit.*, p. 311.
[25] *Op. cit.*, p. 129 f.
[26] *Op. cit.*, p. 75.
[27] *Op. cit.*, p. 150.
[28] J. J. von Allmen has dealt in particular with the rules of sexual and conjugal morality transmitted by Paul as elements of the tradition (*Maris et femmes d'après saint Paul (Cah. théol.* 29, 1951), p. 20, n. 4). Cf. also E. Hirsch, 'Eine Randglosse zu I Cor. 7', *Zeitschr. f. syst. Theol.*, 1925, p. 50 f., who in places approaches our thesis.

and now also had as its subject words of Jesus and narratives from his life. As regards the words of Jesus, this tradition appears already very advanced. They must have played a more important role than the relatively small number of words of Jesus quoted by Paul (I Thess. 4.15; I Cor. 7.10; 9.14) would lead us to suppose. The way in which Paul uses these words, especially in I Corinthians 7, proves that the *paradosis* of these words was already very extensive and sharply marked out: he clearly distinguishes between the instructions which he himself gives as an apostle and those which the Lord gives. Especially instructive is verse 25, where he says that on the subject of virgins he has no instructions from the *Kyrios*. Since Paul emphasizes that in this particular case he has no words of the Lord at his disposal, we may presume that in general the *paradosis* contained such words dealing with the most detailed aspects of conduct.

At any rate it is certain that the words of Jesus which Paul takes from the *paradosis* belong to the same class as the kerygmatic formula in I Corinthians 15.3 and the story from the life of Jesus in I Corinthians 11.23.

All these are cases of traditions which the apostle has received from others and hands on, just as the rabbi received and handed on the traditions of the interpretation of the law.[29] The authority with which the rabbi transmits tradition has here passed over to the apostle. The *tanna* of the Jews is replaced by the *apostolos* of Christ. When, as Paul says, he went to Jerusalem to meet the apostle Cephas (Gal. 1.18), it is more than likely that his object was to receive tradition from him.[30] For just as one rabbi could only receive tradition from another rabbi, so one apostle can only receive tradition at first hand from another apostle. It is true that Paul did not go to Jerusalem until three years after his conversion, but very probably while at Damascus he had already become acquainted with the apostolic traditions as they circulated in that area. It is impossible, however, to distinguish with certainty what traditions Paul may have received at Jerusalem, Damascus or Antioch, and

[29] See on this P. Carrington, *The Primitive Christian Catechism*, 1940, p. 67 f.

[30] P. H. Menoud, 'Revelation and Tradition: The Influence of Paul's Conversion on his Theology', *Interpretation*, 1953, p. 131 f., insists that since Paul's revelation on the Damascus road amounted to a *christological* affirmation, he was bound to combine this revelation with the tradition about Jesus for which he had to refer to those who alone could give it to him. This is correct. But I wish to point out that the connection between revelation and tradition is closer still, because both go back to the same Lord.

we must reckon with all three possibilities.[31] Nevertheless, it must be understood that the legitimate agent of the tradition is the apostle—not only one of the Twelve, but apostle in the wider sense of an eye-witness, one who 'had seen the Lord'. When Marcion cut out the words ὁ καὶ παρέλαβον in I Corinthians 15.3, he did so because he interpreted them as implying Paul's dependence on the Twelve—an interpretation which, in principle, is correct.

The analogy of the Jewish tradition raises the question whether all these traditions about Christ (*kerygma*, words of Jesus, narratives) ought to be considered as the sole true interpretation of the law of the Old Testament. This at any rate seems to be indicated by the words κατὰ τὰς γραφάς in the traditional formula in I Corinthians 15.3 f. And so we must ask *whether Jesus Christ the 'Lord', as the fulfilment of the law, does not take the place of all Jewish paradosis.*

If so, we understand the fact with which we began, and which is by no means intelligible in itself, that Paul applied to the Christian message the very concept of the *paradosis* which Jesus so decisively rejected. For in Christ alone can there be a tradition which is not παράδοσις τῶν ἀνθρώπων.

This brings us to our main problem: How is Paul able to designate the tradition concerning Jesus as *Kyrios*?

(*b*) A contradiction has long been felt between Galatians 1.12, where Paul emphasizes that he did not receive his Gospel 'from man' and passages where he appeals to traditions which he can only have received through mediation. Calvin sought to resolve the difficulty of Galatians 1.12 by suggesting that in Acts 9.10 f. Ananias plays the part of a human mediator, and remarked that direct divine revelation and human mediation, which God uses, go together. But, in my view, the connection is closer than this.

Modern exegetes try to solve the apparent contradiction by distinguishing between historical facts and their theological interpretation. The facts Paul was able to discover only through human mediation; what was revealed to him by a direct *apokalypsis* from the Lord was the theological understanding of these facts, in other words the 'gospel' of which he speaks in Galatians 1.12.

This distinction may stand in itself. In the previous section we have described the content of the *paradosis* as the summary of faith, words of Jesus, and single narratives. Now we can add the εὐαγγέλιον as interpretation of the facts in the sense of Galatians 1.12. But this

---

[31] J. Jeremias, *op. cit.*, p. 131, for instance, assigns the tradition in I Cor. 11.23 f. to the Church of Antioch, J. Héring, *op. cit.*, p. 100, to the Church of Damascus.

is not to be regarded as one element alongside others, since neither Paul nor the early Church made a conscious distinction between different elements of the *paradosis*. Confirmation of this is to be found in the combination of facts and theological interpretations such as we find in the formula of I Corinthians 15.3 f. Here Paul clearly attributes *both* to tradition, and we cannot claim that he received the facts alone through human intermediaries and their interpreta- tion through direct revelation. Of course, Galatians 1.12 does not deal with facts, but with their kerygmatic interpretation. Neverthe- less, interpretation implies the facts, just as these include interpreta- tion.

This is confirmed by the particular *paradosis* which Paul in I Corinthians 11.23 expressly states he has received 'from the Lord'. At first sight this phrase suggests that this *paradosis*, like the revela- tion on the road to Damascus, is going to be a case of theological interpretation; whereas in reality it is a factual account of the last meal of Jesus. Thus we understand why Paul is not aware of any contradiction when he says that he has received his gospel without human intermediaries, despite the fact that he refers to traditions which have been transmitted to him.

Most critics take the words 'from the Lord' to mean that the Lord is merely the first link of a chain to whom others have succeeded up to Paul. 'The Lord', then, is the historical Jesus and not the exalted Lord. In support of this explanation, which is at present the most popular one, it is generally argued that Paul does not use here the preposition παρά, as is usual with the verb παραλαμβάνειν, but ἀπό. But this argument is not as weighty as is usually supposed, for the difference between παρά and ἀπό is not fundamental in this case. If it is said that ἀπό indicates only the *direction* of the origin, and not the *immediate* origin, the same can apply to παρά. Besides, there is at least one example in Paul where ἀπό unquestionably denotes the *immediate* origin of a communication, Colossians 1.7: 'as you learned from Epaphras' (ἐμάθετε ἀπὸ Ἐπαφρᾶ).

In actual fact, then, it is the exalted Christ who is meant, and not the historical Jesus. And yet Paul is not thinking of a special vision nor of the revelation on the road to Damascus, as H. Lietzmann agrees when he says that for Paul 'everything he has heard about Jesus before and after his conversion is fused together and appears to him as a single stream flowing from the revelation at Damascus'.[32] As in I Corinthians 15.3 f., Paul is using a tradition handed down

[32] *Op. cit.*, p. 57. Cf. also *Messe und Herrenmahl*, 1926, p. 255.

THE EARLY CHURCH

to him by intermediaries. The formula of I Corinthians 11.23 refers to the Christ who is present, in that he stands behind the transmission of the tradition, that is, he works *in* it. The words ἀπὸ τοῦ κυρίου can quite well mean a direct communication from the Lord, without it being necessary to think of a vision or to exclude intermediaries through whom the Lord himself transmits the *paradosis*. In the last section of this chapter we shall show that these intermediaries are the apostles, and that their essential function is to be bearers of direct revelation, one being concerned with one fact, another with another, so that they are dependent upon one another. But it is the united testimony of all the apostles which constitutes the Christian *paradosis*, in which the *Kyrios* himself is at work.

In this way we can understand why both the tradition of the words of Jesus and that of narratives of his life are attributed to the exalted Lord. *Kyrios*, when introducing the words of Jesus, is not to be understood otherwise than as in I Corinthians 11.23, which is a narrative. This is also confirmed by Colossians 2.6: 'you received (by tradition, παρελάβετε) Christ Jesus the Lord'. The context deals with instructions of Christ according to which the faithful should 'walk' (περιπατεῖν), and in verse 8 this *paradosis* is expressly distinguished from all 'tradition of men' (παράδοσις τῶν ἀνθρώπων) as it is spread abroad by the heretics. In Colossians 2.6 the *Kyrios* appears as the content of the *paradosis*, but he is at one and the same time *its content and its author*.

This conclusion is also to be drawn from the use of the present tense in I Corinthians 7.10: 'To the married I give charge, not I, but the Lord' (παραγγέλλω). Chr. F. Baur drew attention to this present tense. *It is the exalted Lord who now proclaims to the Corinthians, through the tradition, what he had taught his disciples during his incarnation on earth.*[33]

It is true that the historic tense, the aorist, διέταξεν, is found in I Corinthians 9.14 (in I Thess. 4.15 the question cannot be definitely decided, but the words λέγομεν ἐν λόγῳ κυρίου presuppose likewise the past tense). The alternation between the present and the aorist shows, in this case also, that the exalted Lord and the earthly Jesus are regarded as one and the same person. The exalted Christ himself, after his resurrection, delivers the words he had spoken during his incarnation. In addition one could mention that the verb

[33] There is an analogy in Eph. 4.21, where the readers are referred to Christ *whom they have heard* (εἴγε αὐτὸν ἠκούσατε), although they never met him in Palestine.

παραγγέλλω in I Corinthians 7.10 contains the preposition παρά which is characteristic of the *paradosis* terminology, and that for this reason Paul may have chosen this verb deliberately.

In his study of εὐαγγέλιον, which is important for our subject, E. Molland,[34] following J. Schniewind,[35] has shown that in the expression εὐαγγέλιον Χριστοῦ, in Romans 15.19 and other passages, the genitive Χριστοῦ is subjective, so that here again appears the same complex fact of which we are speaking: the risen Christ is himself the author of the gospel, of which he is also the object. He is both subject and object.

Our conclusion is that the resolution of the difference between Paul's claim to have received the gospel directly from the Lord and the fact established in our first section that he received παραδόσεις from others consists in the belief that the exalted Christ himself stands as transmitter behind the apostles who transmit his words and works. Paul can place on the same level the revelation on the road to Damascus and the apostolic tradition he has received, because in both Christ is directly at work.

(c) It now remains to inquire whether this conception of the *Kyrios* as the author of the *paradosis* of Christ is basic to Pauline theology and whether it is also attested in the rest of the New Testament.

First of all it must be remembered that, according to the Synoptic Gospels, Jesus himself had a definite conception of the παράδοσις τῶν πρεσβυτέρων and of its relation to scripture. He contrasted it as a παράδοσις τῶν ἀνθρώπων with the 'commandment of God' (Mark 7.8). Does he thereby intend to condemn all interpretation of scripture? On the contrary, the antitheses of the Sermon on the Mount prove that he replaces the interpretation offered by the 'elders' by his own which 'fulfils' the ultimate intention of the divine will contained in each commandment. W. G. Kümmel[36] rightly emphasizes that by the words ἐγὼ δὲ λέγω ὑμῖν Jesus opposes to the *paradosis* of the rabbis, which he rejects, the definitive and only valid *paradosis*, namely, the messianic *paradosis*. The former is *paradosis* of men, while the latter, the foundations of which he himself lays in the Sermon on the Mount, has as its author him who speaks as *ego* with the authority of the Messiah. He, the

34 *Das paulinische Evangelium*, 1934, p. 100.
35 *Die Begriffe Wort und Evangelium bei Paulus*, 1910, p. 110. Cf. also *Evangelion. Ursprung und erste Gestalt des Begriffs Evangelium*, 1927.
36 'Jesus und der jüdische Traditionsgedanke', *Z.N.T.W.*, 1934, p. 105 f.

Messiah, as the one who fulfils the law, takes the place of the παράδοσις τῶν πρεσβυτέρων. It can rightly be maintained that, according to the Synoptic testimony, Jesus himself is the sole *paradosis*.

In the extant epistles Paul nowhere draws this conclusion from the attitude of Jesus to the law, but a direct line of connection is nevertheless discernible between the statements of Jesus and Paul's idea of Jesus as the end (τέλος) of the law. In his recent book W. D. Davies [37] has brought out very clearly the idea of Christ as the new law. For Paul, Christ the Lord takes the place of the law. This does not mean that he regards Jesus as *first* the lawgiver or the interpreter of the law, and *consequently* as the incarnation, in his own person, of the new, the messianic law. On the contrary, for Paul, Christ is above all in his person and work the fulfilled new law, and from this is derived his role of lawgiver as one who in his words imparts new *halakhoth* and gives instruction by the example of his life (Phil. 2.5). The latter idea is subordinated to the former, but without there being any opposition between them.[38]

Paul develops the conception of Christ as the new law in II Corinthians 3.4 f. Here it is not Christ but Paul himself who is put on a parallel with Moses. Paul is the 'minister' of the 'new covenant', just as Moses was the minister of the old; but in the new covenant Christ takes the place of the law in the old. To be sure, already in the old covenant the divine *doxa* shone through the law, so that it was reflected in the face of its mediator Moses; but this reflection was only transient, and so Moses put a veil over his face so that the children of Israel should not see this glory passing away. In Christ this veil is taken away (verse 16); in his person the divine glory is visible for all, and verse 18 says that the ministers of this new covenant with unveiled face reflect the divine glory which does not pass away, and that this happens 'from the Lord the Spirit' (ἀπὸ κυρίου πνεύματος).

This reference to the Holy Spirit which lies at the basis of this whole contrast between the old and new covenants in II Corinthians 3 (γράμμα—πνεῦμα) is important for our question. It points to the end-time fulfilled in Christ. Ultimately, according to Jeremiah 31.33, the law will be written in men's hearts; at that time, too, the Holy Spirit will come. Both promises are realized in Christ: he is

[37] *Paul and Rabbinic Judaism*, 1948, especially p. 147 f.
[38] H. Windisch, *Der Sinn der Bergpredigt*, 1929, wrongly contrasts Matthew and St. Paul in this respect.

the new law, and he is also the Spirit.[39] It is not accidental that this bold identification of the Lord and the Spirit stands precisely in this passage about the law (verse 17). Because the Holy Spirit imparts himself, the law can now be inscribed in men's hearts. *Henceforth the Holy Spirit, who is identical with the Kyrios, takes the place of the paradosis of the law.* The revelation of the divine glory which is the result (ἀπὸ δόξης εἰς δόξαν, verse 18) takes place καθάπερ ἀπὸ κυρίου πνεύματος. Of course, the whole of this passage deals only with the interpretation of the law, but there is a line of connection leading to the tradition of the early Church, as we realize when we consider that everything which concerns Christ is ultimately fulfilment of the Old Testament, and when we remember the analogy, including the terminology, between the Christian tradition and the rabbinic tradition.

This, then, appears to be the theological background of our suggested interpretation of the relation between *Kyrios* and *paradosis*. The *Kyrios* Christ replaces the *paradosis* of the law, and imparts himself also, in connection with this function, as Holy Spirit. This explains how the exalted Lord can be active in the actual transmission of the apostolic tradition of his words and works.

Paul does not establish the connection between the ideas of II Corinthians 3 and the tradition of the words and life of Jesus. But the fourth Gospel does; its concern is precisely with the relation between the historical Jesus and the risen Lord. The farewell discourses bring to expression the line of thought which I recognize in Paul, but as an implicit assumption. The passages which most clearly express the notion that the Holy Spirit will impart to the apostles the teachings of the historical Jesus are John 16.13 and 14.26: 'the Comforter, the Holy Spirit, whom the Father will send in my name, he will teach you all things, and bring to your remembrance *all that I said to you*'.

If my interpretation of the Pauline conception of the connection between *Kyrios* and *paradosis* is correct, we have before us an idea which, while not everywhere fully thought out in the same way, can yet be regarded as quite widespread in the early Church.

(*d*) On several occasions we have been led to emphasize the role belonging to the apostle, because of his unique function as a witness, in transmitting the *paradosis* of the *Kyrios*. In II Corinthians 3 the apostle and the Holy Spirit are both spoken of as replacing the

[39] C. H. Dodd, *History and the Gospel*, 1943, p. 55 f. has seen this clearly; cf. *The Apostolic Preaching and its Developments*, 1936, *passim*.

mediators and interpreters of the law of the old covenant. Of course, the Holy Spirit is not a gift reserved for apostles alone. The passages from John mentioned above (16.13 and 14.26), while addressed only to apostles, do not perhaps point solely to them. The Holy Spirit is not reserved for them. Nevertheless, in the transmission of tradition proper, an exceptional place belongs to them as the eye-witnesses commissioned directly by Christ. What distinguishes the *paradosis* of Christ from the rabbinic principle of tradition is this: firstly, the mediator of the tradition is not the teacher, the rabbi, but the *apostle* as direct witness; secondly, the principle of succession does not work mechanically as with the rabbis, but is bound to the Holy Spirit. We shall now deal with these two points.

We have seen that in Galatians 1.12 Paul expressly denies having received the gospel from men. This is fundamental for his apostolic authority. As apostle, as witness, he must stand in direct relation with the Lord. The unique honour of the apostle is that he has received a direct *apokalypsis*. But this concerns not only the theological understanding of the history of salvation, but also the facts of this history in themselves. We may think of the resurrection to which the apostles are to testify as to an actual fact (Acts 1.22; I Cor. 9.1). For the Twelve it is a question besides of testifying to the events which took place in the period when the incarnate Jesus 'went in and out' among them (Acts 1.21). From this point of view the above-mentioned distinction between the communication of facts and the communication of their theological meaning loses still more its justification, for both are revealed to the apostle by the Lord, and of both he is a direct witness.

In early Christianity the word 'apostle' is used in two senses: in the wider sense it denotes simply an eye-witness of the resurrection of Christ, in the narrower sense a member of the group of the Twelve who must bear witness not only to Christ risen but also to Christ incarnate on earth. Consequently every apostle is not able, as a direct eye-witness, to pass on information about *all* the facts. Paul himself cannot report, as an eye-witness, the events of the earthly life of Jesus. And yet he is an apostle since he can give direct eye-witness evidence of the risen Lord whom he has seen and heard on the road to Damascus. For the other events he must rely on the *eye-witness testimony of the other apostles*. We may recall here his meeting with Cephas in Jerusalem (Gal. 1.18), as well as the *paradosis* of I Corinthians 15.3 f., where he makes a clear distinction between the Easter event proper as transmitted by the testimony of other apostles, and the appearance granted to him. It must not be over-looked that in this very passage, after quoting the *paradosis*, he stresses in verse 11 his agreement with the original apostles.

It can now be understood how, in virtue of a real sense of community created by the function of an apostle as witness to Christ, all tradition passed on by apostles could be regarded as directly revealed by Christ. Thus Paul can say that he has received 'from the Lord' a tradition which in reality he has received by way of other apostles. *Transmission by the apostles is not effected by men, but by Christ the Lord himself who thereby imparts this revelation.* All that the Church knows about words of Jesus, about stories of his life, or about their interpretation, comes from the apostles. One has received this revelation, another that. The apostle is essentially one who passes on what he has received by revelation. But since everything has not been revealed to each individual apostle, each one must first pass on his testimony to another (Gal. 1.18; I Cor. 15.11), and only the entire *paradosis*, to which all the apostles contribute, constitutes the *paradosis* of Christ.[40]

In a wider sense the whole apostolic Church performs this function of passing on tradition; and in actual fact the primitive *kerygma* was handed on in this way. At the same time it must be remembered that the theological foundation of the tradition rests on the apostolic office. R. Bultmann rightly remarks that the conception of the apostolate in the early Church was determined by the idea of tradition.[41]

Just as the Jewish tradition comes through the *tannaim*, so the tradition about Jesus comes through the apostles. It is no accident that in the very key-passages for the *paradosis* of Christ, above all Galatians 1.12 and I Corinthians 15.3 f., the apostolate is always dealt with at the same time.

This is also how the pronoun ἐγώ in I Corinthians 11.23 is to be understood: 'I (the apostle) received from the Lord . . .' Attention has rightly often been directed to this *ego*, but it has rarely been explained satisfactorily. Paul could certainly have put this pronoun in the parallel passage, I Corinthians 15.3. The reason why he does so only in I Corinthans 11.23 is that it was vital, in opposition to the false conception of the Lord's Supper current at Corinth, to stress the dignity of his apostolic office as bearer of the correct tradition.

[40] The legend that each of the apostles contributed an article to the so-called Apostles' Creed points, in its own way, to the same idea.
[41] *Op. cit.*, p. 59.

In I Corinthians 7.10 ἐγώ is contrasted with the *Kyrios*, but it is the same ἐγώ of the apostolic consciousness. Here Paul points out that even in cases where the *Kyrios* does not give exact instructions in a *logion* handed down by tradition, the apostle is entitled to give his own opinion. That this ἐγώ may be regarded as that of the apostolic claims is clear fron verse 25: 'Now concerning virgins I have no command of the Lord, but I give my opinion as one who by the Lord's mercy is trustworthy'. This grace to be trustworthy refers to the apostolic office.

This trustworthiness is manifested in a double function: on the one hand, faithfully to transmit the *paradosis* about Jesus—that is the meaning of ἐγώ in I Corinthians 11.23; on the other, to give judgments which are inspired by this *paradosis*, and go beyond it, but must be entirely subordinated to it—that is the meaning of the same pronoun in I Corinthians 7.10. The ἐγώ in this passage derives its authority from that in the first, where the apostle is the legitimate and authorized mediator of the *paradosis* of Christ.

While the Jewish rabbi passes on in what might be called an automatic succession of rabbis the παράδοσις τῶν πρεσβυτέρων, which is, for that very reason, only 'tradition of men' (Mark 7.8), the apostle needs the Holy Spirit and his own call to enable him to perform the task of handing on tradition. In the apostolic age there was not yet any contradiction between succession and Holy Spirit.[42] In Judaism the activity of the rabbi marked the end of prophecy, the end of direct inspiration of the Spirit. The rabbi followed the prophet. The apostle also transmits tradition, but his office depends on the gift of the Holy Spirit.

For this reason the function of the apostle respecting the tradition can be traced back ultimately to that of the *Kyrios* himself, who is the πνεῦμα (II Cor. 3.17). At the beginning of this chapter we asked how Paul could ascribe such high honour to the concept of *paradosis*, when Jesus had rejected tradition as a work of men contrary to the divine commandment in such terms that the very idea of a revelation vouchsafed by way of tradition seemed completely excluded. We have shown that the early Christian view was that a παράδοσις τῶν ἀποστόλων is not a παράδοσις τῶν ἀνθρώπων. On the contrary, the *Kyrios* himself controls its transmission, so that there is no antithesis between apostolic tradition and direct revelation. In Colossians

---

[42] This is not the case in Jewish Christianity; cf. H. von Campenhausen, 'Lehrerreihen und Bischofsreihen im zweiten Jahrhundert', *In memoriam E. Lohmeyer*, 1951, p. 240 f., and also his recent book referred to below, p. 94, n. 62.

2.6–8 Paul distinguishes between the legitimate *paradosis* about Christ Jesus the Lord (παρελάβετε τὸν Χριστὸν Ἰησοῦν τὸν κύριον) and the tradition of men by using the expression παράδοσις τῶν ἀνθρώπων to describe the Gnostic traditions.

Our conclusion, then, is that on the ground of the New Testament there can be only one legitimate tradition, that which is transmitted by the apostles and is designated as *Kyrios*.

Does this favourable estimate of the apostolic *paradosis* justify the attribution of the same normative import to later ecclesiastical *paradosis*? The Catholic Church claims that it does; and this is because it identifies the authority of the post-apostolic Church which preserves, transmits and interprets the apostolic message with the authority of the apostles.[43] But is this identification justified? In order to answer this question we must inquire into the relation of the apostolic office to the Church.

(2) *The Significance of the Uniqueness of the Apostolate*

The problem of the relationship between scripture and tradition can be viewed as a problem of the theological relationship between the apostolic period and the period of the Church. All the other questions depend on the solution that is given to this problem. The alternatives—co-ordination or subordination of tradition to scripture —derive from the question of knowing how we must understand the fact that the period of the Church is the continuation and unfolding of the apostolic period. For we must note at the outset that this fact is capable of divergent interpretations. That is why agreement on the mere fact that the Church continues the work of Christ on earth does not necessarily imply agreement on the relationship between scripture and tradition. Thus in my thesis developed in *Christ and Time*, as well as in my studies on the sacraments in the New Testament, I came considerably nearer to the 'Catholic' point of view. In fact, I would affirm very strongly that the history of salvation is continued on earth (*through the Church*). I believe that this idea is present throughout the New Testament, and I should even consider it the key to the understanding of the fourth Gospel.[44]

---

[43] Cf. J. Daniélou, 'Rép.', p. 111: 'In this transmission and interpretation of the message, the Church enjoys a divine, infallible authority as did the apostles as recipients of revelation.'

[44] *Les sacrements dans l'évangile johannique*, 1951. [English readers may consult Cullmann's *Early Christian Worship*, E.T., 1953, Ed.]

I would maintain, moreover, that the sacraments of Baptism and the Eucharist take the place in the Church of the miracles performed by Jesus Christ in the period of the incarnation. And yet I shall show in the following pages that I subordinate tradition to scripture. *Vice versa*, certain 'Catholic' expositions of the unique role played by the period of the apostles in the story of revelation seem to come curiously near to the 'Protestant' point of view. And yet their authors co-ordinate and resolutely set side by side scripture and tradition by regarding the latter as an infallible interpretation of the former and at the same time as a more complete expression of apostolic teaching. This means that it is necessary to define exactly the temporal relationship to which I have referred.

The time within which the history of salvation is unfolded includes the past, the present, and the future. But it has a centre which serves as a vantage-point or norm for the whole extent of this history, and this centre is constituted by what we call the period of direct revelation, or the period of the incarnation. It comprises the years from the birth of Christ to the death of the last apostle, that is, of the last eye-witness who saw the risen Jesus and who received, either from the incarnate Jesus or the risen Christ, the direct and unique command to testify to what he had seen and heard. This testimony can be oral or written.

All the separate parts of total time derive their meaning from these few years of the revelation. If we want to assign to them a date in accordance with secular chronology, we can only do so approximately, because we do not know the precise year of the birth of Christ or of the death of the last apostle. We can say, however, that they are the years from about the year 1 to the year 70 or 80 of our era, without these being taken as exact limits—all the less so as the witness of certain apostles was fixed in writing only after their death.

If we consider the Christian faith from the point of view of time we should say that the scandal of the Christian faith is to believe that these few years, which for secular history have no more and no less significance than other periods, are the centre and norm of the totality of time. This is a scandal of which our usual manner of reckoning the years from the year 1, regarded as the year of Christ's birth, can be considered as a symbol. It is only from the starting-point of the events of these central years that faith sees the history of salvation unfolding in two directions, backwards and forwards, within secular history. It is only in the light of these years that it speaks of the history of a chosen people which moves towards the incarnation of Christ. It is only in the light of these years that it awaits a fulfilment of all things linked to a return of Christ, and it is above all in the light of these years that it believes, in the present time, in a Church as the body of Christ by which he exercises now his dominion over the universe.

The problem of scripture and tradition concerns the place we give to the period of the Church with reference to the period of the incarnation. This period of the Church is part of the history of salvation. We would deliberately underline this over against a narrow Protestant position which does not assign to the period of the Church any value *sui generis* in the history of salvation, and which recognizes no other possibility of being a Christian than that of living in the past time of the incarnation and the apostles. This is to fail to recognize that Christ reigns now and that the Church is the centre of his universal reign.

But this is not enough. Like every other period in the history of salvation, the period of the Church must be defined and determined from the centre. Just as the past appears to us as the time of preparation (the 'old' covenant), and the future as that of the final fulfilment, so the period of the Church is the *intermediate* period. It is intermediate because, while the decisive event has already taken place, the final fulfilment is yet to come. The miracles of the years 1–70 continue to happen, and yet neither the absolute of the central period nor the absolute of the fulfilment is realized: it is an essentially intermediate period. The Church shares in this intermediate character. It is indeed the body of Christ, the resurrection-body, but being composed of those who are still sinners, it is not simply the resurrection-body. It remains at the same time an earthly body which can not only be crucified, but shares in the imperfections of all earthly bodies.

The period of the Church, then, is a prolongation of the central period, but it is not the central period: it is a prolongation of the period of the incarnate Christ, but it is not the period of the incarnate Christ and of his apostolic eye-witnesses. The Church is built upon the foundation of the apostles, and will continue to be built upon this foundation as long as it exists, but in the present period it can no longer produce apostles.

Indeed, the apostolate is by definition a unique office which cannot be delegated. According to Acts 1.22 the apostle is a unique, because direct witness of the resurrection. Moreover, he has received a direct command from the incarnate or risen Christ. Like the Jewish *shaliach* he is 'as him that sent him'. He cannot transmit to others his completely unique mission. After having discharged it he gives it back to him who entrusted it to him, Christ. That is why in the New Testament the apostles alone fulfil exactly the functions which belong to Christ himself. The missionary charge that Jesus gives them in Matthew 10.7 f. corresponds exactly to the mission which in his reply to John the Baptist (Matt. 11.6) he assigns to his own person as Messiah: to heal the sick, to cast out demons, to raise the dead, to preach the good news. That is why the New Testament attributes the same images as are applied to Jesus to the apostles: 'rocks', and the corresponding images of 'foundation' and 'pillars'. Never are these images used to describe the bishop.[45]

The function of the bishop, which is transmitted, is essentially different from that of the apostle, which cannot be transmitted. The apostles appoint bishops, but they cannot delegate to them their function, which cannot be renewed. The bishops succeed the apostles but on a completely different level. They succeed them, not as apostles but as bishops, whose office is also important for the Church, but quite distinct. The apostles did not appoint other apostles, but bishops. This means that the apostolate does not belong to the period of the Church, but to that of the incarnation.

The apostolate consists in the witness given to Christ. Of course, the Church also bears witness to Christ. But it cannot bear that direct witness which belongs to the apostles. Its witness is a *derived* witness, because it does not rest on the direct revelation which was the privilege of the apostle alone as an *eye*-witness.

The epistle to the Galatians makes the clearest and most explicit distinction between the preaching of the apostle and the preaching of those who depend on the apostles (Gal. 1.1, 12 f.). The apostle alone has received the gospel δι' ἀποκαλύψεως (Gal. 1.12) and not δι' ἀνθρώπου (Gal. 1.12)—by direct revelation without human intermediary. Paul agrees with his Judaizing opponents on this point: an apostle is one who has been called by Christ *without the intermediary office* of another, in other words, outside the succession of a tradition. The Judaizers taunted Paul with having received the gospel through others and therefore refused him the title of apostle. Paul denies this stoutly, but he implicitly acknowledges that he would not be an apostle if he had not received the gospel *directly*

[45] For full details and bibliography see O. Cullmann, *Peter: Disciple—Apostle—Martyr*, E.T., 1953.

from Christ. We have seen [46] that this by no means contradicts his reliance on the tradition designated as *Kyrios*, independently of this direct call and this direct revelation. But it is inherent in the very nature of this apostolic tradition that each of the apostles has received a direct call and with it a direct revelation of the risen Christ.

To affirm thus the unique character of the revelation given to the apostles is not to deny the value of all post-apostolic tradition,[47] but it is to bring it clearly down to the level of a human fact, even though the Holy Spirit can reveal himself through it also. I have shown above that there is an apostolic tradition, and this is identified with the *Kyrios* himself. The apostles compare their testimonies; for the richness of the revelation demands a plurality of apostolic testimonies, as it demands a plurality of written Gospels, and they transmit to one another their unique apostolic testimonies. We have here a tradition, a *paradosis*, which does not fall under the condemnation which Jesus pronounces on *paradosis* in general. There is one normative tradition, that of the apostles considered in its diversity as a unity.

No writing of the New Testament emphasizes so much as the fourth Gospel the continuation of the work of Christ incarnate in the Church. Its very object is to set forth this continuation. But it is this very Gospel which distinguishes clearly between the continuation by the apostles, which is part of the central period, and the continuation by the post-apostolic Church. The high-priestly prayer (chap. 17) establishes this line of descent: Christ—the apostles —the post-apostolic Church. The members of the last are described as those who *believe because of the word of the apostles* (John 17.20).

I have already said that the uniqueness of the apostolate is emphasized, forcibly so, by Catholic theology, but it seems to me that at the decisive moment it does not draw the necessary conclusions. For if one thinks through this important idea of the uniqueness of the apostolate, one necessarily gets to the point of making an essential difference, also from the point of view of tradition, between *the foundation of the Church*, which took place in the period of the apostles, and the *post-apostolic Church*, which is no longer that of the apostles but of the bishops. There is consequently a difference between apostolic tradition and ecclesiastical tradition, the former

[46] Above, p. 66 f.

[47] On the practical value of post-apostolic tradition I hope to write elsewhere in detail.

being the foundation of the latter. They cannot, therefore, be co-ordinated.

If the apostolic tradition ought to be considered as the norm of revelation for all time, the question arises: how can we make alive for ourselves this witness which God condescended, for the salvation of the world, to grant to the apostles at a period which we call the mid-point, the centre of time? The Catholic Church replies: by the apostolic succession, by the infallible teaching-office of the Church, by means of the later, post-apostolic tradition. Thus the objective revelation of God comes to us (1) through the apostles, (2) through the ecclesiastical tradition which hands down and makes explicit the witness of the apostles. But is the *uniqueness* of the apostolate a guarantee of any such thing? It rests, as we have seen, on the immediate character of the revelation granted to the apostles, on the fact that it did not come to them through any intermediary, but δι' ἀποκαλύψεως (Gal. 1.12). The apostle cannot, therefore, have any successor who can replace him as bearer of the revelation for future generations, but he must continue *himself* to fulfil his function in the Church of today: *in* the Church, not *by* the Church, but *by his word*, διὰ τοῦ λόγου (John 17.20), in other words, by his *writings*.

The oral and written word of the apostles is, of course, not identical with the objective revelation, with the divine Word itself, since human language—spoken and written—shares in our weakness, and consequently cannot be an adequate vehicle for the Word pronounced by the omnipotent God. But it is only by this means which is accessible to us that God can speak to us, and he chose the apostles in order that the good news might be transmitted to us through their testimony.[48] In order that *other* human elements should not find entrance into this testimony, the apostolate has this character of uniqueness which can only be safeguarded by the *writings* of the apostles. These writings maintain, on the one hand,

---

[48] J. Daniélou's objection ('Rép'., p. 110), then, does not seem well founded: he says that I speak of apostolic tradition as a theologian, and of ecclesiastical tradition as a historian. On the contrary, I concede that in *both* the Holy Spirit is at work and that in *both* there is the human element inherent in all tradition. Nevertheless, the apostolic tradition alone is the norm, and this for a theological reason. This I stress also over against G. Bavaud, 'Écriture et Tradition selon M. Cullmann', *Nova et Vetera*, 1953, p. 138, who likewise asserts that, quite contrary to the 'liberal' Protestant, who refuses to abase his reason as a 'philosopher' (as regards the Bible), the 'orthodox' Protestant he sees in me is ready to abase his reason as a 'philosopher', but not as a 'historian' (as regards the authority of the Church).

the uniqueness of their mission and, on the other hand, they ensure the direct action of the apostles upon us in the twentieth century.

Since it thus pleased God to *restrict* the transmission of the gospel to this one category of the contemporaries of Jesus, in order to *reduce to a minimum* its deformation by the human element, should the Church not do everything in its turn to respect this reservation? We shall see that the Church of the second century understood this necessity in creating the canon of the New Testament and in taking care to admit only writings of which it could guarantee the *apostolic* origin.

The fixing of the revelation granted by God to the apostles as eye-witnesses took place at the very period which we have called the mid-point of time, the centre of the history of salvation. No word pronounced or written later by other men belonging to the Church was to be placed alongside the apostolic writings which, if not all written by the apostles themselves, nevertheless all claim to be the immediate expression of their testimony as eye-witnesses.

The written witness of the apostles is for us the living element which continually brings us anew face to face with Christ. If we realize the magnitude of this miracle—the *unique* ministry of the apostles who lived at the time of the incarnation actualized in our midst in the twentieth century, not by ourselves or certain of our contemporaries, but by these first-century apostles themselves—we can no longer speak of the dead letter of the Bible. Yet this presupposes that we share the faith of the first Christians, that the apostles are not writers like other authors of antiquity, but men set apart by God for the execution of his plan of salvation by their witness, first oral, then written.

Again and again the Catholic objection is that books cannot confront us with Christ as is the case with the infallible teaching-office of the Church, where the Holy Spirit operates in bringing out the implications of the tradition. This argument recurs in most Catholic reviews of my book on St. Peter.[49] But the conclusion reached in the preceding chapter is that in the New Testament the *Kyrios* Christ *is present* in the tradition of the apostles, and therefore also in this tradition as fixed in the written documents. The believer holds that these documents are not simply historical records (although they are that), but that the Holy Spirit confronts the believing reader directly with Christ.

The scriptural principle, then, is not, as one might think, a simple

[49] And in that of J. Daniélou in *Études*, 1953.

application of the scientific principle stressed by the Renaissance, of the necessity of resorting to the sources in order to study and understand a historical phenomenon.[50] On the contrary, it is based on faith in this essential fact of the history of salvation—the setting apart, at the time of the incarnation, of the apostles as unique instruments of the revelation of God in Jesus Christ. But it is true that through the natural consequences which it implies for theological method the scriptural principle meets the scientific motto—back to the sources. This is the meeting-ground of historical science and Protestant theology.

If we believe with the first Christians that the divine institution of the apostolate had as its purpose the direct transmission of the revelation of God in Christ, by the elimination of all other intermediaries as an inevitable source of deformation, we ought to respect God's plan by reserving to the apostolate this same function in the contemporary Church. The real presence of the apostles in the Church of all periods is given to us in the New Testament. But we shall find it in so far as we seek direct contact with these witnesses and eliminate the intermediaries.

Does this mean that the Church in which we are set by Baptism is not for us the place where the Holy Spirit is at work? This conclusion would be contrary to the faith attested by all the New Testament writings. On the contrary, according to this faith, the Holy Spirit who had previously been reserved for certain men of God became accessible after Pentecost to the whole community of believers. We must take seriously this conviction of primitive Christianity. It implies that the work of the incarnate Christ is carried on in his Church, and the history of salvation continues. There is no gap between the ascension of Christ and his return. The fourth Gospel was written to show that in leaving the world Christ did not abandon it. The Holy Spirit is at work in it. There will still be miracles of faith, as in the period of the incarnation, as in the period of Jesus and the apostles. And the great miracle of the redemptive death and resurrection of Christ is given to the Church in the sacraments of Baptism and the Lord's Supper.

I have been accused, in my attitude to the tradition, of being unfaithful to my own conception of the sacraments in which I acknowledge the present activity of God, because I deny the

---

50 Against J. Daniélou, 'Rép.', p. 110, who describes my attitude as 'the return to the sources, the need of contact with the original document behind the subsequent glosses'. Cf. the last note but one above.

infallibility of the Church's teaching-office and tradition.[51] But can the sacraments and an infallible teaching-office be placed on the same level? I fail to see any justification for this. Infallibility and error are not categories which are applicable to the sacraments. Of course, both in the sacraments and in tradition there is divine activity in the present. The sacraments are an actualization of the work of Christ, but in exactly the same way as in the time of the apostles who observed them as we do. On the other hand, as regards revelation, Catholic scholars are bound to admit that there is a fundamental difference between the apostles and the post-apostolic Church, because in the Church there is no fresh revelation. As regards the sacraments, through their very nature there is no difference between the period of the apostles and that of the Church. I do not, therefore, think that there is any inconsistency between my opposition to the doctrinal infallibility of the teaching-office of the Church and my conception of the sacraments.

We could go still further. Inspiration through the Holy Spirit continues also in the sense that the Paraclete is the Spirit of Truth.[52] And yet the high-priestly prayer makes a clear distinction between the apostles and those who believe 'because of their word'. Perhaps it is for this reason that the fourth Gospel reports a special out-pouring of the Holy Spirit which took place before that in Acts, on Easter day itself, and was experienced by the apostles only (20.22). The revelation of the Word of God continues in the Church, but it will no longer be a *norm* or *criterion*, like the revelation granted to the apostles. Despite the deep gulf between them in other respects, is it not true to say that the Catholic Church, Gnosticism, and ancient and modern sects which claim a superior enlightenment, are at one in denying that scripture is a superior norm for the testing of the genuine activity of the Holy Spirit? The Church will examine every later revelation, individual or collective, but will always take as criterion this norm of the apostolic witness. The Church will therefore not be a superior tribunal able to decree what must be added to this norm. *God speaks to the Church of today through the witness of the apostles.* As long as there is a Church this witness of the apostles will be a *sufficient norm.*

[51] See J. Daniélou, 'Rép.', p. 114.

[52] Here I omit a sentence which stood in my article in *Dieu vivant*, no. 23, p. 54 (and in *Scottish Journal of Theology*, 1953, p. 120 [Ed.]): 'There will still be revelation', for I think it gave rise to a misunderstanding on the part of J. Daniélou ('Rép.', p. 107). The word 'revelation' was there used in the sense of inspiration.

The apostolic witness has a double role: it engenders inspiration and acts as its controller, since in all inspiration there is a risk of other spirits putting themselves in the place of the Holy Spirit. Thus the Church will have the right and the duty to proclaim whatever, examined in the light of the apostolic norm, appears to it as truth. In this way an ecclesiastical tradition is elaborated. It will have great value for the Church, and Protestantism is wrong to underestimate this in principle. But in any case it recognizes it in fact by giving a large place in its teaching to the writings, for instance, of the theologians of the sixteenth century and even to the decisions of the early councils.[53] But whatever the respect owed by the Church to the tradition, and the importance attaching to it in the elaboration and understanding of Christian doctrine, it can never assume the same value as the apostolic norm, and it can never itself become a norm. A norm is a norm because it cannot be expanded. *Revelation* and *criterion of revelation* must not be confused.

In practice the institution of the apostolate, which is unique in the history of salvation, seems to us to be devalued by the infallible teaching-office of the Catholic Church. The uniqueness of the apostolate is annulled by this teaching-norm. The period of the apostles and that of the Church are confused. Of course, the Catholic Church claims only to *interpret*, to explicate the apostolic witness by its decisions which constitute the tradition. But when the ecclesiastical interpretation assumes the same normative value *for all periods* as the apostolic norm itself, does not the affirmation that it is only interpretation become a fiction? Is it not the essence of a true interpretation that it has not the same definitive character as the norm itself? Certainly we must always consult the interpretations of the norm which have been given in order to understand it, but we must always be ready to revise them, and even to abandon them, by setting ourselves before the norm itself, and removing the screen of earlier interpretations.

Moreover, does the Catholic Church not tend to abandon, in fact if not in theory, the fiction that tradition is interpretation of scripture, when in justifying the dogma proclaimed in 1950 it does not spend time giving a scriptural foundation, but relies on the *consensus* of the Church, as if collective inspiration in the Church has

53 On this see the interesting article of J. N. Bakhuizen van der Brink mentioned above, p. 59, n. 7, also J. Courvoisier, 'De la réforme comme principe critique du protestantisme', *Verbum Caro*, 1953, p. 20 f., who also emphasizes the respect of the Reformers for the Church Fathers. Cf. also F. J. Leenhardt, 'Des raisons et de la façon d'être protestant', *Verbum Caro*, 1953, p. 31 f.

no longer any need at all to be controlled by the apostolic witness, and as if the infallible teaching-office of the Pope were sufficient for this purpose? [54]

None the less Catholic theology will always oppose the affirmation of the superiority of scripture to tradition by the argument that the former *needs to be interpreted*. We readily concede this necessity. For, as we have already said, the apostles used the imperfect instrument of human language, and moreover languages and thought-forms different from our own. But neither the need for interpretation nor the errors of individual interpretation justify the claim that the teaching-office of the Church is infallible. Besides, if the conception brought out in the preceding chapter of the presence of the *Kyrios* himself in the apostolic tradition is taken seriously, the watchword of the Reformers, *scriptura sui ipsius interpres*, assumes full importance. The Church ought to take more seriously, than is the case in Protestantism, the teaching-office, the duty of pronouncing as Church in matters of exegesis. The Church ought to take up a position regarding any interpretation proposed by the exegetes, and ought to pray for the help of the Holy Spirit in reaching the right decision. The Church ought to translate the biblical message into the language of today. But in doing this, the Church ought to know that it is fulfilling its duty for its own period, and is not doing something which, like the testimony of the eye-witnesses, binds all the future centuries of the period of the Church, so that future generations will be bound by its decisions in the same way as they are bound by scripture. Earlier decisions of the Church will serve as guides to the exegetes, but not as norms or criteria.

Even when there is the inspiration of the Holy Spirit, there is a human element in all interpretation of scripture. This human element is present also in the apostolic writings themselves, which have transposed the divine Word into human language. But behind them there are the apostles as eye-witnesses. The human element is here reduced to an *inevitable minimum inherent in the very notion of a divine revelation to man*. I readily concede the danger of false interpretations of our own. But if we set between scripture and ourselves as a norm the total collection of official interpretations given in all past centuries by the Church, then errors which are insignificant, when considered singly, are increased by virtue of a

[54] I refer to the reality, not the theory. That in *theory* no claim is made to promulgate a new revelation I readily concede to J. Daniélou ('Rép.', p. 108) and G. Bavaud, *op. cit.*, p. 136.

development which no tradition transmitted by men who are not eye-witnesses can escape. The chronological question necessarily comes into play here: this is why the period of the Church cannot be normative like the period of the *foundation* of the Church.

Otherwise our interpretation would risk coming under the condemnation pronounced by Jesus on the tradition: 'You reject the commandment of God, that you may keep your tradition' (Mark 7.9). The interpretation given by the rabbinic tradition to the commandment to honour father and mother was considered also to be faithful to the divine Word, and to shed light on a written commandment which was not clear in itself. And yet Jesus recommends here, as in the antitheses of the Sermon on the Mount, the necessity of returning to the Word itself to get from it the divine intention without the intermediary of a traditional interpretation. The arguments with which the Jewish rabbis justified their view of tradition as a norm correspond to a considerable extent to those used by Catholic theology in support of a tradition constituted by the Roman Church's decisions in questions of dogma.

But is this not to miss the fact that everything has been changed by the coming of Christ, by the existence of a Church of Christ? Is it not a blasphemy thus to compare the tradition of the rabbis with the tradition of the Church? With this objection we return to our starting-point: the distinction which can be drawn between the period of the incarnation and the period of the Church. For to make this distinction comes to the same thing as saying that there is tradition *and* tradition. There is an apostolic tradition which is a norm because it rests upon eye-witnesses chosen by God, and because Christ speaks directly in it, and there is a post-apostolic tradition which is a valuable help for the understanding of the divine Word, but is not to be regarded as a norm. While accepting humbly the *exegetical and dogmatic directives* of the Church and its teachers, we must be ready to set ourselves directly before the testimony of the apostles, as the apostles themselves were confronted directly with the divine revelation (Gal. 1.12), without any intermediate interpretation.

It is true that the same Holy Spirit who inspired the apostles is at work in the Church, and the Church is the place where Christ manifests his presence. 'Quench not the Spirit', says St. Paul to the Thessalonians, but he knows, too, that other spirits are at work in the Church itself. That is why he adds: 'Prove all things, hold fast that which is good'. To say that inspiration needs to be controlled is not to deny it. Equally, to say that the teaching-office of the Church needs to be controlled is not to deny it; and it must be controlled by the word of the apostles. *The Holy Spirit interprets scripture, but is at the same time controlled by it.*

(3) *The Significance of the Fixing of the Canon by the Church of the Second Century*

To determine the connection between scripture and tradition we began, in the preceding chapters, from the very foundation of the Christian Church, that is, from the period which we call the central period in the history of salvation, the period of Jesus and his apostles. By an examination of the New Testament we have found that the idea of the apostolate, or more exactly of the uniqueness of the apostolate, has led us to the answer which we have thought must be given. By centring the whole discussion on this idea of the apostolate we have only considered so far the New Testament as scripture, that is to say, the direct witness of the apostles to the fundamental facts of the work of the incarnate Christ and their own acts.

Now we are about to deal with the question from the starting-point of the history of the primitive Church, and to discover if this will confirm our results. If we have just been looking for the answer to our problem in scripture, we shall now look for it in the tradition. We shall insist on the fact that *the infant Church itself distinguished between apostolic tradition and ecclesiastical tradition*, clearly subordinating the latter to the former, in other words, subordinating itself to the apostolic tradition.

Catholic theology, in order to combat the thesis of the superiority of scripture, lays much stress upon the chronological priority of tradition to scripture. This is a fact that no one will think of denying, provided, however, that it is made clear that it is the *apostolic* tradition which is prior. But if it can be shown that the Church itself recognized an essential difference between the tradition before and the tradition after the establishment of the canon, the fact of the priority of the oral apostolic tradition over its fixation in writing will prove nothing about the tradition as such. We shall speak first about the origin of the first Christian writings, then about the origin of the canon.

Of course, the oral tradition of the apostles precedes the first apostolic writings. The oral tradition prior to the first writings was certainly quantitatively richer than the written tradition.[55] But we must ask what is the significance of the fact that the apostles, or the mouthpieces who served them as secretaries, at a given moment took up the pen to give this tradition a written form. This is a fact of the very greatest importance *for the history of salvation*. Its meaning can only have been to delimit the oral tradition of the apostles, so as to make of the apostolic witness in this form a definitive *norm* for the Church, at the moment when it was going to expand into the whole world and had to be built up until the Kingdom of God itself was established. If it is allowed that the oral tradition of the apostles had been entrusted as a deposit to the Church in order that, in the course of the centuries, it might draw from it normative elements of equal worth which are not to be found in the apostolic writings, then the composition of writings which have as authors men whom the Church calls 'sacred authors' is completely minimized. The writings of the apostles are devalued to the point of becoming tools, useful indeed, but in no way indispensable. In actual fact the theory of 'secret', unwritten traditions of the apostles was elaborated by the Gnostics, and the Church itself drew attention to the danger of these.[56]

If, on the other hand, the written fixation of the witness of the apostles is one of the *essential facts of the incarnation*, we have the right and the duty to bring together apostolic tradition and New Testament writings, and to distinguish both from the post-apostolic, post-canonical tradition. We shall see that the rule of faith, though transmitted in oral form, was accepted as a norm alongside scripture only because it was considered as having been *fixed by the apostles*. What matters is not whether the apostolic tradition was oral or written, but that it was *fixed by the apostles*.

But did the early Church really distinguish between apostolic and post-apostolic tradition? This is the place to speak about the establishment of the canon by the Church of the second century. This

---

55 This I readily concede to G. Bavaud, *op. cit.*, p. 136, who refers to II Thess. 2.15 ('hold the traditions which you were taught, whether by word, or by epistle of ours'), and concludes that scripture is only a part of the tradition.

56 G. Bavaud, *op. cit.*, p. 137 f. rightly reminds us that, in Catholic teaching, the role of tradition is not only to interpret scripture, but to determine the contents of the apostolic deposit which includes oral traditions as well (I Tim. 6.20; II Tim. 1.14). I took into consideration this function of Catholic tradition in my article in *Dieu vivant*, p. 58. But I assert that the *norm* for determining this apostolic deposit (including matters of rites and institutions) is not ecclesiastical tradition, but scripture. It is here that the fundamental divergence appears.

again is an event of capital importance for the history of salvation. We are in complete agreement with Catholic theology in its insistence on the fact that *the Church itself* made the canon. We even find in this fact the supreme argument for our demonstration. The fixing of the Christian canon of scripture means that *the Church itself*, at a given time, traced a clear and definite line of demarcation between the period of the apostles and that of the Church, between the time of foundation and that of construction, between the apostolic community and the Church of the bishops, in other words, between apostolic tradition and ecclesiastical tradition. Otherwise the formation of the canon would be meaningless.

We must recall the situation that led the Church to conceive the *idea* of a canon. About the year 150 there is still an oral tradition. We know this from Papias, who wrote an exposition of the words of Jesus. He tells us himself that he used as a basis the *viva vox* (φωνὴ ζῶσα) and that he attached more importance to it than to the writings. But from him we have not only this declaration of principle; for he has left us some examples of the oral tradition as he found it, and these examples show us well what we ought to think of an oral tradition about the year 150! It is entirely legendary in character. This is clear from the story that Papias reports about Joseph Barsabbas, the unsuccessful candidate, according to Acts 1.23 f., for the post of twelfth disciple rendered vacant by Judas's treason. Above all there is the obscene and completely legendary account of the death of Judas Iscariot himself.

The period about 150 is, on the one hand, relatively near to the apostolic age, but on the other hand, it is already too far away for the living tradition still to offer in itself the least guarantee of authenticity. The oral traditions which Papias echoes arose in the Church and were transmitted by it. For outside the Church no one had any interest in describing in such crude colours the death of the traitor. Papias was therefore deluding himself when he considered the *viva vox* as more valuable than the written books. The oral tradition had a normative value in the period of the apostles, who were eye-witnesses, but it had it no longer in 150 after passing from mouth to mouth.

The traditions reported by Papias are not the only ones. From the same period we have the first apocryphal Gospels, which were collections of other oral traditions. It is sufficient to read these Gospels, one of which tells of the infant Jesus making living sparrows, carrying water in his apron, and miraculously killing companions

who were annoying him, or to read the numerous apocryphal
Acts, in order to realize that the tradition, in the Church, no longer
offered any guarantee of truth, even when it claimed a chain of
succession. For all these traditions were justified by a chain of transmission reaching back to the apostles. Papias himself also makes
this claim when he says that he got his information from people
who had been in contact with the apostles. The teaching-office of
the Church in itself did not suffice to preserve the purity of the
gospel.

By establishing the *principle* of a canon the Church recognized
that *from that time* the tradition was no longer a criterion of truth.
It drew a line under the apostolic tradition. It declared implicitly
that from that time every subsequent tradition must be submitted
to the control of the apostolic tradition. That is, it declared: here is
the tradition which *constituted* the Church, which forced itself upon
it.[57] Certainly the Church did not intend thereby to put an end to
the continued evolution of the tradition. But by what we might
call an act of humility it submitted all subsequent tradition to be
elaborated by itself to the superior criterion of the apostolic tradition, codified in the Holy Scriptures. To establish a canon is equivalent to saying this: henceforth our ecclesiastical tradition needs to be
controlled; with the help of the Holy Spirit it will be controlled by
the apostolic tradition fixed in writing; for we are getting to the
point where we are too distant from the apostolic age to be able to
guard the purity of the tradition *without a superior written norm*, and
too distant to prevent slight legendary and other deformations
creeping in, and thus being transmitted and amplified. But at the
same time this meant that the tradition that was to be considered as
alone apostolic had to be fixed, for all the Gnostics boasted of secret,
unwritten traditions which claimed to be apostolic. To fix a canon
was to say: henceforth we give up regarding as a norm other
traditions that are not fixed by the apostles in writing. Of course,
there may be other authentic apostolic traditions, but we regard as
an apostolic *norm* only what is written in these books, since it has
been proved that by admitting as norms oral traditions not written
by the apostles we are losing the criterion for judging the validity
of the claim to apostolicity made by the many traditions in circula-
tion. To say that the writings brought together in a canon should

57 This is strongly emphasized by Karl Barth, *Die Kirchliche Dogmatik*, I, 1, p.
109 f., and, following him, by H. Diem, 'Das Problem des Schriftkanons',
Theol. Studien, no. 32, 1951.

be regarded as a *norm* was to say that they should be regarded as *sufficient*. The teaching-office of the Church did not abdicate in this final act of fixing the canon, but made its future activity dependent on a superior norm.

The Catholic Church, to quote Père Daniélou,[58] admits 'that the fixing of the canon marks the place where revelation properly so called ceased, but it denies that the seat of authority is thereby shifted and is transferred from the living Church to the written word'. But we do not speak of transference of authority from the Church to the written word. In actual fact, there was no doctrinal authority properly so called in the period before the canon was fixed. The proof of this is the spate of apocryphal traditions, all of which sprang up within the Church itself. Among the numerous Christian writings the books which were to form the future canon *forced themselves on the Church by their intrinsic apostolic authority*, as they do still, because the *Kyrios* Christ speaks in them.

By setting up the *principle* of a canon (the fixing of its final limits came later) the Church of the second century did not only take up a position with regard to the difficulties that arose at that particular time, especially as regards Gnosticism. *It took a decision that committed the whole future*. It did not fix a norm for others, but for itself, and committed the Church for all future centuries to this norm. In doing this the Church did not deprive itself of its teaching-office. But it gave to this teaching-office its exact character: it will be truly the teaching-office of the Church in so far as it begins by submitting to the ecclesiastical norm of the canon. It derives its efficacy from this submission. The Holy Spirit will be at work in this very submission. *Within this framework* revelation will continue to be granted to the Church.

Is it legitimate to attribute such primary importance in the history of salvation to this act of fixing the canon? Does not this mean attributing an exceptional dignity to the Church of the second century which conceived this idea of a canon? It must be remembered that this was, in fact, a decisive moment for the Church. On the one hand, about the year 150 they were still near enough to the apostolic age to be able, with the help of the Holy Spirit, to make a selection among the oral and written traditions; on the other hand, the bewildering multiplication of Gnostic and legendary traditions had made the Church ripe for this act of humility in submitting *all* later inspiration to a norm. At no other time in the history of the

[58] 'Rép.', p. 109.

Church could the fixing of the canon have been undertaken. It was at that very time that God granted to the Church the grace of recognizing the difference between the period of the incarnation and the period of the Church. Only the clear distinction between these two periods enables the Church to preserve the sublime consciousness of having its own place and its own time in the history of salvation. And it has it in so far as it recognizes that the period of Jesus and the apostles is the mid-point of all time and gives its significance to every period, including that of the Church.

In creating a norm the Church did not desire to be its own norm,[59] since it had discovered that *without a superior written norm its teaching-office could not keep pure the apostolic tradition*. While remaining conscious of its high mission of representing the body of Christ on earth in the present period, the highest mission there is, it understood that it could not accomplish this mission except by submitting to the norm of the apostolic canon. If the fixing of the canon had been carried out by the Church on the tacit assumption that its teaching-office, that is, the *subsequent* traditions, should be set alongside this canon with an *equal normative authority*, the reason for the creation of the canon would be unintelligible. If after as well as before its creation the teaching-office of the Church continued to be a *supreme* norm of equal value, the Church could on its own authority alone always judge afresh as a last resort on the conformity of the teaching of its scholars with the apostolic tradition. In this case the fixing of a canon would have been superfluous. It only has meaning if the Church henceforth exercises its teaching-office in submission to this supreme norm, and continually returns to it. We might even go so far as to say, paradoxically, that the teaching-office of the Church at least approaches real infallibility in so far as, through submission to the canon, it abandons all *claim* to infallibility; and that the tradition created by the Church assumes a real value for the understanding of the divine revelation if it does not claim to be an indispensable screen between the Bible and the reader.

But the canon fixed by the Church of the second century does not contain only the books of the apostles, but also the Old Testament. At the outset it must be said that the Old Testament was admitted only because it was believed that the period of the

[59] Karl Barth, *Die Kirchliche Dogmatik*, I, i, p. 107, puts it thus: 'In the unwritten tradition the Church is not addressed, but is engaged in conversation with itself',

incarnation is the mid-point of time, the mid-point in the history of salvation which begins before the incarnation and continues beyond it. The Old Testament was received into the canon as the testimony to that part of the history of salvation which prepared for the incarnation. This was the way in which Jesus and the apostles understood the history of Israel. Thus the Church was faithful to the apostles themselves in admitting the Old Testament into the *apostolic norm* which is the canon.

Here an objection may be raised. Since the history of the people of God in the Old Testament thus acquires a normative character, why should it not be the same for the people of God in the New Testament, i.e. the Church? Is not a privileged position given to the period of preparation for the incarnation as compared with the period of the unfolding of the incarnation which is the period of the Church?

This objection has actually been made to me.[60] But once again the fixing of the canon must be viewed as an element in the history of salvation itself. The fixing of this norm certainly did not mean, as many Protestants think, that the history of salvation was henceforth to stop until the return of Christ, so that meanwhile all we can do is mark time. Rather, we must boldly assert that the people of the New Testament are in a privileged position as compared with that of the Old, since they already live in the new age, even though the final fulfilment is still to come. For the Holy Spirit which, in the Old Testament, is only manifested in *some* men of God, is now accessible to all the members of the Church. This is the interpretation of the miracle of Pentecost, based on the prophecy in Joel, which is given by Peter in his sermon (Acts 2.16 f.): 'in the last days . . . I will pour out my Spirit upon *all* flesh'.

And yet this period of the Church, in spite of all the graces bestowed upon it, especially in the sacraments, cannot be a *norm*. In answering the objection already mentioned, it must be pointed out that it is wrong to suggest that there is in the Old Testament an infallible teaching-office. The authority of the Old Testament must not be regarded as that of an infallible teaching-office.[61] The Spirit operated in the people of Israel, but there was no infallible teaching-office. The authority of the Old Testament which, for the most part, was already regarded as canonical by the Jews, impressed itself

[60] By Père Daniélou, first in conversation, then in 'Rép.', p. 111 f.

[61] It is this confusion which seems to underlie the objection of J. Daniélou, 'Rép.', p. 111 f.

on the early Church as part of the normative history of salvation through Christ, in the same way as that of the several New Testament books. The Church saw in the Old Testament the activity of the Spirit, and it is for this reason that the primitive confessions of faith lay stress on his speaking through the prophets. This means that for the Church the Old Testament is canonical only in so far as it is explicitly orientated towards the New; in other words, because the time of the incarnation is regarded as normative for the time which preceded it, and as the criterion by which it is to be understood. Thus the apostolic writings are the norm not only of the post-apostolic, but of the pre-apostolic period.

If there is a certain parallelism between ecclesiastical tradition and scripture, it only applies to the *Old* Testament scripture, because both of them have their norm and canon in the apostolic writings of the New Testament. The period of the Church, however, *is not closed* as was the case, in the age of the apostles and of the fixing of the canon, with the period of preparation for the incarnation in the history of Israel.

But, it may be asked, does not the *rule of faith* prove that ecclesiastical tradition is a norm of equal authority with scripture? In the first place, it is of the greatest importance that the idea of giving it a normative authority was conceived *at the same time* as that of giving a normative authority to the canon, that is to say, about the middle of the second century. By misunderstanding the significance of certain declarations of the Fathers of the second century we are too accustomed to contrast rule of faith and canon, as if the former constituted the continuous tradition of the Church, alongside the writings of the apostles. In fact, the definitive fixing of the apostolic rule of faith corresponded exactly to the same need of codifying the apostolic tradition as did the canonization of the apostolic writings. It is not a matter of, on the one hand, the Apostles' Creed and, on the other, their writings. The two form henceforth one block of apostolic tradition over against the post-apostolic tradition. The apostolic rule of faith is the very tradition of which the Fathers of the second century speak.[62] What is important is not that it was first of all transmitted orally, but the conviction that its text has

---

[62] Irenaeus especially should be studied from this point of view. Moreover, our work should be supplemented by a study of tradition in the early history of dogma. The problem has recently been treated in connection with the conception of the ministry in the important book by H. von Campenhausen, *Kirchliches Amt und geistliche Vollmacht in den ersten drei Jahrhunderten,* 1953, p. 163 f.

been *fixed*—just like that of the canonical books of the New Testament—by the apostles. According to the conviction of the Church of the second century it is not a question of a secret or implicit tradition, but of a text already fixed in the period of the apostles, as were their writings.

This creed was a kind of apostolic *résumé* of the books of the New Testament, as it were a rule of apostolic interpretation of all the very different books. The multiplicity of apostolic writings necessitated a short *résumé* of the truths that are common to them for the different needs of the Church.[63] In order to be the norm of interpretation this creed itself must be *apostolic*. Of course, there were still fluctuations as regards the precise and definitive text,[64] but in the main outline the different affirmations were already contained in the symbols of the middle of the second century, and, above all, the principle of the norm of an apostolic rule of faith was admitted by that time. The attribution of each phrase to one of the twelve apostles is a legend. The truth in it is that behind the developed symbols stand the oldest ones, shorter formulae whose text was fixed in the apostolic age, traces of which are to be found in the New Testament.

The role of future creeds of the Church as worked out by the councils is quite different. Certainly they are also necessary in their intention to define an attitude towards the problems of their time and the heresies of the day. They are necessary, and in every age the Church must construct its creed. But these later confessions can never assume the value of a symbol attributed to the apostles; they can never become norms for all time. Here again we must repeat what we have said about the post-apostolic traditions of the Church. They have a very great importance in guiding our understanding of

[63] See O. Cullmann, *The Earliest Christian Confessions*, E.T., 1949.
[64] As I granted in my article in *Dieu vivant*, no. 23, p. 64, where I pointed out that the important thing is the *principle* of an apostolic creed. Moreover, in the book mentioned in the last note, I specified the relation between the already fixed formulae in the New Testament, and the later 'apostolic' symbol. J. Daniélou's objection, therefore, in 'Rép.', p. 115 f., is difficult to understand. Of course, the Apostles' Creed and even the old Roman symbol from which it grew did not exist in the apostolic age. But the principle of the creed and its essential elements are contained in the New Testament formulae. Fluctuations regarding certain of the clauses are of no more importance for our question than the discussions which went on for centuries about the admission of certain books into the canon, since the *principle* of the canon had long since been accepted.

the apostolic revelation, but they are not, like the so-called Apostles' Creed, a kind of last page to be added to the New Testament.

The conclusion, then, is that the difference established between apostolic and post-apostolic tradition is not arbitrary, but that it is *the difference which the Church itself made, at the decisive moment, in the second century, by formulating the principle of an apostolic canon and an apostolic summary of belief.*

All this finds its confirmation in the evolution of patristics. For a long time it has been noted that, apart from the letters of Ignatius, the writings of the so-called Apostolic Fathers, who do not really belong to the apostolic age but to the beginning of the second century—the first epistle of Clement, the *Homily* assigned to Clement, the epistle of Barnabas, the *Shepherd* of Hermas, the epistle of Polycarp—despite their theological interest, are at a considerable distance from New Testament thought, and to a considerable extent relapse into a moralism which ignores the notion of grace, and of the redemptive death of Christ, so central to apostolic theology.[65] It has also been noted that the Church Fathers who wrote after 150 —Irenaeus and Tertullian—although chronologically more remote from the New Testament than the authors of the first half of the century, understood infinitely better the essence of the gospel. This seems paradoxical, but is explained perfectly by that most important act, the codification of the apostolic tradition in a canon, henceforward the superior norm of all tradition. The Fathers of the first half of the century wrote at a period when the writings of the New Testament already existed, but without being vested with canonical authority, and so set apart. Therefore they did not have any norm at their disposal, and, on the other hand, they were already too far distant from the apostolic age to be able to draw directly on the testimony of eye-witnesses. The encounters of Polycarp and Papias with apostolic persons could no longer guarantee a pure transmission of authentic traditions, as is proved by the extant fragments of their writings.

But after 150 contact with the apostolic age was re-established through the construction of the canon, which discarded all impure and deformed sources of information. Thus it is confirmed that, by subordinating all subsequent tradition to the canon, the Church once and for all saved its apostolic basis. It enabled its members to hear, thanks to this canon, continually afresh and throughout all the centuries to come the authentic word of the apostles, a privilege

[65] See T. F. Torrance, *The Doctrine of Grace in the Apostolic Fathers*, 1948.

which no oral tradition, passing through Polycarp or Papias, could have assured them.

We have said that scripture needs to be interpreted. The Church ought to feel itself responsible for this interpretation. It ought, when necessary, to declare its attitude to the exegesis of certain biblical passages put forward by its teachers or by independent scholars. But responsibility in this case consists, as we have seen, in pronouncing judgment in humble submission to the apostolic norm of the canon. Two implications follow: (1) The Church does not impose on future generations the obligation to take as a starting-point and as a norm of their interpretation of the same text the decision that it feels bound to take, but it remains conscious of the superiority of scripture as the immediate testimony of the divine revelation to the interpretation which it feels compelled to give, and which can only be a derivative testimony, in which the human element plays a larger part. (2) The Church decides by confronting the biblical text itself, trusting in the internal witness of the Holy Spirit, and having recourse to the tradition only as a secondary source and as a guide which can give us light if we do not set it above the word of the apostles, and are ready, if need be, to break away from it.

Do we not continually experience afresh a kind of liberation when, after having read a number of commentaries, however good, we read the biblical Word itself, forcing ourselves to forget the very things we have read in the commentaries, with the healthy *naiveté* of the catechumen seeking to hear the apostles speak of what they have seen and heard? Certainly the Bible needs to be interpreted. For its writers were men of their time, and therefore it contains inevitable imperfections inherent in any human word which tries to translate the divine Word. But is it not lack of faith to take our stand on the human character of the revelation transmitted by the apostles and on our own human weakness as readers exposed to all kinds of mistakes, in order to claim that we are no longer capable of hearing their testimony without passing through a long chain of intermediaries in which the human element, moreover, plays a greater part because they are not eye-witnesses like the apostles? Certainly we ought to undertake the reading of the biblical Word with the philological knowledge that we have acquired, and we ought to give certain directives to the common man to whom it is not available. But in order that the exegete, like the common man, should become capable of hearing, in this twentieth century, the very voice of the apostles, and thereby the *Kyrios* himself, they must be certain (and must communicate this certainty to others) that the eye-witnesses, while expressing themselves in the language of their time, are still able to speak to us *directly*, when we are ready to confront their word with this faith in the Holy Spirit who is able to dispense with intermediaries.

Conclusion

Is the gulf which separates Catholic doctrine and Protestant doctrine on the relation between scripture and tradition unbridgeable? Perhaps so, as regards the theory. In practice the two attitudes have come curiously near to one another. We have said that Protestants have always recognized a tradition as guide—the decisions of the first ecumenical councils and the writings of the Reformers. But for some time now Protestant theology has been turning, more than in the past, to the study of patristics. Thus we are beginning to understand on the Protestant side what an immense treasure there is in the work of the Fathers, and we have begun to break away from that strange conception of Church history and Christian thought which supposed that between the second and the sixteenth centuries there was, with the exception of certain sects, a complete eclipse of the gospel.

On the other side, we are witnessing today a Catholic interest in the reading and study of the Bible greater, perhaps, than at any previous period. The work of Père Lagrange, to name only one; the encyclical *Divino afflante spiritu*; the extraordinary energy of the Biblical Institute in Rome and of the Biblical School of the Dominicans in Jerusalem; the publication of the excellent translation in the *Sainte Bible*, known as the Jerusalem Bible; do these not prove that the most valuable Catholic contributions to the understanding of the Bible are due, despite the theory of tradition, to a direct, immediate contact with the biblical text in the original? And the 'Catholic variations' in the appreciation of certain exegetical problems—for instance, the famous *comma Johannis* (I John 5.7)— are these revisions of previous judgments not a proof that on many occasions the Catholic Church has been able to set scripture above its tradition?

In mentioning these *rapprochements* that can be noted on the practical level, we do not seek to minimize the great divergence of doctrine which nevertheless exists. But we think that they ought to incite us to discuss the old theoretical problem of 'scripture and tradition' without any polemical intention, and with an absolute frankness and calmness which can do nothing but good in furthering interchange of views among the Christian communions.

The great divergence between Protestants and Catholics concerns especially the question whether the unique testimony of the apostles can be actualized by the written word. Our answer has been, Yes. It is scripture which actualizes this testimony, as it is the sacraments which actualize the redemptive work of Christ. *The divine Word and the sacraments: these are the two great contemporary miracles in our midst, in the Church!*

And why is scripture not a dead letter, but a source of life in which Christ is present? Because, on the one hand, the *Kyrios* speaks directly through it, as we saw; and, on the other, the actualization of the revelation, in spite of our human imperfection and the possibility of errors in interpretation, is guaranteed by the Holy Spirit, for we live already in the new age, which is the age of the Spirit. The *Kyrios* is present in scripture, and the Holy Spirit is present in the reader who has faith.

As an illustration of what I have wished to bring out in this work, I may conclude by referring to the story of the disciples on the road to Emmaus in Luke 24.13 f., three verses of which stand at the beginning of this study. While the disciples are questioning together and their unknown companion is speaking to them of Moses, all the prophets, and all the scriptures (verse 27), suddenly their eyes are opened and they know the Christ seated before them.

V

The Kingship of Christ
and the
Church in the New Testament

Translated from *Königsherrschaft Christi
und Kirche im Neuen Testament*, 3rd
edition, 1950, Zollikon-Zürich

Foreword

THE PRESENT STUDY is the result of the reshaping and expansion of a lecture which I gave on the occasion of the first meeting of students of all the evangelical theological faculties in German and French Switzerland, which was held in Gwatt near Thun on April 27th, 1940.

Several fundamental studies on the Church in the New Testament and its relation to the Kingdom of God have appeared in recent years. My purpose in this essay is to develop and deepen the insights already achieved, by introducing a third New Testament concept, the *Regnum Christi*, which, while differing from these other two concepts, is nevertheless closely bound up with them. My treatment of the question of the relations between the *Regnum Christi* and the Church is also intended to illuminate, as far as its ultimate New Testament roots are concerned, the much-discussed problem of Church and State which is anchored in the very nature of Christianity.

In accordance with the original framework of the lecture I have proceeded by way of synthesis and have attempted to work out the common elements in the New Testament statements on our theme, but the method is not intended to efface the differences established by analysis. The tacit assumption behind the enquiry is that the various New Testament writings deal with the same questions from different points of view, just as, inversely, the tacit assumption on which analytical studies of problems of New Testament theology are based is that the writings of the New Testament are all united by a common theme.

The Kingship of Christ and the Church
in the New Testament

(1) The Problem

In the New Testament we find the classical expression of the belief in the kingship exercised by Christ in the present era in all those passages which refer to Christ 'sitting on the right hand of God' and to the 'subjection of all his enemies',[1] following the prototype of Psalm 110, which is taken as referring to the kingship of Christ. The supreme expression of the belief is to be found, however, at the close of that creed-like early Christian psalm, probably first composed in Aramaic[2] which appears in Philippians 2.6 f.: '. . . wherefore God also highly exalted him and gave him a name which is above every name, that in the name of Jesus every knee should bow, of things in heaven, and things in earth, and things under the earth; and that every tongue should confess that Jesus Christ is Lord, to the glory of God the Father'.

The fact that from a particular moment in time God conferred on Jesus Christ the title 'Lord' (Hebrew: *Adonai*; Greek: *Kyrios*), which belongs to him alone (Phil. 2.10), means that Christ rules as King not only over us men but over the invisible powers in heaven, on earth and under the earth. The 'enemies' to whose subjection Psalm 110 refers are related to the invisible hostile powers.

One of the oldest Christian creeds consists of the three words: *Kyrios Jesus Christos*: Jesus Christ is Lord. For the first Christians this meant that Christ is not merely the true ruler of men, as the Roman emperor claimed to be, but ruler of the whole visible and invisible creation. It is essential to remember this to grasp the whole range of meaning contained in this first early Christian creed. In the epistle to the Romans what St. Paul calls 'confessing with the

---

[1] Rom. 8.34; I Cor. 15.25; Col. 3.1; Eph. 1.20; Heb. 1.3; 8.1; 10.13; I Peter 3.22; Acts 2.34; 5.31; 7.55; Rev. 3.21; Matt. 22.44; 26.64; Mark 12.36; 14.62; 16.19; Luke 20.42; 22.69; see also I Clem. 36.5; Barn. 12.10.

[2] E. Lohmeyer, 'Kyrios Jesus' in *Sitzungsberichte der Heidelberger Akademie der Wiss., Phil.-hist. Kl.*, 1927–8, no. 4, and J. Héring, 'Kyrios Anthropos', in *R.H.P.R.*, 1936, p. 196 f.

mouth' also consists in a confession that Jesus is the *Kyrios* (10.9). Wherever this short creed is elaborated in greater detail the subjection of the invisible powers to Christ is always mentioned explicitly, as in the passage from the epistle to the Philippians already quoted.

There is evidence that in an early form of the later Roman Apostles' Creed, with which we are familiar, the subjection of the powers and principalities to Christ was specifically referred to after the 'sitting on the right hand of God'. Apart from Philippians 2.10 we may mention I Peter 3.22, where in a context which is clearly confessional it is stated: ' . . . who has gone into heaven, and is at the right hand of God; angels and authorities and powers being made subject to him'. To this may be added I Timothy 3.16: 'seen by angels'. Outside the New Testament these 'powers', the ἐπουράνια, the ἐπίγεια and the ὑποχθόνια, are expressly mentioned in the second century in the epistle of Ignatius to the Trallians (9.1), which contains a version of the creed corresponding to some extent *verbatim* to the second article of the later Apostles' Creed, and in the epistle of Polycarp (2.1), whilst in the writings of Justin Martyr [3] and Irenaeus [4] we still find clear indications that the confession of belief in Christ the 'Lord' embraces his kingship over all the powers of the visible and invisible creation. It should also be noted that at the close of St. Matthew's Gospel the risen Lord introduces the command to baptize all nations, which also gave rise to confessional formulae, with the words: 'all power (πᾶσα ἐξουσία) has been given to me in heaven and on earth'.

This belief in the present rule of Christ over all things, which was the strong centre of the whole faith of the early Christians, accords with the fact that in the New Testament Christ also appears as the mediator of the original divine work of creation: ' . . . by him (Christ) were all things created that are in heaven and that are in

[3] *Apol.* I, 42, ἐβασίλευσεν and especially *Dial. with Trypho*, 85, κύριος τῶν δυνάμεων. The context appears to suggest that the use of the creed in exorcizing demons helped to establish the reference to Christ's dominion over the 'powers'.

[4] *Adv. Haer.*, 1.10. It is typical of Irenaeus that he places this rule over the powers exclusively in the period following the *parousia*, whereas the old creed which he uses here probably implies the present dominion of Christ. This is related to the fact that Irenaeus does not take the present *Regnum Christi* into account at all. The strictly linear conception of time which Irenaeus developed in his struggle against Gnosticism, the almost exaggeratedly uninterrupted straight line leading from the creation to the last things means that the whole process hastens towards the final eschatological fulfilment with such speed that there is no time for an intervening *Regnum Christi*. Cf. below, p. 137.

earth, visible and invisible, whether they be thrones, or dominions, or principalities, or powers: all things were created by him and for him: and he is before all things and in him all things consist' (Col. 1.16). The same thought is expressed in I Corinthians 8.6 and in the prologue to St. John's Gospel: 'all things were made by him', and in the epistle to the Hebrews: 'by whom also he made the worlds' (1.2 f.).

It is therefore natural that at the end of time, when God will create a 'new heaven and a new earth', Christ will also be the mediator of that new creation. The coming of the final catastrophe which the early Christians were awaiting, when Christ will appear again, will take place by a sovereign act of God corresponding exactly to the creative act 'in the beginning'; with a command (I Thess. 4.16) that can only be compared with that first command: 'Let there be light'. Christ was the mediator of creation 'in the beginning'; Christ is to be the mediator of the new creation at the end of time.

The original Christian confession of belief in Christ the 'Lord', according to which Christ now rules over the whole creation, visible and invisible, in heaven, on earth and under the earth has to be understood in this context. We shall have to examine to what period of time this effective exercise of the *Regnum Christi* refers, and in what way the subject powers are governed in this space of time.

How does the Church fit into this whole complex of problems in the New Testament? In what relationship does the Church of Christ stand to this *Regnum Christi* which we still have to define more closely? That there must be a remarkably close connection between them is due to the very nature of the two concepts, and the New Testament does, in fact, reveal an intimate connection between them, inasmuch as the Church of Christ is also mentioned in some of the key-passages concerning the *Regnum Christi*. In Colossians 1.14 f. Christ appears not merely as the creative mediator of all 'visible and invisible things' but also as the one who effects the 'reconciliation' with God 'of all things, whether they be things in earth or things in heaven', and in this wide cosmic setting we read in verse 17 that Christ is also the head of the body, the Church. In the epistle to the Ephesians the solidarity between Church and creation is expressed even more clearly: 'he has put all things under his feet and has made him the head over all things for the Church' (1.22). And according to Hebrews 1.14 even the angels are sent out to serve under Christ 'for the sake of those who are to inherit salvation'.

From these passages it is quite clear that the *Regnum Christi* and the Church of Christ are essentially correlated in the New Testament, and that the question of the relationship between them which we are raising in the present essay is not one that has to be imported into the New Testament. We are, in fact, concerned with a particular aspect of the more comprehensive problem of the relationship between redemption and creation. The creation is discussed not only on the first page of the Old Testament but throughout the Bible, right up to the very last page of the New Testament.

The fact that he is created in the image of God raises man, whom God created in the beginning, above all other creatures; but it also means that the whole creation has been drawn into the drama occasioned by man's sin. The earth is cursed for the sake of Adam. This is stated not only in the book of Genesis but also in the epistle to the Romans (8.20). But for the same reason the redemption of man by Christ's death on the cross also affects the whole creation. According to the Synoptic Gospels the earth grew dark when Christ's sufferings reached their climax; and according to the Gospel of Matthew (27.51) the earth shook at the moment of his death, in which all things are reconciled to God through the blood of his cross (Col. 1.20). In this sense we may speak of the spell cast on Good Friday on the evidence of the New Testament itself.

In particular, however, creation also shares in the present hope, in the waiting and 'groaning' of man for perfection (Rom. 8.21 f.), precisely because of what took place on the cross in the first place for man, but also for creation. This groaning of the whole creation is an intimation of the new creation in which there will be no more death and decay.[5] The whole of nature is still waiting but one can also say, has been waiting already, since the all-important event has already taken place.

The New Testament relationship between the kingship of Christ and the Church of Christ is grounded in the solidarity which binds the whole creation to man. One is, therefore, not surprised that at the end of St. Matthew's Gospel (28.18) the risen Christ at the very time when he issues the summons to establish the Church which is implicit in the command to baptize all nations, which we have already mentioned, also reminds his disciples of the power over the whole

---

5 Papias sketches a drastic picture of renewed and liberated nature. See Irenaeus, *Adv. Haer.*, V, 33.3 f.

creation which has been given to him: 'All power is given to me in heaven and on earth'.

As *Kyrios* (*Adonai*) Christ is, in the first place, Lord of creation; as βασιλεύς, King of the Jews,[6] King of Israel,[7] he is above all Lord of the Church. But the title of *Kyrios* also refers to his dominion over Israel and over the Church, wherever there is resistance to the Roman emperor's claim to be *Kyrios*. And, inversely, Christ's kingship covers his rule over creation when he is described as 'the King of kings and Lord of lords' in I Timothy 6.15, and in the reference to his kingship in I Corinthians 15.24 and especially in Matthew's Gospel which emphasizes Christ's kingship over Israel from the very first chapter onwards,[8] and ends with an unsurpassably emphatic reference to his power over heaven and earth. Here, too, then, we have the same close connection between the kingship of Christ and the Church.

(2) *The Time of the Regnum Christi and the Time of the Church of Christ*

We are assuming that the *Regnum Christi* and the Church of Christ, these two closely related but not identical factors, both belong to the same limited period of time. This is what differentiates them from the Kingdom of God. Therefore, however close their relationship, the *Regnum Christi* and the Kingdom of God are no more interchangeable concepts than the Church and the Kingdom of God.

It is quite true that the *Regnum Christi*, the Church and the Kingdom of God all belong to the end of time, but the *Regnum Christi* and the Church of Christ coincide with a chronologically limited phase of this time, namely, the phase which has already begun and in which we are living, the beginning of which is behind and the end of which is before us, whereas the Kingdom of God is a purely future quantity.[9]

The endless discussion as to whether the Kingdom of God is a

[6] Matt. 2.2; 27.11, 29, 37; Mark 15.2, 9, 12, 18, 26; Luke 23.3, 37; John 18.33, 37, 39; 19.3, 14, 19, 21.

[7] Matt. 27.42; Mark 15.32; John 1.49; 12.13.

[8] J. Wilkens rightly considers this motif the key to an understanding of St. Matthew's Gospel in his *Der König Israels. Eine Einführung in das Evangelium nach Matthäus*, 1934 (*Die urchristliche Botschaft*, edited by O. Schmitz).

[9] There is far-reaching agreement on this point today. See Schmidt, article βασιλεία, in G. Kittel's *T.W.N.T.*, i, p. 562 f.

present or future quantity in the New Testament [10] might have
taken a different turn if a clear-cut chronological distinction had
been made between the βασιλεία τοῦ υἱοῦ, that is to say, the *Regnum
Christi*, and the βασιλεία τοῦ θεοῦ, that is to say, the Kingdom of
God. St. Paul makes the clearest possible chronological distinction
between them. In I Corinthians 15.23 f. the Son to whom 'the
Father has subjected everything' will subject himself to the Father
only after his second coming and after all the events connected with
it, and will then surrender all authority to God the Father. This will
happen when he 'shall have destroyed all rule and authority and
power'. Only then will come the time of the new creation, the
time of the Kingdom of God the Father. 'For the son must reign as
king' we read in the same passage, in free imitation of the psalm:
'until he has put all enemies under his feet'. But this kingship is not
to begin sometime in the millennium, in which it will continue
after Christ's second coming,[11] but has begun already. We are
already in a βασιλεία, namely, the *Regnum Christi*. In so far as we
share his dominion, we already form this βασιλεία on the basis of
redemption (Rev. 1.6).

In the epistle to the Colossians (1.13), too, the beginning of the
Son's kingship, which is clearly distinguished from the Kingdom of
God, lies in the past: '(God) delivered us from the power of dark-
ness, and translated us into the kingdom of his dear son'. Thus
Christ already exercises his authority over all the subject powers.
For the βασιλεία of the Son the Christian can already thank God
(Col. 1.12 f.); but for the coming of the Kingdom of God he must
still pray: 'Thy Kingdom come'. The original Christian creed:
Kyrios Jesus Christos simply means: The *Regnum Christi* is here, 'Jesus
Christ reigns as King, all things are subject to him'. One can see
why Christians were willing to die for this faith. In Thessalonica
(Acts 17.7) they were already accused of 'saying that there is another
king, one Jesus'. And it is even easier to see how 'serious' it was for
them (to use the words of the heathen imperial official from
Smyrna in the year 155) to say *Kaisar Kyrios* (*Martyrdom of Polycarp*,
8.2). If there was another *Kyrios* besides the one to whom
God had given this name which is above all other names, then
the *Regnum Christi* would simply not yet exist at all, Christ

10 As far as the Gospels are concerned a good account is given by W. G. Kümmel,
  'Die Eschatologie der Evangelien', *Theol. Blätter*, 1936, p. 225–41. Cf. G. Gloege,
  Reich Gottes und Kirche im N.T. (*N.T. Forsch.*, edited by O. Schmitz), 1929.
11 See below, p. 111 f.

would not be reigning, and we should be back at the stage of mere waiting. The Christian waits for the Kingdom of God, but he waits for it because he knows that the *Regnum Christi* has already begun.

Christ laid the foundation of his kingship in his death and resurrection, through which he secured the victory over the powers that are henceforth subject to him. Even though the final destruction of the enemies is reserved for a future phase, of which we shall speak later on,[12] in which the 'last enemy', death, will be destroyed along with the other hostile powers (I Cor. 15.24, 26), the decisive defeat of death has already been accomplished in the death and resurrection of Christ (II Tim. 1.10), and the apostle can write: 'Death is swallowed up in victory. O death, where is thy victory? O death, where is thy sting?' (I Cor. 15.55). It is the risen Lord who tells the disciples that all power has been given to him in heaven and on earth (Matt. 28.18). Christ's death and resurrection provide the basis for the present realization of the *Regnum Christi*.

The effective beginning and the appropriation of his kingly power took place in the ascension, when Christ set himself at the right hand of God. In the New Testament what the much-quoted Psalm 110 says in the Jewish messianic interpretation of the messianic king of the future: 'Sit at my right hand until I make thine enemies thy footstool', is transferred to the present phase which has already begun: '(Christ) is gone into heaven, and is on the right hand of God; angels and authorities and powers being made subject to him' (I Pet. 3.22). That Christ has already sat down at the right hand of God is a recurring *leitmotiv* in the New Testament.[13] According to the passage in I Peter just quoted, the subjection of the 'enemies' prophesied in Psalm 110 has already taken place. This does not conflict with Hebrews 10.13 and I Corinthians 15.25, where it is pointed out that their destruction will only be consummated in the future, in the last stage of the *Regnum Christi*.

For just as the *Regnum Christi* has a beginning, so too it has an end. Because the end is in the future it cannot be assigned a historical date like the beginning. But the New Testament does at least indicate the future event which will initiate the final phase of the *Regnum Christi*: the second coming of Christ. It began with the ascension of Christ; it will end with his second coming. Therefore, in the words of the 'two men in white apparel' the author of the Acts of the

12 See below, p. 112 f.
13 See above, p. 105, n. 1.

Apostles (1.11) also stresses the external correspondence between these two facts which constitute the framework of the *Regnum Christi*: 'this Jesus . . . shall so come in like manner (that is, on the clouds) as you saw him go into heaven'.

It should be noted very carefully, however, that according to the Revelation of John and I Corinthians 15.23 f. the second coming of Christ and the eschatological events associated with it have still to be regarded as the final act of the *Regnum Christi*. For the Son will 'deliver up the kingdom to God' only when the final struggle has been successfully fought, after Christ's second coming. Thus the final act of the *Regnum Christi* projects into the beginnings of the coming age, the αἰών μέλλων, the new creation; it belongs not only to the present but also to the eschatological future. In that final act what has already happened and what is still happening in the present phase of the *Regnum Christi* will be repeated in a final and concentrated form: the victory over Satan and the 'powers', their bondage and the release for final destruction.

That part of the *Regnum Christi* projects into the future age is evident from the whole of the Revelation of John and also from the concept of the millennium (20.4 f.) which represents the Church as it will be in that final act,[14] and which is usually misleadingly described as an *interregnum*. The millennium and the apocalyptic events which precede it represent the part of the *Regnum Christi* which began with the ascension and which overlaps into the future age.[15] The term *interregnum* would be better applied to the whole of the *Regnum Christi*, the whole period between the conclusion of the work achieved by the historical Christ and the conclusion of the work achieved by Christ at his second coming. The millennium must, therefore, not be identified with the whole *Regnum Christi* or

---

[14] As expounded correctly by Karl Ludwig Schmidt in 'Le problème du christ-ianisme primitif', *Quatre conférences sur la forme et la pensée du Nouveau Testament*, 1938, p. 84, n. 4. We would, however, wish more emphasis to be placed on the connection of this final act with the *Regnum Christi* which began with the ascension.

[15] J. Héring, *Le Royaume de Dieu et sa venue, Objet de l'espérance de Jésus et de St. Paul*, 1937, p. 176, rightly stresses the contemporaneity of the messianic king-dom in St. Paul's thought, as against Albert Schweitzer, *The Mysticism of Paul the Apostle*, E.T., 1931. But he does not allow its due importance to the final phase of this kingdom, which Paul also conceives as projecting into the coming age and which both crowns and recapitulates the messianic kingdom, when he merely mentions in a subordinate clause, 'that the messianic kingdom pro-jects slightly into the time fixed by the *parousia*'.

with the present Church.[16] The *Regnum Christi* is the more comprehensive concept, for this reign began almost two thousand years ago and will continue for an indefinite time in this age, whereas the millennium belongs to the final act of the *Regnum Christi* initiated by the *parousia*, in which the Church will play a specially important part.

In chronological terms, the theme of the whole drama described in the Revelation of John as far as and including chapter 20 is not the Kingdom of God but the *Regnum Christi*, or rather the final act of this reign of Christ.[17] At the very beginning we hear that Christ has power over death and Hades (1.18), that he is the ruler of the kings of the earth and, later, that he rules all nations with a rod of iron (12.5; 19.15), that his name is 'King of kings' and 'Lord of lords' (19.16).

Thus the faithful Christian is subject at present to a rule which, though it still belongs entirely to the present age, will continue for a while within the future age of which the apocalyptist speaks. Nevertheless, the whole *Regnum Christi* forms a unity, as is already evident from the fact that the phase which precedes the *parousia* merely represents a kind of recapitulation of the phase which is to follow it.[18] This is the reason for the curious tension between present and future which runs right through the New Testament and which is typical of the Christian situation. The *Regnum Christi* is the meeting-ground of the two great ages of the universe into which the New Testament, along with late Judaism, divides the whole course of time. The rule of Christ occupies both the final period of the present age and the beginnings of the future. Although it still belongs entirely to this age, our present age is already a final period since a reign has already begun which will still exist in the *parousia* and the events associated with it: the *Regnum Christi*.

The eschatological problem of the New Testament is contained in this tension. Any attempt to remove the tension would mean

---

[16] This latter assumption, maintained by the Donatist Tyconius and made famous by Augustine, is in contradiction to the whole of the New Testament.

[17] The literary and historical problem of the sources of the materials used in the Revelation is not under discussion here and may be passed over.

[18] For this reason, that is, because the two phases of the *Regnum Christi* form a unity, every generation which belongs to the phase of the *Regnum* preceding the *parousia* may see in contemporary events the signs of the end described in the Revelation. But no generation must assert that such events are the final sign from which the actual date of the end can be worked out. For we do not know how long this first phase is to last. The New Testament lays special emphasis on the fact that we do not know the date of the *parousia*.

annulling the situation created by Christ. It derives in the last resort from the fact that judgment has already been passed within the present age in the death and resurrection of Christ, and that it must be made once again after the present age has disappeared.[19] This is why the subjection of the hostile powers precedes the ascension in I Peter 3.22 whereas, according to the writer of the epistle to the Hebrews, the Christ who sits at the right hand of God still waits for it (10.13). That is also the reason for the characteristic relationship between the 'subjection' and 'destruction' of the powers. The verb καταργέω, which the New Testament is fond of using in this context, has both meanings: 'subject' and 'destroy'. It is used in II Timothy 1.10, which refers to the victory over death which Christ has already achieved on the cross, and also in I Corinthians 15.26 where the reference is to the victory over death which will only be attained after Christ's second coming (see also Rev. 20.14). On both occasions the victory is final but, whereas the first time death merely has the 'power taken from it', to quote Luther's faithful translation of the verb in II Timothy 1.10, the second time it is destroyed.[20] Between the two victories the 'powers' are tied to the power of Christ, but the line to which they are attached varies in slackness from time to time.

Is this a case of the cyclic, that is, the Greek concept of time, according to which everything recurs in an eternal revolution, and redemption consists in a release from the compulsion of time and is therefore outside time? To accept that view would mean mistaking the very essence of New Testament eschatology, which presupposes a linear concept of time,[21] and in which redemption takes place

19 Schweitzer, *The Mysticism of Paul the Apostle*, E.T., 1931, p. 64, recognizes that Paul represents the future redemption 'as having already begun to come into operation', but he still thinks it remarkable (p. 66) that a struggle with the invisible powers will take place in the coming age. The reason why he evidently perceives a contradiction in Paul's thought which he cannot explain is that the character of the present *Regnum Christi* is not defined in its relationship to the future age.

20 Barth, *Rechfertigung und Recht* (Theol. Studien, no. 1), 1938, p. 16, rightly draws attention to the double meaning of καταργεῖν, but translates the verb in I Cor. 15.24 as 'subject', whereas the meaning here is 'destroy', no less certainly than two verses later where it is a question of death (cf. Delling in *T.W.N.T.*). The verb also has the sense of 'destroy' in II Thess. 2.8, where it is a question of the events which will take place in connection with the *parousia*.

21 Cf. on the problem of 'time and eschatology', F. Holmström, *Das eschatologische Denken der Gegenwart*, 1936 (cf. my review in *R.H.P.R.*, 1938, p. 347 f.). Cf. also Barth, *Die kirchliche Dogmatik. Die Lehre von Gott*, 1st Halbband, 1940, p. 685 f.

within the process of time controlled by God. Admittedly, God is the Lord of time and it was possible for the decisive victory over Satan and the 'powers' to be perfectly achieved on the cross; yet it was still possible for the eschatological unfolding of the drama of redemption (ushered in by this victory) to be reserved for a later time. It must not be inferred from the fact that Christ's death is the central, all-inclusive event in the New Testament that there is no process of salvation in time. According to the New Testament the death of Christ includes everything before and after, both the Old Testament from the creation onwards and the New Testament with its eschatological vision of the Kingdom of God the Father. But this does not involve a denial of the temporal, chronological nature of world history as a linear and unrepeatable process; far from denying the linear nature of history it is asserted more fully in the New Testament than ever before, in a reaction to Greek Gnosticism.

All the characteristic and often misinterpreted 'anticipations' of the future in the New Testament arise from the fact that Christ's death includes everything that precedes and follows it, though the drama of salvation is a forward-striving process developing in time. Thus, for example, in the Synoptic Gospels Jesus sees Satan cast down from heaven even before his death (Luke 10.17). When Jesus, who came to achieve the victory by his death, dwelt on earth such an anticipation was natural,[22] as was his proclamation that the Kingdom of God had already come (Matt. 12.28; Luke 11.20).[23] This is why the linguistic distinction between the βασιλεία of the Father and that of the Son is not sustained consistently in New Testament

---

[22] The formula of Christ as the αὐτοβασιλεία which was created by Origen (Migne, *P. G.*, Series I, T. XIII) refers to this. Cf. P. Feine, *Theologie des N.T.*, 1910, p. 100; G. Kittel, *Die Probleme des palästinischen Spätjudentums und das Urchristentum*, 1926, p. 130 f.; K. L. Schmidt, article βασιλεία in Kittel's *T.W.N.T.*, i, p. 591.

[23] In Luke 10.17 Jesus communicates the vision of the fallen Satan to the returning Seventy, who have reported to him with joy that the demons were subject to them through his name. The words 'through your name' are all-important for the Synoptic testimony. The driving out of the demons could not be connected in itself with the vision of the fallen Satan. Jesus himself recognizes that even Jews cast out demons (Matt. 12.27). He is able to infer that the Kingdom of God exists already from the fact that he, the Son of Man returning on the clouds, casts them out and has them cast out in his name.

usage.[24] This does not alter the fact that the chronological differentiation between them is unequivocally implicit in the New Testament. In substance the *Regnum Christi* is no more separate from the Kingdom of God the Father than the Son is separate from the Father, but from the point of view of time it represents a power of its own; it began with the ascension, and will end in the opening phase of the future age.

The time of the Church can be defined in just the same way. It, too, has a beginning and an end, and its duration coincides with the same phase of the end of time as that of the *Regnum Christi*. It was initiated by the same central fact of the death of Christ. For the Church of Christ the cross is also the *terminus a quo*. Only the cross makes the existence of the Church possible, though a church already existed in the Old Testament in the form of God's chosen people and then as the 'remnant' of Israel, which turns back and which, according to the prophets, God has chosen to save.[25] The history of man's salvation, which Christians now interpret retrospectively as preceding the Church of Christ, began in Old Testament times.

Christian understanding of this fact is born in the light of the cross. But this insight into what has gone before does not necessarily obliterate the chronological frontiers of the Church of Christ.[26] The fact remains that the Church which was prepared for in the Old Testament is only realized as the Church of Christ in that final phase of time ushered in by the death of Christ.

According to the Acts of the Apostles the only chronological difference between the beginning of the *Regnum Christi* and that of the Church is that the *Regnum Christi* was born at the ascension and the Church at Pentecost.

Pentecost is the beginning of the Church, the opening stage of the realization of the people of God in the end of time. The Spirit overcomes the separation of nations divided by language. But the Spirit is the element of the future Kingdom of God. The miracle of

---

24 See K. L. Schmidt, article βασιλεία in G. Kittel's *T.W.N.T.*, i, p. 581 f., though he is forced to conclude, ib., p. 582, 'that one must not speak of the βασιλεία of Christ without that of God'. In fact, it is impossible to separate them as far as their content is concerned, though chronologically it is absolutely essential to differentiate them.

25 See Schmidt, article βασιλεία in *T.W.N.T.*, i, p. 502 f.; id., 'Die Kirche des Urchristentums' (*Festgabe f. A. Deissmann*), 1927.

26 On the relation between the Church of Christ and the Old Testament see below, p. 128–131.

Pentecost is that this future element which is to provide the material of the new creation takes hold already of a part of the old sin-corrupted creation in the present age, without being able to transform its outer framework. The miracle occurs from now on in the Church. That which took place at the ascension for the whole creation on the basis of death and resurrection, the subjection to Christ in the end-time, here takes place for the people of God, on whom the highest mission in creation devolves: the realization in the end-time of a fellowship in Christ ordained by the Spirit of God —both on the way to the Kingdom of God.

Peter's speech at Pentecost (Acts 2.14 f.), which is based on the prophecy of Joel, clearly refers to the fact that now that the Spirit has laid hold of the community, the 'last times' are being made manifest (ἐν ἐσχάταις ἡμέραις, verse 17). When he calls the Spirit that already exists in the present the 'first-fruits' (ἀπαρχή, Rom. 8.23) and 'earnest' (ἀρραβών, II Cor. 1.22), St. Paul is recalling that the Spirit represents part of the future that is already present. Seeing that the Church of Christ was founded by the Spirit at Pentecost as the Church of the end-time, it is significant that in the later creed Spirit, Church and expectation of the future are combined in the third article.

The sacrament of Baptism, by which the believer becomes a member of the Church, leads to a sharing in the Spirit: 'By one Spirit we were all baptized into one body' (I Cor. 12.13). On the other hand, in Romans 6.3 Paul emphasizes that Baptism means being taken up into the death and resurrection of Christ, which are the precondition of the Church's existence. Since the birthday of the Church coincides with the coming of the Spirit, it not only introduces the end-time, but presupposes the death of Christ in time. For, according to the Gospel of John, the Spirit can only appear after this event and after Christ has been 'glorified' (John 7.39). And according to the farewell discourses in this Gospel the promise of the Spirit can only be fulfilled as a sequel to Christ's death, so that the Church of Christ cannot arise before that event has taken place.

If we proceed from the other crucial New Testament definition of the Church we shall reach the same conclusion. According to Ephesians 2.20, the Church is 'built upon the foundation of the apostles and prophets'.[27] Paul recognized that as much as did the early Church itself. According to him the apostolate supplements

[27] In view of 3.5 and 4.11 it can hardly be disputed that New Testament prophets are meant in this passage.

the Spirit as a constitutive element of the Church.[28] But, in the New Testament, being an apostle means having witnessed the resurrection of Christ, having seen the risen Lord, which is another way of saying that the Church can only be translated into reality after the death and resurrection of Christ.

So far as this is true, the disciples can only be said to have constituted the foundation of the Church in Jesus's own lifetime. First of all, they had to become apostles, witnesses of Christ's resurrection. And it is significant that baptism, the sacrament of reception into the Church, was first instituted by Christ after his resurrection.

Nevertheless, it was the earthly Jesus who laid the foundations of the Church before his death. There is no reason to doubt the authenticity of the words about the Church which Jesus spoke to Peter in Matthew 16.18 or to regard them as a later insertion of the early Church. But it should be noted that the Greek rendering of Jesus's words uses the future tense: οἰκοδομήσω, 'I *will* build my Church'. The context shows that the evangelist used the future tense to underline the necessity of Christ's death as the precondition of the Church's existence. It can hardly be a coincidence that in the very passage in Matthew in which he predicts the coming of the Church, he also foretells his passion for the first time and that the evangelist deliberately underlines the connection between the two prophecies: 'from that time forth', ἀπὸ τότε, that is, after Christ had referred to the future Church, 'he began to show to his disciples how that he must suffer many things . . . and be killed, and be raised again the third day'.

It is not, however, merely a common point of departure which the Church shares with the *Regnum Christi*. It also has the same duration, and the parallel is so close that, like the kingship of Christ, the Church also fills the whole final period of the present age which

28 In Karl Holl's suggestive article 'Der Kirchenbegriff des Paulus in seinem Verhältnis zu dem der Urgemeinde' (*Ges. Aufsätze zur Kirchengeschichte*, ii, 1928, p. 44 f.) the contrast between the foundation of the Church on the apostolate (the concept of the Church held by the Church in Jerusalem) and the foundation of the Church on the Spirit (Paul's concept of the Church) is exaggerated. (The same applies to Maurice Goguel, 'Le problème de l'Église dans le christianisme primitif', in *R.H.P.R.*, 1938, p. 293 f.). In fact, the Church in Jerusalem did know that the Church is founded on the Spirit (otherwise one would have to dispute the historical authenticity of the account of Pentecost with Maurice Goguel, 'La conception jérusalémite de l'Église et les faits de pneumatisme', *Mélanges Cumont*, 1936, p. 209 f.), and with St. Paul the foundation of the Church on the apostolate is more than a 'residue' (see Gal. 2.2: 'lest by any means I should run, or had run, in vain').

has still to run its course and then projects into the opening phase of the future age, after which it will yield to the Kingdom of God. In the first place the Church of the New Testament is bound up with the present age, but it will appear as part of the coming age in that final act when Christ, returning on the clouds, will be encompassed by those who have for ever formed his Church on earth, when the apostles will sit on twelve thrones (Matt. 19.28), when they will reign with him (Rev. 5.10; 20.4; II Tim. 2.12), and when the 'saints', that is, all the members of the Church, will judge the 'angels' (I Cor. 6.2 f.). The millennium will be the Church of this final phase.

This will be the end of the Church as it will be the end of the *Regnum Christi*. And so the Church also shares in the tension between present and future. And here again it would be wrong to attempt to resolve the tension, for it is part of the very nature of the Church, as it is part of the nature of the *Regnum Christi*. The Church already belongs entirely to the end and still belongs entirely to the present.

This duality of the Church's existence is particularly apparent in the possession of the Spirit by which the Church is constituted. We have seen that the Spirit is an element of the future age, an element which will constitute the new creation of the Kingdom of God within and without. This constituent of the future Kingdom of God is already present in the Church, but only as an 'earnest' (II Cor. 2.22), as the 'firstfruits' (Rom. 8.23), because it is not yet able to break the outer framework of the present age in which the Church must live.

Thus despite its possession of the Spirit the Church still belongs to the present and has to wait for the time when God's Spirit will embrace all things, when God will be 'all in all' and when its own time will have run its course, after it has fulfilled a particularly important task as a 'co-ruler' in the final act. It is still waiting, but it may also be said that it has been waiting already, for its waiting is grounded in the Spirit which it already possesses (Rom. 8.23 f.).

Though it is already true that the 'gates of Hades shall not prevail against it' (Matt. 16.18), it must constantly fight against the power of hell, just as Christ in his kingdom still has to overcome the 'powers', though he has already vanquished them.

The Church and the *Regnum Christi* show the same tension between present and future time because they coincide in time.

Notable differences between them only appear when one examines their respective spheres and membership.

(3) The Sphere of the Kingship of Christ and the Sphere of the Church

The Greek word for dominion, βασιλεία, has three meanings. It means (1) the exercise of power, government; (2) the sphere, the territory or area governed; (3) the community of those who are governed. All three meanings are applicable to the βασιλεία of God, and the same is true of the βασιλεία of Christ except that the intermediate character of this βασιλεία modifies the usual meaning in each of the three cases. As far as the exercise of kingship is concerned, we have already seen how, in the Kingdom of Christ, it is marked by that peculiar provisional 'binding' of the 'powers', which still allows for their temporary release from bondage to Christ and the unleashing of their demonic violence.

It is in this light that the sphere and the membership of the *Regnum Christi* have to be defined. As regards the sphere of the kingdom, we have already noted that the kingship of Christ extends to the whole of creation: 'all authority has been given to me in heaven and on earth'; 'that in the name of Jesus every knee should bow, of things in heaven, and things on earth, and things under the earth; and that every tongue should confess that Jesus Christ is Lord' (Phil. 2.10); the reconciliation of all things to himself, whether things on earth or things in heaven (Col. 1.14-20).

It is, therefore, not true that Christ now exercises his kingship only in heaven or the invisible world. Christ also rules on earth and over the state as well as the Church.[29]

Admittedly, he does not rule over the states of this world directly, but only through the mediation of the 'powers and authorities' which he has subjected and which are provisionally attached to him. These invisible powers are active on earth. It is impossible to know how the various earthly spheres of influence are distributed among them since we do not know if the various terms: ἀρχαί, ἄρχοντες τοῦ αἰῶνος τούτου, ἐξουσίαι, δυνάμεις, θρόνοι, κυριότητες, ἄγγελοι were synonymous in New Testament times or whether, as appears likely, there were differences in meaning among them. But at any rate the earthly power of the state belongs to the sphere of these

---

29 When the Johannine Christ declares 'My kingdom is not of this world' (John 18.36), he merely means that it is not an earthly state. That it is not *of* (ἐκ) this world does not mean that its influence does not extend to this world.

angel-powers. They were already behind the state authorities who brought Christ to the cross. They are the ἄρχοντες τοῦ αἰῶνος τούτου, who crucified the 'Lord of glory' in their ignorance of the 'hidden wisdom of God' (I Cor. 2.7–8). Herod and Pilate were merely their executive organs. If the invisible powers which stood behind them had known the divine plan of salvation they would not have crucified Christ, as the apostle writes in this passage of I Corinthians. For—this must have been the train of thought in Paul's mind—by this crucifixion they brought about their own defeat at the hands of Christ.

It is also evident from I Corinthians 6.3 that these invisible 'powers' are behind the earthly states. Paul justifies forbidding Christians to use secular courts for lawsuits between Christians on the ground that, at the end of time, in the final act of the *Regnum Christi*, the members of the Church will judge the 'angels'.

Apart from Titus 3.1 reference must be made, above all, to the main passage in which the state is discussed, Romans 13.1 f. Here Christians are commanded to be subject to the 'powers', ἐξουσίαι. The context shows that Paul is referring to the state. All the same, the expression ἐξουσίαι should be translated 'powers', to make it clear that the basis of the argument is the New Testament view that state authorities are the executive organs of the invisible powers.[30] Since these powers have been subjugated by Christ and are bound to him in this final phase of time, everyone is to be subject to them. For the duration of this period, the period of the *Regnum Christi*, they are 'ordained by God' and the fact that the New Testament associates the state so closely with these powers does not in any way imply, as has sometimes been thought, a disparagement of the state.[31] On the other hand, the fact that the powers have already been overcome and yet have to be overcome once again, that, in particular, the ἐξουσίαι, ἄγγελοι, ἄρχοντες τοῦ αἰῶνος τούτου which stand behind the state are able to free themselves temporarily from their attachment to Christ during the *Regnum Christi* and become demonic, just as Satan will be let loose from his prison in the final

[30] On the problem of the explanation of the ἐξουσίαι as angel-powers, see the appendix at the end of this essay.

[31] Karl Barth's study, *Rechtfertigung und Recht* (*Theol. Studien*, no. 1), 1938, p. 14 f. shows how positively the state can be appraised on the assumption that the ἐξουσίαι of Rom. 13.1 refer to the angel-powers. It must not be forgotten, however, that however positively it is valued, even the lawful state is 'provisional and inconclusive' for the Christian in the New Testament (K. L. Schmidt, *Die Polis in Kirche und Welt. Eine lexikographische und exegetische Studie*, 1940).

act (Rev. 20.7), is one aspect of the whole duality of the *Regnum Christi*. For these things that are to be concentrated at the close of the *Regnum Christi* are, as we know, typical of the whole *Regnum Christi*, even in so far as it belongs to the present age.

As soon, however, as even a temporary release of the 'powers' behind the earthly states takes place, they reveal their demonic nature, violence is unleashed, and the authority of the state becomes a 'beast'. The self-deification of the state which bids the world set up and worship an 'image of the beast' (Rev. 13.14 f.) is the sure sign of this release from the ties which bind it to the *Regnum Christi*.

Attention has often been drawn to the contradictory attitude of Christians to the state as expressed in Revelation 13.1 f. on the one hand and in Romans 13.1 f. on the other. In the one case the state is 'ordained by God', 'servant of God'; in the other it is 'the beast'. In fact, there is no contradiction. The different approach is conditioned by the whole tension which characterizes the *Regnum Christi*, in which the subject powers and their executive organs, the earthly states, are subject to the rule of Christ and yet still able to obtain occasional release. The Christian attitude is perfectly clear: the most loyal subjection to the state as such, granting it everything that is its due and which it needs for its existence and security, but relentless opposition once it deifies itself. That an unleashing of demonic power is still possible does not alter the basic fact that Christ has already been given all power over the earth. There is no sphere of the divine creation in heaven and on earth which is excluded from the present rule of Christ. He also reigns over the 'groaning' creation of the earth that is waiting for final redemption.

The βασιλεία of Christ is everywhere, but it does not necessarily coincide spatially with creation, as will be the case with the βασιλεία of God. For not only are the 'powers' merely 'bound' throughout the visible and invisible world, but, although already conquered, the terrible power of the σάρξ and the 'last enemy', death, still persists on earth. The divine Spirit is already at work on earth, but it has not yet taken hold of earthly bodies; it will only transform them at the end (Rom. 8.11, 23; I Cor. 15.35 f.). So if it is only possible to describe the βασιλεία of Christ as a place, the place of the whole sphere of creation, with certain reservations, this is not to be taken as meaning that a part of creation, such as the earth, is excluded and that the present kingship of Christ is only in the invisible world, but rather that (1) the whole place is inhabited by the σάρξ and death which have been overcome by Christ but are still hostile; and (2) every part of this place, whether in heaven or on earth, can release itself temporarily, as happens in the demonic unleashing of the power of the state. On the other hand, it is a mistake to believe that these unleashed powers can really escape from the rule of Christ. In fact, the line to which they are attached is merely lengthened sufficiently for them to cross the boundary. But the line remains.

In Colossians and Ephesians the image of the 'head' is used to describe the rule which Christ exercises over the visible and invisible creation. 'Christ is the head of all principality and power' (Col. 2.10). God has resolved to give history its fulfilment by summing up (ἀνακεφαλαιώσασθαι) everything in Christ, things in heaven, and things on earth (Eph. 1.10).

In both letters, however, Christ is also described as the head of the Church (Col. 1.17 and Eph. 1.22). From this point of view the Church might appear to be a mere section of the *Regnum Christi*, Christ being head of the Church because he is head of the whole creation, of which the Church itself is a part. At first sight this seems to be confirmed by the fact that the Church's sphere of influence is confined to the earthly world. In the New Testament that is part of the very nature of the Church. Its origin and its goal, Christ, the head, is beyond the earthly world, but the place where the rule of the Church is exercised is the visible world, and, within that world, an earthly community of human beings. The place in which the Church is set is much narrower than that of the *Regnum Christi*, and yet it would be wrong to infer that the Church therefore occupies a subordinate position within the all-embracing *Regnum Christi*. This concentration on one definite point of creation, the earthly world and, within this world, a human community, signifies rather that the Church is the heart and centre of the *Regnum Christi*. It is not merely a section but the only point from which the whole of the *Regnum Christi* can be seen, and whatever happens in the Church has a decisive influence throughout the *Regnum Christi*, just as the unique work of the earthly, incarnate Christ was decisive for the subjection of the whole creation.

This central position of the Church in the *Regnum Christi* is expressed in the New Testament in the description of the Church as the body of Christ. The Church is the earthly body of the risen Christ, who sits in heaven at the right hand of God in the fulness of his glory. The fact that Christ is at the same time described as head of the whole creation and, therefore, of the Church appears to occasion a certain incongruity inasmuch as for the Church he is now both head and body, and the body 'grows up' into the head (Eph. 4.15–16).[32] But this incongruity is, in fact, typical of the curious relationship between the Church and the *Regnum Christi*, and is related to the fact that, on the one hand, the Church is part of the whole sphere of the *Regnum* of which Christ is the head and, on the other hand, Christ himself is present in this limited part of the kingdom in quite a different way from elsewhere.

The term 'head' is an image of the whole Christ who rules over his kingdom, whereas the term 'body' is more than a mere image in the New Testament, since the bodily nature of the Church is conceived in a quite concrete sense,[33] not merely in Colossians and Ephesians but also in I Corinthians 12.27 and Galatians 4.19, where Paul writes that Christ must be 'formed' in the Galatian Churches (as in every Church). The early Christians may have seen this view prefigured in such words of Jesus as Matthew 10.40: 'He that receives you, receives me'. In the above-mentioned passage in Galatians (4.14) Paul writes that the Galatians had received him as Christ Jesus when they entered the Church and, inversely, in the Acts of the Apostles (9.4; 22.7; 26.14) on the road to Damascus the risen Lord says to Paul who is persecuting the Church: 'Why do you persecute me?'[34]

In this connection, too, the Church exhibits a duality and a tension which is particularly acute at this point: the Church is, on the one

[32] H. Schlier, 'Zum Begriff der Kirche im Epheserbrief', *Theol. Blätter*, 1927, col. 12 f., and *Christus und die Kirche im Epheserbrief*, 1930, has referred to Gnostic-mythological conceptions to explain the images; they do certainly afford parallels and contribute to the understanding of the language of Ephesians, but they do not illuminate the theological meaning of the concept of the Church as the body of Christ which is presupposed in this epistle. The same applies to Traugott Schmidt, *Der Leib Christi, eine Untersuchung zum urchristlichen Gemeindegedanken*, 1919, who quotes Stoic descriptions of the body as an organism; and also E. Käsemann, *Leib und Leib Christi, eine Untersuchung zur paulinischen Begrifflichkeit*, 1933, who tries to explain the Pauline conception of the body of Christ on the basis of Gnostic speculations on aeons.

[33] F. J. Leenhardt, *Études sur l'Église dans le Nouveau Testament*, 1940, p. 40, takes a different view, however, and interprets the term as merely a 'concept of relationship'. The relation between the Church and the Danielic Son of Man which Leenhardt rightly stresses in connection with F. Kattenbusch's important work, 'Der Quellort der Kirchenidee', *Festgabe für A. v. Harnack*, 1921, p. 14, by saying 'this community is inseparable from its leader, the Messiah-Son of Man, who is at once both its head and its embodiment', leads to a much more concrete conception of the statements on the σῶμα Χριστοῦ.

[34] The decisive argument for my conception of the σῶμα Χριστοῦ can only be given in the following section in connection with the idea of substitution.

hand, the body of Christ himself, the highest thing possible on earth, yet, on the other hand, it is ruled by Christ the head, like all the other parts of the creation to which his kingdom extends.

This dualism influences the life of the Church as the body of Christ: it is the suffering, crucified body, because it shares in a world where the σάρξ and sin still exist and where the subject-powers can still break free; but it is also the body of his resurrection, since Christ is already risen from the dead.[35]

That as the body of Christ on earth the Church is the body of the crucified is made particularly clear in the important passage in Colossians 1.24, where Paul writes: 'in my flesh, I complete what is lacking in the afflictions of Christ for the sake of his body, the Church.'[36] That the believers in Christ become one with Christ, become 'joint-heirs' with him, means, according to Romans 8.17, that they must share his sufferings if they are to share his glory. What every Christian individually experiences at Baptism when he enters the Church (Rom. 6.3 f.), dying with Christ and being raised up with him, characterizes the whole life of the Church. In so far as it is the body of Christ on earth it is the lowly and suffering Church—'drawn by the exalted Lord, it goes the way of the humiliated' (Kierkegaard).[37]

On the other hand, it is also the body of the risen Lord, a spiritual body (σῶμα πνευματικόν, I Cor. 15.44), since it was constituted by the πνεῦμα at Pentecost; πνεῦμα is its substance, and so everyone that is received into the Church in Baptism enters even now into a spiritual body, the only spiritual body that is already in existence, the Church, the earthly body of the exalted Christ. 'By one Spirit we were all baptized into one body' (I Cor. 12.13), and the Eucharist is already a concrete sharing in this spiritual body of the Church through the eating of the bread: 'The bread which we break, is it not a participation in the body of Christ? seeing that we, who are many, are one bread, one body' (I Cor. 10.16 f.).[38] Since the body of Christ is incorporated in the community of the Church no man must eat for himself in the Eucharist (1 Cor. 11.20 f.).

[35] In connection with the Eucharist this duality of the meaning of the body of Christ is very well brought out by A. Schweitzer, *The Mysticism of Paul the Apostle*, E.T., 1931, p. 270 f.

[36] The στίγματα τοῦ Ἰησοῦ mentioned in Gal. 6.17 should also be remembered in this context.

[37] S. Kierkegaard, *Einübung im Christentum*, *Ges. Werke*, vol. 9, 1924, p. 181.

[38] See, in addition to the passage in Schweitzer already mentioned (n. 35), especially J. Héring, *Le Royaume de Dieu et sa venue*, 1937, p. 228 f.

It is because it is the spiritual body of the risen Christ that such unworthy eating is so evil, and he is guilty who fails to 'discern the body' (I Cor. 11.27 f.). Paul even goes so far as to say that it is because of unworthy partaking of the Eucharist, that is, the risen body of Christ as he is incorporated in the Church, that there are so many 'weak and sickly' in the Corinthian Church and a number that 'sleep' (1 Cor. 11.30).

The tension between present and future in the Church is not only due to the fact that it is the persecuted, suffering and crucified body of Christ and at the same time the resurrection-body, the spiritual body of Christ. It goes much further and also arises from the fact that, though as a gift offered by God the spiritual body of Christ is a reality in the midst of the earthly world doomed to destruction, it cannot exert its full influence owing to the unworthiness of its own members, so that this body in which nothing corruptible should remain still contains sin, disease and death. The reason is that the Church is made up of human beings who are still living in the carnal body, still living in sin. This brings us to the question of the membership of the Church which we intend to examine in relation to the question of membership of the *Regnum Christi*. The answer to this question will shed light on the ultimate relationship between the *Regnum Christi* and the Church. We shall have to proceed from the result which we have just reached: the Church of Christ forms the narrowly confined earthly setting of the *Regnum Christi* which Christ, the head of the whole creation, has chosen for his earthly body.

(4) *The Members of the Regnum Christi and the Members of the Church*

The fact that Christ, the head, has chosen and marked out the fellowship of the Church, one small part of creation, must have a special significance for the *Regnum Christi* as a whole. The members of the Church, who are at the same time members of the whole *Regnum Christi*, must participate in his government in a special way.

To be a member of a kingdom always means, on the one hand, being ruled and, on the other hand, sharing the government with the head, though being subordinate to him. Now we have here a supremely important difference between the *Regnum Christi* and the Church. As we have seen, all beings in heaven, on earth and under the earth belong to the *Regnum Christi*. All those invisible powers and authorities and their executive organs, the earthly states, are therefore members of this kingdom too. They are part of the *Regnum*

Christi and entitled to obedience and active support, especially from all those who are aware of the existence of the *Regnum Christi*. All earthly, material institutions which, while disengaged from the *Regnum Christi*, are extremely questionable and demonic, such as the bearing of the sword (Rom. 12.4), are ennobled, and state officials become 'God's servants', λειτουργοὶ θεοῦ (Rom. 13.6)[39] on receiving a place in the *Regnum Christi*. These earthly institutions are the things which 'are Caesar's' and which, according to the words of Jesus (Mark 12.17), are to be given to Caesar, as God is to be given the things that are God's. But this does not mean that the state has any independent right of its own.[40] The only reason why Caesar is to be given the things that are Caesar's is because he is included in the divine order of the *Regnum Christi* and God has given him power over these things so long as the present age lasts. The Church must not be an earthly state itself; for the Christian's 'state' is in the future, in heaven (Phil. 3.20; Heb. 11.10, 13–16; 12.22; 13.14; Rev. 21.2). But for that very reason the Christian knows that the earthly state, though not ultimate and divine in itself, is nevertheless a member of the *Regnum Christi* by the will of God, in so far as Christ's kingdom belongs to the present age.

Thus the angel-powers and their organs, the state authorities on earth, are governed by Christ and participate in his provisional kingdom in the way marked out for them. Nevertheless, they are members of his kingdom only very indirectly, since they are not necessarily aware of their role. Everything that Paul and Jesus say about subjection to Caesar and the state refers to a pagan state, which has no knowledge of Christ and his kingdom and of God the Father of Christ.[41] But even a pagan state such as Rome can play a divinely ordained part in the *Regnum Christi* so long as it carries out its own task and thereby makes it possible for the Church, which

[39] The connection with the angel-powers is confirmed to some extent by the fact that in Heb. 1.14 the angels are called λειτουργικὰ πνεύματα εἰς διακονίαν ἀποστελλόμενα.

[40] G. Kittel, *Christus und Imperator. Das Urteil der ersten Christenheit über den Staat*, 1939, p. 17, holds the opposite view.

[41] One is entitled to ask, however, whether a pagan state can remain within its proper confines as a state at all. Otto Eck, *Urgemeinde und Imperium*, 1940, p. 105 f., answers the question on the basis of the late-Jewish conception that the Torah was well-known to the heathen and that 'all political order is an outcome of the Torah'. Keeping more closely to the New Testament, F. J. Leenhardt, *Le chrétien doit-il servir l'État?* 1939, has made the interesting attempt to consider Christian love of neighbour as the Christian basis of all secular justice, precisely in relation to Rom. 13.

is of such importance to the *Regnum Christi*, 'to lead a quiet and peaceable life' (I Tim. 2.2).

According to the New Testament the Christian must never oppose a state simply because it is pagan, but only if the state forsakes its proper task and deifies itself. The state that remains within its proper sphere belongs to the kingship of Christ, though all unwittingly. Since only the Christian is aware of the fact, such a state means more to him than to any other citizen. Inversely, the state's transgression of its rightful boundaries, though witnessed by non-Christians as well as Christians, will mean a much more terrible lapse from the Christian point of view, for the Christian will see it as a defection from the *Regnum Christi*, the unleashing of demonic power, the uprising of the 'beast'.

The fact that the members of the Church are conscious of all this, that they know that Christ rules, and are therefore members of the Kingdom of Christ consciously, is what distinguishes them as a Church from all the other members of the *Regnum Christi* who may be its servants unconsciously.

The central position which the Church occupies within the whole *Regnum Christi* should now be fairly clear. To grasp it completely, however, we must first see how from the very beginning the whole process of events led up to the Church. The whole witness of the Bible presupposes a divine scheme of salvation with the Church as the final goal: man was intended to rule over the rest of creation. He fell, and his fall involved the whole creation in the divine anathema: 'For your sake' (Gen. 3.17; Rom. 8.20). From sinful humanity God chose a community, the people of Israel, for the salvation of the world. Within this people, however, a further reduction took place, first of all, to a still smaller community, the 'remnant of Israel', the *qehal Yahweh* on whom devolves the role appointed by God. This 'remnant' was still further concentrated and reduced to one man who was alone able to assume the role of Israel, that is, the 'Servant of Yahweh' in Deutero-Isaiah, the 'Son of Man' in Daniel, who represents the 'people of the saints' (Dan. 7.13 f.). This one must enter history in the Son of God, Christ, who is to achieve by his vicarious death that for which the people of Israel have been chosen by God. Until the coming of Christ the scheme of salvation, therefore, took the shape of a progressive reduction: from humanity at large to the people of Israel and from the 'remnant of Israel' to Christ, in whom the whole process attains its centre, though it has not come to an end in him. It is now a matter of travelling in the opposite direction: moving from the one to the many, so that the many may represent the one. The way now leads from Christ to those who believe in him, who know they are redeemed by faith in his vicarious death. The way now leads to the Church, which is the body of Christ, and which is now called to fulfil for the whole of humanity the task of the 'remnant', the 'people of the saints', and which, therefore, applies to itself the name of the 'remnant': qehal Yahweh, the Hebrew equivalent for ἐκκλησία, Church.

The process of salvation proceeds in two directions: from the many to the one: that is, the old covenant, and from the one to the many: the new covenant. The decisive fact of the death of Christ stands exactly midway between the two movements.

This is not merely a retrospective reconstruction of what has happened. The process is clearly documented in Galatians 3.6–4.7, where Paul takes as the starting-point of his argument the promise made to Abraham, and then points out that this promise to Abraham's offspring was fulfilled in the promise to the one, meaning Christ (3.16), who through his vicarious death redeemed those who were under the law (4.5). For the first time the way was clear for all who believe in Christ to become the descendants of Abraham (3.26). Through Baptism (3.27) they all enter into the promise which was given to the one. Now there are many, but these many are 'all one', πάντες εἷς, in Christ Jesus (3.28). Thus all are to become sons and heirs (4.4–7).

This is the history of the origin of the Church as the body of Christ considered within the context of the whole scheme of salvation. The Church as the body of Christ and the part it has to play in the Regnum Christi and later on in the Kingdom of God can only be understood on the basis of the concept of vicariousness which, in fact, provides the key to an understanding of the whole biblical concept of the scheme of salvation. The election of the people of Israel was already based on the idea of vicariousness: vicarious sacrifice for the human race which has fallen away from God. It then became concentrated in the tiny 'remnant', and still further in the figure of the 'Servant of Yahweh' on the one hand, and the 'Son of Man' on the other.

Since the 'Servant of Yahweh' fulfils the role which should have been fulfilled by the many, this figure of Ebed Yahweh is exceedingly variegated in Deutero-Isaiah, and Old Testament scholars have never completely solved the problem whether the 'servant' is an individual,

9

or the whole people of Israel, or merely the 'remnant'. The question is tied up with the fact that a concentration or reduction based on substitution took place before it was realized in a historical personality.

We find the idea of vicariousness recurring in the figure of the Son of Man. According to Daniel 7.13–27,[42] the Son of Man represents the 'people of the saints'. It is significant that this is the very description which Jesus applied to himself, since it is based on the idea of vicariousness: by proclaiming that 'the Son of Man must suffer many things' (Mark 8.31), and that he came 'to serve and to give his life a ransom for many' (Mark 10.45), he realized and combined in his person the Son of Man and the Servant of Yahweh, both of whom are rooted in the common conception of the representation of the many by the one.

As 'Son of Man' and 'Servant of Yahweh' Christ represents the 'people of the saints', the 'remnant of Israel', and therefore the whole of Israel and humanity, since Israel was chosen as representing the whole of humanity. The fact that Christ represents the whole of humanity is indicated by the term 'Son of Man' itself, for 'Son of Man', Aramaic bar-nasha, simply means 'human being'. The Pauline description of Christ as the second Adam (Rom. 5.12 f.; I Cor. 15.45 f.) is based on a similar idea.

We are now in a position to appreciate why the Church of Christ must be the body of Christ. Substitution by Christ, in whom the human race is summed up, remains the leading principle in the return from the one to the many. So the Church must be a human fellowship in which Christ, the one, is 'formed' (Gal. 4.19), in which he becomes incarnate, and this, too, is of outstanding significance for the whole creation because of the importance which, according to the divine plan, belongs to man within the creation, which is in any case grounded in Christ from the very beginning: 'in him were all things created' (Col. 1.16).[43]

---

42 F. Kattenbusch, 'Der Quellort der Kirchenidee', Festgabe f. A. v. Harnack, 1921, has the merit of being the first to have applied the idea of the Son of Man= people of the saints to the Christian concept of the Church. T. W. Manson pointed out the connection of the Son of Man with the 'remnant' and the Ebed Yahweh in his very notable work, The Teaching of Jesus, 1935. On the relation to the body of Christ, see the short exposition on p. 232 f.

43 In the New Testament it is merely presupposed that the dominion of man over creation, which was intended in the beginning at the creation of the world, will be realized in the new age, but it is stated expressly in the epistle of Barnabas, 6.18 f.

We have outlined the biblical scheme of salvation to show the surpassing importance of the Church within the *Regnum Christi* as a fellowship of human beings. In the last section we saw that the Church is the centre of this kingdom because it has been chosen to be the earthly setting of the body of Christ. It is now clear that the Church forms the centre, because it is the body of Christ as a human community which is the goal of the divine plan of salvation. The dominion which was prophesied for the Son of Man=people of the saints in Daniel 7.27 is fulfilled in the Church as the body of Christ.

The members of this fellowship are, therefore, not only aware of the position held by the other members, such as the state, within the *Regnum Christi*: they are aware, above all, of their own position as believers in redemption by the death of Christ; as believers in the kingship of Christ and in the Church as the body of Christ, which they themselves constitute. Therefore the fact that the Church is governed by the head and the Church shares in his government is more important for the *Regnum Christi* than the participation of all its other members. And this explains why in the final act of the *Regnum Christi* the members of the Church will reign in particularly close association with Christ and in the kingdom of a thousand years (Rev. 20.1), and also why they will sit in judgment on the other members of the *Regnum Christi* (I Cor. 6.3). They will also 'reign with him': συμβασιλεύσομεν (II Tim. 2.12).[44]

But we have already seen that everything that is to take place in a concentrated form in that final act is typical of the whole previous and present kingship of Christ. Thus, according to I Corinthians 4.8, 'reigning with Christ' is to be conceived as a fact already,[45] and to this extent we ourselves already constitute a βασιλεία (Rev. 1.6).

That the human community of the Church exists is important for the creation which is summed up in the *Regnum Christi*, just as the fall of the first human beings had important consequences for creation in general. As Christ himself worked and suffered as man among men in his incarnation and died on the cross, and yet conquered the invisible powers and principalities by this earth-bound activity, so everything that happens in the body of Christ, that is, the Church of those who believe they are redeemed by the death of Christ, projects into the world of ἐπουράνια: through the Church

[44] Cf. *Epistle of Polycarp*, 5.2.
[45] Rightly explained by K. L. Schmidt, *T.W.N.T.*, article συμβασιλεύειν, i, p. 592, as a reigning 'with Christ',

the manifold wisdom of God is now made known to the principalities and powers in the heavenly places (Eph. 3.10)—the wisdom of which it is written in I Corinthians 2.8 that 'the rulers of this age' did not know it when they 'crucified the Lord of glory'. It is the Church's destiny only to fight against the visible manifestations of the hostile powers but, according to Ephesians (6.12), this, too, is a fight 'against the principalities, against the powers, against the world rulers of this darkness, against the spiritual hosts of wickedness in the heavenly places', that is to say, against the powers that have freed themselves from the ties binding them to the Kingdom of Christ.

Although the Church only works among men, except in the final act which will take place in the coming age, all its activity is important for the *Regnum Christi*, and the influence works both ways, since all the 'service' which the subject-angels perform in this kingdom is on behalf of 'those who are to inherit salvation' (Heb. 1.14). Likewise, according to Acts 5.31, God raised Christ up to his own right hand 'to give repentance to Israel and forgiveness of sins', a further token of how everything is concentrated on the 'little flock' in whom Christ is 'formed' (Gal. 4.19). The *Regnum Christi* is promoted by this concentration, regardless of the visible success or failure of the Church, but not independently of the Church's faithful fulfilment of its task, of which we still have to speak.

(5) *The Church's Task in the Regnum Christi*

We have seen that as the body of Christ himself the Church is God's supreme gift, but the tension inside it is almost unsurpassable because it shares in the dualism inherent in the whole situation between the resurrection and the second coming of Christ: sin and death are present in the Church because it consists of human beings who though redeemed by faith are still sinful. Hence the paradox that whilst the body of Christ which represents the pivot of the *Regnum Christi* is given to us in the Church, we ourselves, sinful men, form this body! Thus the Church is not only the supreme gift of God, but is faced with a supreme task. The body is never completed but has to 'grow up into the head' (Eph. 4.15 f.; cf. also Col. 2.19). This growth is effected by God and the Spirit that constitutes the body, but it has to take place in human beings, and that is the real problem that faces the Church. It flows from the definitions of the Church's function which we reached in the previous chapter.

Since it is an essential mark of the Church that, in contrast to the other members of the *Regnum Christi*, those whom Christ rules and who rule with Christ have knowledge of him, so the first task of the Church is to preach the gospel. Christ rules in the Church and through the Church by the witness that is borne to him. 'He who hears you, hears me'. The Church's preaching is concerned with the Kingdom of Christ; Christ has redeemed us by his death and resurrection by overcoming the powers and principalities. He reigns as *Kyrios Christos*. The Church has to strengthen its own members in this faith by preaching, and also in Baptism and in the Eucharist in which its nature as the body of Christ is shown forth with particular clarity.

The state supports the Church in all the tasks which it fulfils, consciously or unconsciously, as a member of the *Regnum Christi*; but where it prevents the free preaching of the gospel and demands a *Kyrios Kaisar* the Church will resist it courageously in its preaching and declare that it has fallen away from the *Regnum Christi*. It will openly confess its faith in the lordship of Christ. Since all power in heaven and on earth has been given to him, no sphere must be excluded from Christian preaching.

The preaching of the gospel must cover the whole period of the Church between Christ's ascension and second coming. For the end will only come when the gospel has been preached to all (Mark 13.10; Matt. 24.14).[46] This does not mean that all must be converted before the Kingdom of God can come, but that all must have at least heard the gospel. The coming of the Kingdom of God does not depend on whether the Church is great or small on the day which God has appointed for the end of the age. But the Church must do that to which it is called, preach the gospel to all.

It is always working to extend the space occupied by the Church in the *Regnum Christi* but it knows, all the same, that the further exercise of the kingship of Christ and the coming of the Kingdom of God are not dependent on the success or failure of its preaching. Nevertheless, it is important that the voice of the Church should never be wholly silent, even though it may be quite a small flock in whom Christ is formed. The 'growing of the Church into the

[46] See my article, 'Le caractère eschatologique du devoir missionaire et de la conscience apostolique de St. Paul', in *R.H.P.R.*, 1936, p. 210 f., for a discussion of Paul's testimony to the same idea.

head' need not necessarily be a quantitative increase (Matt. 24.12), but it must be an ever-increasing insight, expressed in word and deed, into the significance of the Church for the rule of Christ.

The rule of Christ is preached in deeds as well as words, in the exercise of love and in suffering. The fact that Christ reigns is shown forth in the suffering of the Church. Christ has already overcome all the invisible powers by the cross, and the victory that he has achieved is also shown forth in the suffering of the Church, which is caused by the powers that free themselves for a time from their bondage to the *Regnum Christi* and manifest this in their attitude to the Church which is the centre of the *Regnum Christi*. The suffering of the Church refers back to the conquest of the invisible powers that has already taken place and it points forward to their final defeat.

Even should the Church shrink more and more in numbers, according to the New Testament it is all-important that the body of Christ should exist even in a small Church, that is, in the community of those who know and believe that in spite of everything Christ will continue to reign over everything that is in heaven, on earth and under the earth. It is vitally important for the rule of Christ that this knowledge should be preached to the world. No failure need discourage the Church in its work, since the greatest earthly failure that ever was is at the very centre of the faith of the New Testament: the cross of Christ, which, to the Christian, means victory over all hostile powers and the eschatological beginning of the present kingship of Christ, which can only be superseded by the Kingdom of God.

APPENDIX [47]

On the interpretation of ἐξουσίαι *(Rom.* 13.1 *f.) as angel-powers*

It is true that the correctness of our present findings does not depend on taking the ἐξουσίαι in Romans 13.1 f. to mean the angel-powers (p.120 f.), and it does not stand or fall on that interpretation. But the relation between the *Regnum Christi*, the state and the Church which has been suggested here does provide additional support for the assumption that this interpretation of the ἐξουσίαι is correct.

This interpretation of the ἐξουσίαι of Romans 13.1 f., as stated by M. Dibelius in *Die Geisterwelt im Glauben des Paulus*, 1909, and later

[47] See now also Dr. Cullmann's article, 'Zur neuesten Diskussion über die ἐξουσίαι in Röm. 13.1', *Theologische Zeitschrift*, Sept.–Oct. 1954, p. 321 f. [Ed.]

recommended by H. Schlier, 'Mächte und Gewalten im N. T.', *Theol. Blätter*, 1930, col. 292, and argued more comprehensively by G. Dehn, 'Engel und Obrigkeit', *Theol. Aufs. f. K. Barth*, 1936, and adopted by K. Barth (most recently in *Rechtfertigung und Recht, Theol. Studien*, no. 1, 1938) and K. L. Schmidt ('Das Gegenüber von Kirche und Staat in der Gemeinde des Neuen Testaments', *Theol. Blätter*, 1937, col. 1 f.), has been violently disputed by G. Kittel in *Christus und Imperator. Das Urteil der ersten Christen über den Staat*, 1939, in a special supplement, p. 48 f., and by F. J. Leenhardt in *Le chrétien doit-il servir l'État?* 1939, p. 36 f.; and, finally, Otto Eck in his *Urgemeinde und Imperium (Beiträge zur Förderung christlicher Theologie* 42, 3), 1940, p. 35, in a footnote (no. 3), imagines that it is sufficient to call these ἐξουσία theories 'adventurous' and 'completely absurd' without giving any reasons for this summary judgment.

The arguments produced by Kittel and Leenhardt against the interpretation do not seem to me to be valid. In particular I am not convinced by Kittel's reference to the fact that out of ninety cases (wrongly quoted as nineteen by Leenhardt, p. 35, n. 1), in about eighty in which the word ἐξουσία is found, only the normal sense of 'any kind of power that a person has' is implied (p. 50). That the singular is, in fact, used in this sense is not in dispute. We are merely concerned with the plural ἐξουσίαι or the plural use of the singular πᾶσα ἐξουσία, and in this respect the statistics are quite definitely in favour of the meaning 'angel-powers'.

Kittel's reference (p. 50) to the fact that, according to W. Förster, *T. W. N. T.*, article, ἐξουσία, ii, p. 559 f., there is evidence of the singular and plural being used by secular writers in connection with ἀρχαί in the sense of 'secular authority' is more important. On the other hand, this is not valid as an argument against considering the ἐξουσίαι of Romans 13.1 as a reference to the angel-powers, since Kittel joins Förster in citing the other authentic fact that the late Jewish and New Testament conception of ἐξουσίαι as angel-powers is quite unknown in secular Greek.

When Paul spoke, in Romans 13.1, of the state being the executive organ of these angel-powers, he probably had in mind the secular meaning of ἐξουσίαι (state). But for Paul the important thing is that the powers are ordained by God. In I Corinthians 2.8 he was probably thinking of the secular meaning of ἄρχοντες, that is, Herod and Pilate, though undeniably it is the invisible rulers, the ἄρχοντες τοῦ αἰῶνος τούτου, who are meant in the first place.

There is no question here of an alternative and certainly not of a 'metaphysical drama unrelated to historical events' (Leenhardt, *op. cit.*, p. 39, n.).

It must also be stated that Kittel is wrong to regard my interpretation of the ἐξουσίαι as a 'devaluation' of the state *in malam partem* (p. 50). He proceeds from this false presupposition when he states that the passage in I Peter 2.13–17, which refers to Romans 13.1 and offers as it were the first exegesis of the Pauline statement, excludes the possibility of this interpretation, since such high honour is conferred on the ἀνθρωπίνη κτίσις, to which the author of I Peter assigns state authority in this context. This honour is, however, perfectly compatible with the character of *exousia*. In Romans 13.4 the almost incomparable dignity implied in the description of the state as 'God's servant' must be taken quite seriously even though and just because we know that the angel-powers ordained by God are behind the state.

The passage from the *Martyrdom of Polycarp* (10.2) in which, according to Kittel (p. 52, cf. also p. 32) it is impossible to understand ἐξουσίαι as angel-powers, does not appear to me to contradict my interpretation in the slightest. For, like Paul in Romans 13, Polycarp supports the case for the most loyal possible Christian attitude to the ἀρχαί and ἐξουσίαι, which are 'ordained by God'. But the fact that the same Polycarp, who wants the state to be shown every honour so long as it really stays within the τάξις, the 'order' of God (τεταγμέναι ὑπὸ τοῦ θεοῦ, 10.2), resists the same state unto death when it requires the κύριος Καῖσαρ of him (8.2), that is to say, when it falls away from this 'order' and its demonic power is unleashed, is particularly easy to understand if one construes the ἐξουσίαι as the angel-powers, but does not interpret their role dualistically, but as we have done in the present study, in the sense of the *Regnum Christi* to which these powers are subject, but from which they are able to obtain temporary release. An approach like Polycarp's is exactly parallel to the New Testament attitude to the state which presupposes an awareness of the angel-powers which stand behind the state and the part which they play in the *Regnum Christi*.

The whole of Kittel's argument is based on a false dualistic conception of the angel-powers, which leaves out of account the fact that there is an intervening *Regnum Christi* in which angel-powers are present, though subject to Christ. The concept of the *Regnum Christi* excludes any form of dualism.

The same must be said of Irenaeus, to whom Kittel refers and who only rejects this construction because he interprets it dualistically, which is just what it is not. The first to refer to the passage quoted by Leenhardt, *op. cit.*, p. 40 n. (*Adv. Haer.*, V, 24.1) in the context of this discussion was Harald Fuchs in *Der geistige Widerstand gegen Rom in der antiken Welt*, 1938, p. 59. This passage, which does, in fact, expressly reject the application of ἐξουσίαι in Romans 13.1 to angel-powers, only concerns a false, heretical, because dualistic interpretation of this explanation, as though the state thereby became an institution inimical to God, whereas to a correct interpretation of this explanation, it is God's servant just because it is the organ of those ἐξουσίαι which are subject to Christ, in other words, because it is a member of the *Regnum Christi*.

That Irenaeus only interprets the explanation (ἐξουσίαι=angel-powers) dualistically, that is to say, misinterprets it, is related to the fact that in his struggle against Gnostic dualism he exaggerates the rectilinear development from creation to redemption and completely leaves the present *Regnum Christi* out of account. We have seen that even in a confessional text which came down to him (*Adv. Haer.*, I, 10.1) he interprets what is said there about the present reign of Christ, in particular, his reign over the invisible 'powers' eschatologically. From this point of view Irenaeus can only understand the interpretation of ἐξουσίαι as angel-powers in the form in which it had been advocated by the Gnostic heretics.

In conclusion, I should like to say with great emphasis that the view that angel-powers are behind the state is stated so clearly by Paul in I Corinthians 2.7 f. and 6.3, quite apart from Romans 13.1, that it would be quite unthinkable that he should have used the word ἐξουσίαι in Romans 13.1 in any other sense than that of angel-powers with which he was familiar. I think I have shown in the present study that it is impossible to banish the idea of angels and powers to the periphery of Pauline theology as has been done by Kittel, *op. cit.* (p. 51) and Leenhardt, *op. cit.* (p. 36).

VI

The Return of Christ

The New Testament Hope

Translated from *Le Retour du Christ*,
3rd edition, 1948, Neuchâtel

The Return of Christ[1]

IT CONNOTES a wrong approach to the problem of the hope of
the New Testament to reduce it to the question: what is the
date of the return of Jesus Christ? That is how the hope of the
New Testament is usually distorted by the sects. They make this
question of the date of Christ's second coming, which cannot
possibly be regarded as central from the standpoint of the gospel as
a whole, and which should, in fact, be reserved for God and not
concern us at all, the exclusive theme around which all their discussion of the hope of the New Testament is made to revolve.
Unfortunately, the Church has too often imitated the sects: it has
investigated the problem of the date of Christ's return as though
that was the all-important question. Even theology has made the
same mistake. In reality, though the question is certainly raised now
and then in the New Testament, it remains, as we shall see, on the
periphery; it never constitutes the centre or the nucleus of the apostolic
teaching on hope. To make it the starting-point and nerve-centre of
this teaching is to obtain a disordered, distorted and disfigured hope
which is not the hope of the New Testament at all.

That is why we shall not take as our own starting-point those
sayings of Jesus which seem to fix the irruption of the Kingdom of
God more or less chronologically, as is the case with the so-called
school of 'thoroughgoing eschatology', but we shall deal with them
in their place and in accordance with their true importance.

In the four chapters that follow we shall try to answer the following four fundamental questions:

1. What is the place of hope in the New Testament?
2. Why is this hope a hope in the return of the Lord?
3. What is the fundamental significance of the proclamation of
   the nearness of the Kingdom of God?
4. What conclusions must be drawn from this hope for our
   Christian life in the Church?

[1] A lecture delivered to the old members of the Christian associations of students
in German-speaking Switzerland in 1943 (but first published in French [Ed.]).

(1) *What is the place of Hope in the New Testament?*

All thinking about hope is futile if it is not seen in its due place within the framework of the total witness of the gospel. The sects which discredit the Christian hope by their teaching rely on passages which do, in fact, occur in the New Testament. Their mistake, their heresy, is not that they introduce extra-biblical elements, but that they isolate certain truths and remove them from their context. Now it is impossible to speak accurately about hope without taking as one's point of departure the decisive event that has already taken place, and the faith which looks to the past and which also sees in the present the accomplishment of the divine plan of salvation. Furthermore, the source of nearly all the heresies is that they uproot a particular element of the truth of the gospel, isolate it and set it up as an absolute. The history of the Church provides ample instances in support of this statement. The element which is thus set at the centre of things is usually a genuine, sound and trustworthy element, but by being suddenly isolated it becomes a source of heresy. The apocalyptic sects which have always existed have wrongly isolated the Christian hope in this way. The harmony of the Gospels is thereby destroyed because these sects speak of a hope directed towards the future and ignore the faith which looks to the past and the present: in other words, they ignore the whole history of the plan of divine salvation. In the New Testament hope is, on the contrary, based on the faith which rests partly on the historical facts of the expiatory death of Christ and his resurrection, and partly on the present fact of the invisible kingship of Christ. Any hope that is not the final link in this chain, the final assurance based on this story of salvation, is not hope as understood by the New Testament.

Merely to wait, without believing in the decisive events which have already taken place in the past and the present, without knowing that because of these decisive events man has entered into a final epoch, is to misuse the New Testament, however great the number of isolated verses which can be quoted in support of this false mode of hoping. Such waiting destroys the harmony of the gospel. Hope cannot function without faith in the death and resurrection of Christ, without faith in the kingship of the Lord in his Church, in which the work of his love is pursued. To speak accurately of hope there is no need at all to isolate it and thereby run the risk of falsifying and dechristianizing it. Each element has its own particular place in the good news of salvation, and together they form a harmony which must be respected if heresy is to be avoided. To indicate the special place of hope within this total harmony it is sufficient to recall the words of the apostle Paul in I Corinthians 13.13: 'And now abide faith, hope, love'. Faith comes before hope and love comes after it as the crowning of the three. This is the order, the chain in which hope must be set as a link.

But we must now mention the opposite danger: to eliminate hope, to endeavour to be contented with faith and love, to consider hope a mere concession to the time-bound thought of the apostolic age is to do just as much violence to the gospel message as setting up hope as an absolute. To reject hope is to mutilate the New Testament message of salvation in which every element is essential to the whole. This message begins with Creation and ends with the new creation on the last day, which is its goal and end. Between these two moments there is set the decisive event of the cross, which is past history for us but the basis of our salvation. Between these two moments is set all the intermediate time of the Church in which we ourselves are living.

This general history of salvation may be outlined as follows. God created the world as well as man. He has instituted man as lord over his whole creation, but the fall and its consequence, death, which has established its rule on earth, has made necessary a history of salvation which develops, according to the divine plan, by periods which are clearly determined by the two principles of election and substitution: the election of the people of Israel for the salvation of humanity, the election of a remnant of this people which is intended to represent the whole of Israel, the election of a unique 'man', the suffering 'Servant of God', who takes upon himself the sins of the world, the election of Jesus Christ, whose death on the cross and resurrection constitute the centre of the history of salvation. Henceforth the course of the story is inverted: it no longer proceeds from plurality to unity but from unity to the plurality of the saved. The Church is the body of this one and only Christ; it aspires to embrace the whole of humanity, and it will itself be followed by the final act of divine omnipotence, when God, as in the first creation, will decide in his sovereign act (κέλευσμα, I Thess. 4.16) to constitute the *new creation* by means of the spirit of life. The Christian expectation of the end, the Christian hope for the future are part of the unfolding of this story, they are situated on the line which, starting from creation and passing through the people of Israel, the remnant, through Christ, the one, through the gospel and converted and ransomed humanity, opens out on the new creation. This line is a temporal line and it is characteristic of the Christian revelation.

It is, however, absolutely foreign to Greek thought. The only time known to the Greeks is cyclic time which returns eternally in an infinite circle. Thus the Greek thinker is unable to conceive that salvation can and must be accomplished in time. For him salvation always means liberation from time, an escape from the framework of the eternal return of all beings and all things. The Bible teaches that the unfolding of time itself is determined by the history of God in time. The New Testament lays even stronger emphasis than the Old on this concept of linear time. The New Covenant throws this process of salvation in greater relief than the Old by introducing the present as an interim period with its own autonomous and essential significance between the decisive past event of the death and resurrection of Christ on the one hand, and the final fulfilment of the return of Christ on the other.

In the Church of Christ, eschatology is, in fact, an absolutely chronological concept, and it cannot be conceived as the expression of 'our permanent availability for existential decision' (Bultmann). Eschatology must not be interpreted so metaphysically as to dispel its substance altogether.[2] The eschatology of the New Testament, the hope of the Church of Christ, is not a hope in some kind of reality which is always available to us in the world beyond. It is not hope in a 'beyond' as opposed to a 'below', but hope in a 'then' as opposed to a 'now'. It awaits the age which is to come, which is to succeed the present age. It is essential to recognize the specifically temporal character of eschatology. It is vital to maintain the temporal character of the Christian hope. It can never be stated too clearly or too loudly that in the New Testament time is not a reality hostile to God but, on the contrary, the means of grace by which God intends man's salvation.[3]

---

[2] Cf. Folke Holmström, *Das eschatologische Denken der Gegenwart*, Gütersloh, 1936.

[3] This neglect of the value of time brings in its train the three heresies which usually go together: (1) the rejection of the Old Testament, that is, its historical and contingent facts; (2) Docetism, that is, the refusal to attach any importance, from the point of view of salvation, to the unique and historically common-place event of the incarnation of Christ or his shameful death on the cross; (3) the rejection of eschatology. Once the biblical concept of linear time is replaced by the Greek concept of cyclic time, once the metaphysical dualism of the 'here below' and the 'beyond' takes the place of the biblical dualism of the 'present age' and the 'age to come', one inevitably succumbs to each of these

To the question which forms the theme of this opening chapter we can therefore reply: according to the New Testament hope can only be discussed within the unity of the history of salvation of which it forms an indissoluble and essential element, since the history of salvation embraces past, present and future.

(2) *Why is the New Testament Hope a Hope in the Return of the Lord?*

We have already answered this question by showing how the whole history of salvation is directed towards Christ the Lord. From the creation to the new creation the whole course of the work of God has Christ as its centre. He is the mediator of salvation for his people, Israel. But his mediatory work is not confined to man. He is the mediator for the whole of creation, including the human race that inhabits it, because the human race, created in Adam in the image of God, is intended to reign over all the earth, as ordained by his Lord. This human solidarity with creation was manifested at the time of the fall, when the earth was cursed because of the sin of Adam and Eve. That is why the deliverance of creation is bound up with man's salvation, with the work of Christ, who thus becomes the Saviour of the world.

In the New Testament the story of salvation is therefore identical with the story of Christ. This assertion is based on the line that runs through the whole Bible and constitutes its unity: Christ saves all men in his incarnation, in his suffering and death, because from the very beginning he was, according to God's eternal plan, the Saviour

three heresies. It will suffice to quote as examples not only Gnosticism, but also all the modern philosophical distortions of the New Testament. The rejection or, at least, the allegorical interpretation of the Old Testament goes hand in hand with an elimination or a falsification of biblical eschatology as well as a Docetist christology. It must not be imagined that the liberal interpretation of Jesus Christ as purely man is sufficient to eliminate Docetism. In reality this heresy is not primarily concerned with the human or divine character of Jesus, but with the value for salvation of his historical incarnation as such. Docetism is, in the last analysis, a negation of the meaning of time for man's salvation. It begins as soon as the attempt is made to single out from the traditional elements of the story of Jesus, those which are important for our salvation and those which are not. Such an attitude betrays a failure to grapple with the historical facts before forming one's standards of judgment and selection. As an exegete and historian, Albert Schweitzer has rightly discerned and denounced this error committed by so many modern historians of the life of Jesus. But as a dogmatist he has rendered himself guilty of the same error by trying to eliminate eschatology from the gospel, after having recognized its capital importance.

of the world, who fulfils the intention which God has towards the
creation and towards man, made in his image.

The fundamental passages in the New Testament in which
Christ is described as mediator are John 1.3, 'all things were made
through the Word (=Christ), and without the Word was not anything made that was made'; Hebrews 1.2, 'Through the Son also
he made the worlds'; I Corinthians 8.6, 'But to us there is one God,
the Father, from whom are all things, and for whom we exist, and
one Lord, Jesus Christ, through whom are all things, and through
whom we exist'. This last text is the origin of all the creeds, which
were later divided into several parts: the two articles are not yet
separated as they were to be later on, as though only God himself
and not Christ, too, had a part to play in creation.[4] In Colossians 1.16,
too, we read: 'In him (Christ) were all things created, in heaven and on
earth, visible and invisible, whether thrones or dominions or principalities or authorities'. Thus the testimony of the New Testament
affirms unanimously that Christ has participated in the whole plan
of divine salvation from the very beginning and at all times. He was
at the beginning of creation. By his redemptive act he stands at the
centre of the history of salvation, which has the whole of creation
as its setting and object. This is what the Gospels mean when they
tell how the earth itself trembled at the moment of the redemptive
death. This death of Christ, who triumphs over death and hell,
proclaims the reconciliation achieved between God on the one side
and humanity, or rather, the whole *cosmos*, on the other. Henceforth the invisible powers themselves are subject to God. Colossians
1.19, 'For it pleased the Father that in him should all the fulness
dwell; and, having made peace through the blood of his cross,
through him to reconcile all things to himself, whether on earth or
in heaven'. The old confession of faith quoted by Paul in Philippians
2.6–11 tells that God has 'highly exalted' the Christ who humbled
himself even to the death of the cross, that he has made him Lord
over all things, that, 'in the name of Jesus every knee should bow,
of things in heaven, and things on earth and things under the earth'.
Similarly we find in I Peter 3.22 a confession of faith according to
which Christ has ascended to heaven, with all the angels and
authorities and powers made subject to him.

Thus, according to the New Testament, just as Christ already
participates in creation as mediator, so the work of redemption
which he has accomplished for man extends to the whole universe.

[4] Cf. O. Cullmann, *The Earliest Christian Confessions*, E.T., 1949.

This is why the new creation, towards the fulfilment of which the whole plan of divine salvation tends, also depends on Christ. The decisive event has already taken place, it is true, but the end has not yet arrived. It is still possible for the forces and powers that have already been vanquished to manifest themselves within certain limits. Sin and death have not yet been destroyed and if the Holy Spirit is already at work, it has not yet re-created the substance of the world. This is why we are all waiting, and, according to Romans 8.19, the whole creation, as well as man, shares in this waiting. 'The whole creation waits with eager longing for the revelation of the sons of God. For all creation was subjected to vanity, not of its own will, but because of him who subjected it (Adam). We live in the hope that the creation itself will be set free from bondage to corruption, to share in the glorious freedom of the children of God. For we know that the whole creation groans in a common travail until now.'

And so, according to the New Testament, all things are involved in the process of salvation of which Christ is the centre and the promoter. The creation, redemption, and also the expectation of the final consummation, depend on the death of Christ. This fulfilment will be nothing less than the creation of a new heaven and a new earth (II Pet. 3.13).

This is why Christ will return to earth. The decisive event, like the first decisive event which took place under Pontius Pilate, will take place on earth, because matter itself has to be re-created.

It is true that the New Testament tells us nothing about this return, but speaks of an arrival of Christ who comes, and not of Christ who returns. Only in the farewell discourses of St. John's Gospel do we find the assertion: he will come again. All the other passages simply say, he will come. In secular usage both the Greek words used in these verses (παρουσία and ἐπιφάνεια) mean the appearance of a king in his glory. Now the New Testament makes a perfectly clear distinction between the coming of Christ in his glory and his first coming in humility. Substantially, if not formally, we are entitled to speak of a return of Jesus Christ. It is he who, as always, in association with the divine plan of salvation, will usher in the final act by triumphing definitively over the authorities and powers (I Cor. 15.24 f.) which he had already stripped of their power in his resurrection (II Tim. 1.10).

The hope of the New Testament can, therefore, only be a hope in the return of the Lord if, as we have tried to show, the whole message of the New Testament, of which it is one of the elements, culminates in Christ, the Saviour of man and of the *cosmos*, the beginning, centre and fulfilment of the whole history of salvation from the first to the new creation. Christ as mediator in the past and present must also be mediator in the future. It is only after everything, absolutely everything, has been subjected by him to the Father that the Son will, according to I Corinthians 15.28, 'become subject to him who made all things his subjects, so that God may be all in all'. Only then will his role of mediator come to an end. Like the first decision of the cross and resurrection, these final events must take place on earth. Christ must therefore return as the glorious Saviour, this time surrounded by his own, to inaugurate the new age (I Thess. 4.14). We might therefore reply to the question which forms the subject of this chapter, in the words of Hebrews 13.8: 'Jesus Christ is the same yesterday, today and for ever', that is to say, until the new age which is to come. At the beginning of this new period, when time will yield to eternity, he will still play the part of fulfiller and judge.

To know the real hope of the New Testament it is therefore not necessary, as has unfortunately happened only too often, to set out from a selfish point of view, asking, What will my fate be? Rather, it is necessary to consider the plan of salvation which God is pursuing *vis-à-vis* the world as a whole. How ironical that the Christian Church is constantly reproached with concentrating all its interest on the selfish happiness of the individual in the world beyond! To imagine that such a caricature does justice not only to Christianity but to the New Testament itself is to display total ignorance, since, unlike the belief in the immortality of the soul professed by Greek philosophy, the biblical hope of resurrection sees the destiny of the individual merely as a consequence flowing from the total work of Christ. That is why the resurrection of our 'mortal bodies' (Romans 8.11) will only take place at the end of time: individual death will not be followed by an immediate escape from time. To be sure, the secure eschatological possession of the Spirit is already a real event in the Church. Those who have died and who die in Christ are in a new state: they are raised up to Christ and are 'with him' 'in Paradise' (Luke 23.43; I Thess. 5.10; Phil. 1.23; II Cor. 5.8). But they still remain in time, they are waiting (cf. the question of the martyrs in Revelation 6.10: 'How long, O Lord, holy and true?'). It would be a distortion of the New Testament conception of time to say: Those who have died in Christ are already living outside time and are already participating in all that the Church expects for the end of the world, that is, the resurrection of the body and the putting on of the σῶμα πνευματικόν which really depends on the return of Christ to earth and the re-creation of matter itself.[5]

The line of the history of salvation which we sketched in the first chapter is therefore identical with the line of the work of Christ himself. He fulfils his role of mediator for man and therefore for the whole universe. According to the New Testament, to hope can only be to hope for his return.

(3) *What is the Fundamental Significance of the Proclamation of the Nearness of the Kingdom of God?*

We have already mentioned the tension which characterizes the unfolding of the history of salvation in the New Testament. The decisive event of the resurrection of Jesus Christ has already taken place; but the end has not yet arrived. This statement explains the New Testament conception of the present time, or, to put it more precisely, it enables us to understand the relation of present to future time. We have established that the unfolding of the divine plan takes place and that God uses time to fulfil his intention on the earth and for the earth. God is the Lord of time (Rev. 1.4), of the past and the future as much as the present; we must therefore not attempt to usurp his Lordship with our computations of the date of the irruption of his kingdom. Let us remember, rather, the warning which is repeated so often: 'Watch therefore, for you do not know on what day your Lord is coming' (Matt. 24.42). The master of the house does not know when the thief will come (Luke 12.39); the virgin does not know when the bridegroom will come. Paul reiterates this in I Thessalonians 5.2: 'the day of the Lord comes like a thief in the night'. It is God who in his omnipotence and by his Word will fix and ordain the final moment (I Thess. 4.16). As in the first act of creation, the new world, too, will appear at his command: 'Let there be light!' And all our human activities cannot possibly bring about this final moment. Modern exegetes are almost unanimous on this point, that the kingdom will come from God alone, quite independently of human desires and actions. Human knowledge has no more access to this 'Day of the Lord' than human

[5] For this question cf. O. Cullmann, 'La foi en la Résurrection et l'espérance de la Résurrection dans le Nouveau Testament' (*Études théologiques et religieuses,* 1943, p. 3 f.)

will. 'But of that day or that hour no one knows, not even the angels in heaven, nor the Son, but only the Father' (Mark 13.32). This verse is a clear and solemn declaration, and all the more important because it is stated elsewhere in the New Testament (Matt. 11.27) that none knows the Father truly except the Son. Nowhere is man's inability to fathom the divine mysteries stated with such force. The risen Christ himself replies to the inquisitive and impatient questions of the disciples in a similar way: 'Lord, will you at this time restore the kingdom to Israel?' He said to them, 'It is not for you to know times or seasons which the Father has fixed by his own authority' (Acts 1.6, 7). How, in the face of such statements, have the sects been able to make the computation of the date of the coming of the kingdom the very centre of the hope of the New Testament? How have the exegetes and theologians been able to regard this point as the very essence of biblical eschatology? The error they have committed is unjustifiable.

Nevertheless, it cannot be denied that at the beginning of and throughout the whole preaching of the gospel we are told: 'the Kingdom of God is at hand'. What does this sentence mean? Does it tie down the coming of the kingdom to a definite date or to an event in the history of salvation, the consummation of the work of Christ? Does it simply mean that the kingdom will come in a given age and generation? If so, it would contradict all the other very explicit passages in the New Testament about our inability to know the date of the coming of the kingdom. It is *a priori* hardly likely that the fundamental point about the announcement of the imminence of the kingdom would be an indication of the moment of its irruption. Nevertheless, three verses, all of which record some words of Jesus himself, do seem to contain an indication of that kind. They are as follows. Mark 9.1, 'Truly, I say to you, some of those standing here shall not taste death before they see the Kingdom of God come with power'; Matthew 10.23, 'Truly, I say to you, you will not have gone through the cities of Israel, before the Son of Man comes'; Mark 13.30, 'This generation will not pass away before all these things take place'.

It is not easy to interpret these statements, and there exists, in fact, a whole series of different explanations. We can only mention the main ones here.[6] Do not let us forget in any case the

6 A. Schweitzer is not the first to have realized the problem these verses present. But he has attached an importance to the problem out of all proportion to the truth of the New Testament. To realize that the question had been seen for a

overwhelming number of clear, explicit statements already quoted concerning the impossibility of knowing the date of the end. If we bear in mind the texts of which the meaning is perfectly clear we shall not attach unwarranted and exaggerated importance to the problem presented by these three controversial passages.[7]

To begin with, I should like to mention the recent explanation that has been provided for Matthew 10.23, according to which there is no question here of any indication of the date. Like St. Paul in Romans 11.25, Jesus is setting the conversion of Israel in relation to the end of time. He is content to say: you disciples, you will not achieve this conversion: that is why you flee from one city to another.[8] On the other hand, however, according to Schweitzer, Jesus believed that the kingdom was to appear in his own lifetime, when the disciples would still be on their journeys. Quite recently, two new exegeses of Mark 13.30 have been suggested. According to the first, the γενεά (race or generation) mentioned in the text also refers to the Jews who will be preserved until the end, when they will be converted (Rom. 11.25).[9] According to the second, γενεά has the same meaning as in the verses in which Jesus speaks of this corrupt and perverse generation. The word has the general sense of 'sort of men' and proclaims that the evil nature of man will last to the final day.[10]

There may be an element of truth in some of these suggestions. At any rate they show that the meaning is anything but obvious. But none of them is entirely satisfactory. The word γενεά used in Mark 13.30 certainly has a chronological sense and the three passages undoubtedly refer to the generation alive at the time of Jesus. Even

long time before Schweitzer it is only necessary to consult one of the old editions of the Meyer series. For example, in his sixth edition of 1876 H. A. W. Meyer devoted a long paragraph to Matt. 24, and he did not evade or minimize the difficulties. In opposition to the Tübingen exegetes, Baur, Hilgenfeld, Zeller, who sought to extend to the year 130 and even beyond the generation (γενεά) mentioned in Matt. 24.34, during whose lifetime the destruction and the *parousia* were to come, Meyer asserts explicitly that the generation in question was the one living when Jesus delivered his discourse.

[7] The so-called school of 'thoroughgoing eschatology' commits a similar error of perspective.

[8] Cf. J. Schniewind on this passage in *Das Neue Testament Deutsch*. W. Michaelis also adheres to this explanation in an article against M. Werner, 'Die grosse Enttäuschung', *Kirchenfreund*, 76th year, 1942, p. 226 f.

[9] Cf. J. Schniewind on this passage in *Das Neue Testament Deutsch*.

[10] Cf. W. Michaelis, *Der Herr verzieht nicht seine Verheissung*, Berne, 1942, p. 30.

if Matthew 10.23 and Mark 13.30 could be given a different interpretation, there would still be Mark 9.1, which indicates quite explicitly that 'some of those standing here' will still be living when the kingdom arrives. It must be noted, however, that the text has τινες (some). This term rules out Schweitzer's view that the kingdom was to arrive during Jesus's own lifetime.[11] In fact, Jesus seems to have envisaged the lapse of at least several decades before the arrival of the kingdom, since he says that 'some' of his comtemporaries would survive to see it. Other references in the Gospels also presuppose a certain passage of time between the death of Christ and his return. In Mark 14.62, before the high priest, Jesus distinguishes between the moment when the Son of Man will sit at the right hand of God and the moment when he will return. According to Mark 13.10 and parallel passages the gospel must be preached to all nations before the end.

Be that as it may, it must be recognized that in the early Church, just as much as in Mark 9.1, Matthew 10.23 and Mark 13.30 no one reckoned on the period between the ascension and the return of the Master lasting for centuries.

Does this chronological limitation of the *parousia* constitute the nucleus of the hope of the New Testament, as is claimed by the so-called school of 'thoroughgoing eschatology'? We have already seen, particularly in the light of Mark 13.30, that this is by no means the case. Certainly Jesus did not reckon on the period of waiting lasting more than a few decades: but this does not affect the essence of the hope of the gospel. The announcement of the proximity of the kingdom has quite a different bearing for Jesus and early Christianity. As far as St. Paul is concerned, we have evidence of this in the evolution of his thought regarding the question: will the kingdom come while I am still alive? When writing I Thessalonians he believed that Christ would return during his lifetime ('Then *we* who are left alive, shall be caught up together with them in the clouds to meet the Lord in the air' 4.17). When he wrote Philippians and II Corinthians he no longer reckoned on this possibility. But this evolution in his thinking did not affect the content of his hope in the slightest, nor did it modify his certainty that the kingdom was still imminent. The question of the actual date is not decisive. The same is true of II Peter. This late letter quotes Psalm 90 in this connection: 'A thousand years with the

11 In *Der Herr verzieht nicht seine Verheissung*, W. Michaelis particularly insists on this point.

Lord are as one day'. This quotation allows for the possibility that the expectation may last for centuries and that man knows nothing about its duration. Yet the hope has lost nothing of its pristine freshness and intensity. We may therefore conclude that the limitation of the expectation of the *parousia* to the generation alive at the time of Jesus is not essential, though it is attested by various passages in the New Testament.

What, then, is the fundamental meaning of this nearness of the kingdom which is reaffirmed so often in the gospel? It means that the kingdom has, in fact, drawn nearer with Christ, that time has made a bond with him in advance of the event, that with him we have entered into the final period of time in the present world. 'The kingdom is at hand' means that it has come near (that is the exact meaning of the Greek perfect used in this sentence). The appearance of Christ is a decisive event in the time-table of the divine plan. We are in the final phase of the period, the duration of which we do not know. Thus the preaching of the nearness of the kingdom determines the present more than it characterizes the future. Such was in all probability the certainty which Jesus himself entertained. According to Jesus himself, his death is the decisive event which ushers in the coming of the kingdom. The prophecies of the passion repeat that 'the Son of Man must suffer' (Mark 8.31, etc.); he must play the part of the Servant of God for the sake of humanity; he inserts his own death into the framework of the history of salvation. According to Matthew 12.39 the only sign that will be given to man is the sign of the prophet Jonah. Let us remember, finally, the words of the Last Supper.

Taking the certainty, so clearly attested, of Jesus himself, we might even wonder if in the three verses we have quoted he was thinking equally of the contemporary generation as the generation which was to witness the decisive event of his death.[12] Be that as it may, whether or not Jesus considered that the actual date of his death would coincide with that of the irruption of the kingdom, according to the witness of the Synoptics he certainly did see in his passion and death the fulfilment of his earthly work of preparation for the kingdom. The essential element in the nearness of the kingdom is therefore not the final date but the certainty that the

[12] A. Schweitzer admits that this meaning is only found again in a few other words of Jesus. He believes that at the close of his ministry he changed his opinion: the kingdom would not come in his own lifetime but would coincide with the moment of his death.

expiatory work of Christ on the cross constitutes the decisive stage
in the coming of the Kingdom of God.

Such was the certainty of the New Testament as a whole, including the epistles of Paul and the other writings. There is no
hiatus between the hope of Jesus and that of the early Church. That
is why these three solitary and unique sentences, handed down by
tradition, which speak of the imminence of the kingdom, almost
giving the precise date, did not confront the early Christians with
an insoluble problem, since they turned the eye of faith not to the
periphery, to this restriction of the expectation of the kingdom to
the present generation, but to the centre, to the decisive act of the
death and resurrection of Christ. The only difference between the
hope of Jesus himself and the hope of the New Testament derives
from the fact that when the Gospels and Epistles were written the
decisive event had already taken place.[13]

13 One final point remains to be cleared up: if the promise of Jesus and the hope
of the early Church accord with one another, since the death and resurrection
of Jesus constitute the decisive events for both of them, it must nevertheless be
admitted that in the three statements of Jesus which we have studied, the first
and the last divine decision are not distinguished. From this point of view it
does seem that there is a hiatus between the eschatological promise of Jesus and
the hope of the early Church.

I should like, however, to recall once more that certain eschatological references of Jesus interpose a possible interim period between his resurrection and
his return. Above all, it is important to see that the temporal tension between
the two motifs 'all is finished' and 'the end is not yet come', which are so
characteristic of the time of the Church, is already to be found during the historical ministry of Jesus. In his own lifetime he sees Satan falling from heaven,
though he knows that he will only triumph over the powers at his death.
Before him death must already retreat, *before* his resurrection the Holy Spirit
is already at work: the sick are healed and the dead return to life. No doubt those
who returned to life, such as the young man of Nain and Lazarus, will die
again; no doubt the risen bodies of many saints, to which Matt. 27.52 refers,
are not yet σώματα πνευματικά. Nevertheless, an anticipation of the end
already exists wherever Jesus is present. 'If by the finger of God I cast out
demons, then the Kingdom of God has come upon you.' This does not prevent
Jesus believing in his return on the clouds of heaven after his death.

The question of the demoniac in Matt. 8.29 is clear evidence that the same
tension which characterizes the time of the Church already existed at the time
of the ministry of Jesus. 'Have you come here to torment us *before the time*?'
(πρὸ καιροῦ) the man possessed with demons asks. When Jesus is present
the end irrupts into the very heart of the present. Thus his transfiguration is
an anticipation of his bodily resurrection.

In Jesus, but only in him, the temporal tension which exists between the
present age and the age to come is already abolished, though his work continues to develop in time. That is why the Gospel of John mingles the three

It is from him that henceforth fulfilment is expected and hoped for. The whole time which is in progress at present—and we do not know how long it will last—is henceforth the end-time, the time in which in the Church the decisive and final moment of the death and resurrection of Christ develops. This *leitmotiv* of the hope founded on the resurrection cannot be reduced or eliminated by the delay of the *parousia*. Although we admit that early Christianity did not reckon on a delay of several centuries, and although this fact has a real psychological significance, it does not affect the theological truth of the irreducible sequence of the various periods of salvation: the historical incarnation of Christ—the present but invisible lord-ship of the κύριος—the return of the Lord. There may be impatience and disillusionment, but in the light of the resurrection the divine plan remains firm and unshakeable. That is why the question of the duration of the final phase cannot annul the certainty of the bond of faith in the past and present with hope in the future. And in the light of the divine plan as revealed and realized, the New Testament sets aside all the impatient and indiscreet enquiries into the χρόνοι and the καιροί as unsound (cf. Acts 1.7 and the two epistles to the Thessalonians).

The essential thing to remember is: 'Children, it is the last hour' (I John 2.18).

It is the action of the Holy Spirit which testifies that from now on we are living in the last age of time. This last age is a fragment of the future, the only part of the coming age which exists in the present age. It is the Holy Spirit who will transform matter at the end of time, who will re-create a new world and clothe us in a spiritual body. He will give life to our mortal bodies (Rom. 8.11), but he is already at work in the Church. It is true that for the moment only one spiritual body exists, that of the risen Christ, but through him the Holy Spirit is already working in the Church, which thus continues the work of Christ. This is why in Acts 1.7 the risen Christ replies thus to the impatient questions of his disciples: 'It is not for you to know times or seasons . . . but you shall receive the power of the Holy Spirit'. He is the first-fruits, the

modes of the Lord's return: his coming as the risen one, his coming in the Paraclete, and his coming at the end of time. This third eschatological coming in the fourth Gospel must not be suppressed; such a mutilation would entail the arbitrary suppression of a great number of verses.

In any case it is important to underline the fact that for the historical Jesus the coming of the kingdom is already linked up with the fulfilment of his task. independently of the question of knowing the final date of this fulfilment.

earnest (II Cor. 1.22; Rom. 8.23). According to Peter's speech at Pentecost, he is the sign of the last days when God will pour out his Spirit upon all mankind (Acts 2.17). These last days—today we should say these last centuries—constitute the time between the resurrection and the return of the Lord. The victory of Christ over sin and death has ushered in this reign of the Holy Spirit on earth. This reign still belongs to the present age, but to the end of this age, since the Holy Spirit which belongs to the coming age, is already at work in it. The conquered powers still possess a certain strength; sin and death have not been abolished, though they are irremediably doomed to destruction by the death and resurrection of Jesus Christ and the work of the Holy Spirit. This is why the New Testament is able sometimes to speak of the conquered forces as well as of the forces which still have to be conquered, of the purity already achieved and the purity which will be ours only at the end. Only an understanding of this tension in which the Church lives can prevent the gospel from looking like a tissue of contradictions.[14]

Christ reigns today invisibly except to the eye of faith, but when the final struggle and the last judgment which precede the beginning of the coming age take place, he will reign before all eyes. What will happen then can be described only imperfectly and in images. The Revelation, conscious that our human language is only made for this world, uses figurative language borrowed from the Jewish apocalypses. The seer of Patmos respects the object of which he is trying to express the presence by saying: 'I see as though . . .' The millennium of which he speaks is simply an image used to suggest the participation in the final act of those who belong to Christ. All the questions regarding the details of these images are questions which the Revelation certainly raises, but they do not constitute the essence of the hope of the *parousia* which is now being discussed.

The events of the Revelation belong to the beginning of the world to come, when the present but invisible lordship of Christ will become visible. In both periods it is the same lordship. The New Testament gives us in the Synoptic and Johannine apocalypses or in the apocalyptic passages of Paul's epistles some signs announcing the approaching end: cosmic catastrophes, wars, persecutions of the Church, a final appeal to repentance. These signs will appear in many ways, in a concentrated manner, at the end of the present

14 Cf. 'The Kingship of Christ and the Church in the New Testament', no. 5 in this volume.

age, when the coming age is about to arrive. And because the present time, though extending over several generations, constitutes an eschatological unity, all these signs, which will occur at the very end of this present time, already belong to this last phase in which we have been living since the resurrection of Christ (Col. 1.13). The early Church did not believe, as we have shown, that this interim period would last several generations. But such a possibility was latent in the very heart of the hope of the Church, which did not fix a date for the end of the work of Christ. We shall be true to the New Testament if we say that, since the expectation lasts for several generations, these preliminary signs that the Revelation shows us at the very end of the interim time are already typical of the interim period as a whole. They can assume different forms in accordance with the different generations. And if the Reformers saw antichrist in the Pope, other epochs in the Church's history will see him in other figures. None of these interpretations, however, can claim to have discovered the final sign of this age which is drawing to its close, unless a computation of the date of the kingdom were to be established again by the roundabout way of the preliminary signs, and were to replace the true meaning of the hope.[15]

All the signs remind us that the present is itself an eschatological period, however long it is to last. Events which, without Christ or before Christ, would have been bereft of importance acquire the significance of 'signs' in the light of the Church's faith; they unite faith in the present with faith in the future without providing any opportunity for spurious computations.

The preaching of the gospel which God proclaims to the heathen through the medium of the apostles and the Church is thus a sign of the end, a sign that has lost none of its significance, despite what the Reformers believed: they apparently imagined that the apostles had already preached the gospel to all nations. No, the gospel must be preached by the Church *in every generation* as a sign of the approaching end. But the Church cannot calculate the date of the end, nor hasten its coming by fulfilling this duty which is assigned to it in the divine plan.

[15] At the beginning of this war [1939–46] there were some attempts to interpret it as the apocalyptic sign of the end, and the harder times become the more the temptation to do so will increase. But the intensity of the horror is no criterion of the approach of the end. If the war ends without the return of Christ, the 'scoffers' mentioned in II Peter 3.3 will laugh at the disappointment of those who expected the end on this date. But their mockery will be directed at a false hope, not the hope of the New Testament. [This was written in 1943. Ed.].

This waiting for the return of Jesus Christ—will it not hinder the Church in the fulfilment of its task, since it cannot by any action of its own influence the unknown plan determined by God? How does hope, in fact, determine the work of the Church? That will be the subject of our fourth chapter.

(4) *What conclusions must be drawn from this hope in the return of the Lord for our life in the Church?*

How wrong and dangerous it is to separate hope from faith and isolate it from the message of the New Testament as a whole is now clear. A hope that is directed entirely to the future paralyses action in the present. It calculates dates but it forgets that Jesus will return when God decides, and not when we try to attract him, to bring him back to earth by our actions or our knowledge. Paul fought against this kind of hope in his own age, when it appeared in the Church in Thessalonica. These men had stopped working because they believed they knew the day of the return of the Lord and they therefore despised all earthly labour. Some generations later Montanism represented the same trend in Asia Minor, and the 'fanatics' and 'enthusiasts' of Münster at the time of the Reformation also imagined they were being faithful to the gospel by refusing to work. They forgot that the essential thing about hope is not the computation of the date of Christ's return but rather the certainty that he will come in glory to fulfil his work at the end of time, that he has begun this work and is pursuing it today, though in ways hidden from our eyes. Hope in the future cannot be separated with impunity from faith in the past and the present, since one thereby runs the risk of losing the third constitutive element of the Christian message, which is love.

After all, it is not surprising that the same people who wrongly regard hope as a calculation of dates want at the same time to reject this hope, and reproach the Church with escaping from the world and turning aside from the human duties of the present. But their reproaches only apply to the false hope which seeks to compute dates, which stirs up a demoralizing eschatological fever, and paralyses all true activity by replacing the service of the Church in and for the world by an unhealthy activism. Their reproaches do not apply to the hope of the Gospels.

We have tried to show that hope is, on the contrary, not concerned merely with the future but also with the present; the Holy Spirit, this earnest, this portion of the world to come, has already been given to us; it helps us to live within the present framework of the imperfect world, which is a provisional state but willed as such by God. That is why we accord a real value and dignity to this world despite its problematical nature. Certainly, the fashion of this world passes, but we know that according to the plan of God we must work in it and that God has judged it good for us to do so.

In I Corinthians 7.30 Paul thus exhorts the Christians: 'let those who weep be as though they wept not, and those who rejoice as though they rejoiced not, and those who buy as though they had no goods'. But he does not insist on the second part of the sentence merely to obscure the first part, which is also important: 'Be men who weep, who rejoice and who buy'. Is that the definition of an 'interim morality'?[16] Yes, certainly. But that does not mean that for us it is a morality that has now been abolished, or is merely relative, since our interim age, too, is provided for in the plan of divine salvation and we have to live in it according to the will of God.

The Church, for which the present time is its own time, must be conscious of the value and dignity of the present time. It must pursue in this present age the work of Christ by living according to the Holy Spirit which has been given to it. For Christian faith the present is more than a trivial and indifferent passage of time. It is the time of grace, the end-time, the passing age. The Church must preach the gospel in this present time in word and deed, since, according to Matthew 24.14, the end will come only after the gospel has first been preached all over the world.[17] Acts 1.6 f., which we have already quoted on several occasions, provides us with the clearest and most definite statement of this condition. To the inquisitive and impatient disciples the risen Lord replies: 'It is not for you to know times or seasons which the Father has fixed by his own authority. But you shall receive the Holy Spirit, and you shall be my witnesses to the end of the earth'. Questions about the date must not be asked; all eyes must be fixed rather on the present in which the Holy Spirit constrains the Church to preach the gospel of salvation without pause or rest.

[16] Schweitzer, *Skizze des Lebens Jesu*, 1901; *Geschichte der Leben Jesu Forschung*, 2nd edn., p. 504: 'interimistische Ethik'.

[17] Cf. O. Cullmann, 'Eschatologie und Mission im Neuen Testament', *Evangelisches Missionsmagazin*, 1941, p. 98 f.; 'Le caractère eschatologique du devoir missionaire et de la conscience apostolique de saint Paul,' *R.H.P.R.*, 1936, p. 410 f.

The eschatological determination of the present does not entail a paralysis of the Church's activity; on the contrary, it inspires and encourages it in the most effectual way. We have evidence of this in the simultaneity of the living hope and the intensive missionary preoccupations of the early Church. To be preoccupied with the expectation of the Lord's return is not a waste of time, and does not imply a turning aside from important duties.

The Church acts with power when, conscious of its faith in the past and the present and of its hope in the future, it preaches Christ in word and deed, and thereby testifies that past, present and future are most intimately united one with another. It believes by hoping and it hopes by believing. It interprets present events in the light of this faith and this hope. It shows us that events seen thus do not allow us to calculate the end, but they do enable us to understand our own age as the last epoch of the αἰών οὗτος, in which Christ already possesses all power in heaven and earth, in which he reigns over the invisible powers and is represented by his body the Church, but in which the hostile powers have not yet been destroyed. This age is already wholly determined by the hope of the future, since the main element of this future, the πνεῦμα (Spirit), is already here as ἀρραβών, ἀπαρχή (earnest) of what is coming.

Conclusion

We have now seen what, according to the New Testament, is the basis of the Church's hope in the return of Christ. We have endeavoured in particular to show the indissoluble unity of hope in the future with faith in the past and the present. This unity explains why hope cannot be eliminated arbitrarily from the total message of the New Testament as if it were merely a contingent, transient and secondary element. To sacrifice the hope of the Church or to replace it with another hope—a Platonic hope, for instance—is to abandon the true faith, since it involves destroying the pattern of the history of salvation which constitutes the beginning, the centre and the culmination of the Bible.

The final act of the drama of the history of salvation cannot be neglected without disparaging the previous acts. If the death and resurrection of Christ are not to be consummated in the future, they cease to be the central event in the past, and the present is no longer located in the space between the starting-point and the consummation of christology.

Inversely, however, it must be noted that a weakening of faith in the past and faith in the present entails a deadening and diminishing of the hope in the return of Christ. This became evident very early in the history of the Church. The Christian message lost its eschatological content because the death and resurrection of the Lord ceased to be at the centre of the faith, as they are in St. Paul. Christians no longer considered the present the final period of this age. The concurrent absence of these two elements is typical of the Apostolic Fathers, who abandoned the Pauline concept of grace anchored in the cross and resurrection, as well as almost the entire hope of the New Testament. They replaced the latter with apocalyptic reflections and speculations similar to those of Judaism and completely unrelated to the true faith. Speculations of this kind, which fail to take into account the history of salvation, are absolutely foreign to the eschatology of the Church.

Fortunately faith and hope based on the divine plan of salvation have never disappeared entirely. The presence of the open Bible in the Church has recalled the divine history of which it is the witness from generation to generation. This knowledge of the faith has always been obscured, most of all by the Gnostics of all times, who have been deeply influenced by Hellenism. This suggests that the Greek concept of cyclic time is the real cause of the neglect of the true history of salvation in theology and the Church. Hellenism collided with and modified all the religions of antiquity, and everywhere it appeared it brought a crisis in its train,[18] but its influence on Christianity has been greater than on any other religion. Hellenism and Christianity are destined to clash by their very nature, since only the Church of Christ has drawn the ultimate conclusions from the concept of linear time which comprehends and unites past, present and future. It is radically opposed to all modes of Greek thought, ancient and modern. If the hope of the Church is to be restored to currency, the Hellenic concept of time must be cleared from our minds.

But to rediscover the vigorous faith of the early Christians it is even more important to restore our own period of time to its place

[18] Martin Werner, in *Die Entstehung des christlichen Dogmas*, 1941, has completely misunderstood this aspect of the question in his explanation of the birth of Christian dogma. He has inverted the true relation between Hellenism and the surrender of the eschatological perspective by making the first a result of the second: according to him the delay of the *parousia* occasioned this surrender, which led to the hellenization of Christianity; whereas, in fact, this surrender issues from the progressive hellenization of Christian thought.

11

within the whole history of salvation, to see it as the end-time, between the resurrection and the return of Christ. The time of the Church is founded on the cross and resurrection. It lives in expectation of the Lord's return.

It needs courage to consider our history in this way, but that is precisely what is implied by the faith of the New Testament. On this road, which leads from the suffering and risen Christ to the Lord of glory, our hope will no longer be a vague remembrance of outworn concepts but a living certainty that Christ is the same yesterday, today and in the age to come. Following the example of the Church of the New Testament we *preach* Christ who was *crucified in the past*, we *acknowledge* courageously that Christ is the Κύριος who *now reigns* hidden from our eyes, we *pray* in truth to the Christ who *is to return*: Maranatha!

VII

The Proleptic Deliverance of the Body according to the New Testament

Translated from 'La délivrance anticipée du corps humain d'après le Nouveau Testament', *Hommage et Reconnaissance, recueil de travaux publiés à l'occasion du soixantième anniversaire de Karl Barth,* 1946, p. 31–40, Neuchâtel

The Proleptic Deliverance of the Body
according to the New Testament

OUR BODIES will not rise immediately after death, but only at the end of time. This is the general expectation of the New Testament which, in this respect, differs not only from the Greek belief in the immortality of the soul, but also from the view that the dead live even before the *parousia* beyond time, and thus at once enjoy the fruits of the final fulfilment. Neither the saying of Jesus, 'Verily, I say to you, today you will be with me in Paradise' (Luke 23.43), nor the story of the rich man and the beggar Lazarus who, after death, was carried by the angels 'to Abraham's bosom' (Luke 16.22), nor the desire of Paul 'to depart and be with Christ' (Phil. 1.23), nor his account of the state of 'nakedness' (II Cor. 5.1 f.) supports the idea that those who die in Christ before the *parousia* are immediately clothed with a resurrection-body. These passages simply state that belonging to Christ has consequences also for those who sleep, and II Corinthians 5.1 f. shows in particular that the 'earnest of the Spirit' (verse 5) given to believers removes from the state of nakedness of the dead who die before the *parousia* every cause of fear. Through the πνεῦμα they will be 'with the Lord' already during this intermediate period, which is described as 'sleep' (I Thess. 4.13) or as a place of privilege 'under the altar' (Rev. 6.9). The whole account in I Thessalonians 4.13 f. of the lot of those who die in Christ before the *parousia* is deprived of any meaning if we attribute to Paul the idea of a resurrection of the body following the death of each individual believer.

In fact, there is only one body already raised up and existing now as σῶμα πνευματικόν, *that of Christ*, who is thus the firstborn from the dead (Col. 1.18; Rev. 1.5). By this resurrection the decisive victory over death has already been won (Acts 2.24). While death still has power over men, it has already decisively lost its omnipotence (II Tim. 1.10).

With the resurrection of Christ the power of life, the Holy Spirit, has entered the world. The Spirit is the present great anticipation of the end, the ἀρραβών (II Cor. 1.22; 5.5) or ἀπαρχή (Rom. 8.23). In Romans 8.6 f. Paul shows that the Holy Spirit is the great adversary of the flesh as the power of death. Flesh (σάρξ) means death (θάνατος). The Spirit means life (ζωή). When the Holy Spirit appears, death disappears. Everything it touches loses as by magic its perishable, mortal nature. The Holy Spirit is the creative power of God himself. Every action of the Spirit is a life-giving miracle. To the despairing cry of Romans 7.24, 'Who will deliver me from this body of death?' (ἐκ τοῦ σώματος τοῦ θανάτου τούτου) the whole New Testament replies, 'the Holy Spirit'.

Yet, although the Holy Spirit is already at work, men continue to die after Easter and Pentecost as they did before. The body remains mortal and liable to disease. Although death is already conquered and deprived of its omnipotence (II Tim. 1.10), it will only be annihilated at the end of time as 'the last enemy' (I Cor. 15.26; Rev. 20.13). Only then will the Holy Spirit transform bodies of flesh into spiritual bodies (σώματα πνευματικά, I Cor. 15.44). This is the new creation, when the mortal substance will be replaced by an immortal one. At the present time the πνεῦμα renews day by day only our inward man (II Cor. 4.16; Eph. 3.16). The fact that it dwells in us in this way even now is the guarantee that in the eschatological future it will quicken our mortal bodies. 'If the Spirit of him who raised Jesus from the dead dwells in you, he who raised Christ Jesus from the dead shall quicken also your mortal bodies through his Spirit which dwells in you' (Rom. 8.11). But at the present time the σάρξ, the power of death, remains indissolubly bound to our σῶμα.

Does this mean that there is a whole sphere, that of our bodies, which is completely untouched by the *present* action of the Holy Spirit? Does its life-giving power still remain condemned to impotence before our body of death? Has the existence of a resurrection-body, that of Christ, no significance for our bodies of flesh?

We shall show that according to the New Testament the Holy Spirit, while unable to change our carnal bodies into spiritual bodies before the *parousia*, by anticipation extends its activity here and now into the sphere of the σῶμα and repels death in the very place where it is most firmly established. We shall show, first, that this proleptic activity on the body is revealed during the earthly ministry of Jesus in the miracles of healing and raising from the dead; second, that since the Church is the body of Christ, the σῶμα πνευματικόν on earth, the carnal bodies of the members who constitute this spiritual body feel its repercussions now. For on the one hand, the bodies of the apostles share in the suffering of Christ's body, and on the other, the life-giving power of the glorified body of Christ influences the bodies of believers, especially in the sacraments of Baptism and the Eucharist. We shall see, moreover, that marriage relationships are compatible with this connection between the body of Christ which is the Church and our bodies, but that sexual relations outside marriage destroy it.

(1) Since Christ has lived on earth himself in flesh and blood, the proleptic redemption of the body has taken place in his person. The fourth Gospel says that the Spirit has only existed since the glorification of Christ. 'The Spirit was not yet given, because Jesus was not yet glorified' (John 7.39). While Jesus was on earth the living power which later acted through the Holy Spirit was incarnated in him. As Paul says, 'The Lord is the Spirit' (II Cor. 3.17). A proleptic transformation of the body was realized, for a short time, in the fleshly body of Jesus himself in the transfiguration (Mark 9.2 par.) witnessed by three disciples. The christological significance of this incident is that it is a sign demonstrating in advance that Jesus has come into the world as the power of life clothed with a mortal body, in order to defeat the power of death over the body.

Thus death recoils (one might say, almost automatically) before Jesus: the blind see, the lame walk, the lepers are cleansed, the deaf hear, the dead are raised up (Matt. 11.5). All disease is but a particular form of death. That is why miracles of healing and miracles of raising from the dead are mentioned alongside one another. Between them there is only a difference of degree. In both cases it is death which is repulsed and retreats before the power of life. In Matthew 12.28 Jesus himself says that he casts out the demons by the Spirit of God; and even if the variant 'by the finger of God' in Luke 11.20 is more primitive, Matthew's interpretation is correct. The healing miracles mark the triumph of life over death, of the πνεῦμα, the power of life, over the σάρξ, the power of death. For this reason the healing miracles are on a par with the forgiveness of sins, since death, to which the σάρξ is fettered, is the result of Adam's sin ('the body is dead because of sin', Rom. 8.10). Thus every disease, while not indeed an individual punishment for some particular sin (John 9.2 f.), is, like death, a symptom of the state of general sin in which all humanity is involved. Every healing means the opening of a breach in the domain of death, and consequently in that of sin. That is why Jesus accompanies healing with the promise of the forgiveness of sins.

It is true that death only recoils in these healing miracles. There is no question of its annihilation. In this respect the healings are hardly different from the miracles of raising from the dead. The latter do not put a final end to the grip of death upon the bodies of those who are restored to life. The daughter of Jairus, the young man of Nain, and Lazarus must die and rise afresh, for while Jesus still lives on earth, they are raised up with a mortal body and not with a σῶμα πνευματικόν.

Matthew (27.52 f.) says that at the moment of Christ's death, that is, at the very instant when death suffered its decisive defeat, the bodies of many of the dead came out from the tombs. The evangelist regards this event, too, as only an anticipation consequent upon Christ's victory, and not as a final resurrection of the bodies of the saints. Otherwise it would be impossible to understand why only many (πολλά) and not all the bodies of the saints should be raised at that time. Just as death was bound to retreat before Jesus when he lived on earth, so also, as we expect, it retreats when the most important event for the history of death takes place, when, that is, the irrevocable verdict of condemnation to annihilation is pronounced, although it is not yet carried out.

(2) Since the death and resurrection of Christ his Church is the sphere of the Spirit's activity, and here and now he seeks, by anticipation, to bestow incorruptibility on our mortal bodies in the miracles performed by the apostles.

Paul supplies what may be called a theological basis for this. He says that the Church is the body of Christ on earth, and so the only σῶμα πνευματικόν in existence at the moment. But this resurrection-body of Christ, the Church, consists of believers still clothed with bodies of flesh. Hence the paradox: on earth the faithful together form a resurrection-body, Christ's body, and yet none of them individually possesses a resurrection-body, since all are still clothed with a body of flesh.

We shall attempt to find in Pauline thought the idea which, it seems to me, is fundamental, that *to constitute the spiritual body of Christ has, by anticipation, present consequences for the bodies of the faithful*.

This idea, bold though it seems and at variance with modern idealism, can be traced throughout Paul's writings. As at the end we shall be 'conformed (σύμμορφοι) to the image of his Son' (Rom.

8.29) and the Lord 'shall fashion anew the body of our humiliation, that it may be conformed (σύμμορφος) to the body of his glory' (Phil. 3.21), so now the μορφή of the body of our humiliation is already influenced by Christ who must 'be formed' (μορφωθῇ, Gal. 4.19) in his Church.

The paradox of the Church here is that there is the *body* and the *bodies*, the spiritual body of Christ and the fleshly bodies of men. References to the Church as the body of Christ are not confined to Colossians (1.18, 24) and Ephesians (4.12; 5.30), but are also found completely developed in I Corinthians, where it is the main theme ('you are the body of Christ, and individually members of it' [12.27]), and in Romans ('we, who are many, are one body in Christ' [12.5]). Since the person of the incarnate Christ replaces the temple and since the saying of Jesus about the temple not made with hands certainly refers to the community of the disciples, the fourth Gospel, in the narrative of the cleansing of the temple, can compare the body of Christ with the temple (John 2.19 f.).

We find this complex of temple, Church, body of Christ in I Corinthians 3.16: 'Do you not know that you are God's temple and that the Spirit of God dwells in you?' Obviously what is meant is the Church as the spiritual body of Christ. It is very important to notice that in 6.19 the same thing is said of the individual, fleshly bodies of the faithful who make up the Church. 'Do you not know that your body is a temple of the Holy Spirit which is in you, which you have from God? You are not your own.' This curious application of the same word in the same epistle to two such different objects as the Church and the individual human body can only be explained by the connection we are trying to bring out between the *body* and *bodies*.

The whole argument of I Corinthians 6 depends on the basic idea that it is not a matter of indifference for our body of flesh that it is incorporated in another body, the resurrection-body of Christ, which is the only σῶμα πνευματικόν so far in existence. That is why the bodies of members of the Church are henceforth invested with special honour. They are no longer their own, and Paul exhorts his readers to glorify God in their bodies (I Cor. 6.20). This is the christological foundation of all Paul's teaching on sexual morality. He can even say: 'Do you not know that your bodies are members of Christ?' (τὰ σώματα ὑμῶν μέλη Χριστοῦ ἐστιν, I Cor. 6.15; cf. also Eph. 5.30 μέλη ἐσμὲν τοῦ σώματος αὐτοῦ).

But this glorious body of Christ, as far as it is identical with the

Church on earth, is at the same time also the *crucified* body, since it is set in a hostile world. Consequently, the incorporation of our bodies of flesh in the Church as the body of Christ wears two different aspects corresponding to the twofold character of the body of Christ—as a crucified body and as a glorified body. As a member of the crucified body the body of flesh shares in its suffering: ' . . . always bearing about in the body the death of Jesus, that the life also of Jesus may be manifested in our body' (II Cor. 4.10). It is to be noted that Paul only refers to his own suffering, so that he seems to restrict this effect of the body of Christ to the body of an *apostle*, in accordance with his special status in the Church. Thus he writes in Philippians 1.20: 'Christ shall be magnified in my body, whether by life or by death'. In Galatians 6.17 he speaks of the 'marks' of Jesus which he bears on his body. But the most explicit statement of this conception occurs in Colossians 1.24: 'Now I rejoice in my sufferings for your sake, and complete in my flesh what is lacking in Christ's afflictions for the sake of his body, which is the Church'. Here the connection between the Church as the body of Christ and the apostle's body of flesh is clearly stated.

But Paul is more interested in the effect of the *glorified* body of Christ on the bodies of those who constitute the Church, because it concerns all believers. This effect operates pre-eminently in the sacraments of Baptism and the Lord's Supper. The sacraments occupy the same position in the Church as the miracles in the ministry of Jesus, for they, too, are miracles of the Holy Spirit. Of course, miracles in the stricter sense also continue after the resurrection. But within the body of Christ which became the Church when the Holy Spirit was poured forth on the day of Pentecost, the miracles of the Spirit are identified more and more with the efficacy of Baptism and the Lord's Supper.

Baptism imparts to each individually the Holy Spirit which at Pentecost was poured out on the whole Church. By entering the Church a man is brought under the immediate influence of the σῶμα πνευματικόν. 'In one Spirit we were all baptized into one body' (I Cor. 12.13). This body is the glorified body of Christ, and so, according to Acts, whose accounts of Baptism do not fail to emphasize the fact, Baptism to a certain extent has an immediate effect on men's bodies. This effect, however, is manifested first only as speaking with tongues, which is but an attempt of the Spirit to break through the limits set to human speech by the body, and to find a more direct kind of utterance, the language of angels (I Cor.

13.1). But the attempt is in vain, because speaking with tongues, confined as it is within physical means of expression, only issues in 'groanings' which Paul in Romans 8.23 f. explains as signs that the redemption of our body (ἀπολύτρωσις τοῦ σώματος, verse 23) is already glimpsed and eagerly awaited, but not yet accomplished.

It is in the Lord's Supper that the relation between the risen body of Christ and the fleshly body of a man who belongs to it is most clearly seen. The Eucharist may be called the sacrament of the Church, the body of Christ. I Corinthians 10.16 f. is often quoted, but perhaps insufficiently considered. Here Paul says clearly that the bread which we break in the Eucharist is the body of Christ consisting of us 'who are many'. In breaking the bread we therefore enter into direct and immediate contact with the σῶμα πνευματικόν of the risen Christ, and this σῶμα is at the same time the community of the faithful. This mysterious identity of the Church and the body of Christ is especially efficacious in the sacrament of the Supper, and if we wished and were able to try to determine the place and time in the life of Paul at which this identity was revealed to him, we should probably think of these eucharistic meals which he shared with the brethren.

In any case it can be asserted with confidence that to Paul the spiritual body of Christ present in the company gathered for the meal exerts influence upon the human body. At first sight this might seem rather offensive. But verses 29–30 in chapter 11 are quite explicit about it, and since the narrative of the institution earlier in the chapter is so often quoted, we cannot pass them over in silence. 'He that eats and drinks, eats and drinks judgment to himself, if he does not discern the body. For this cause many among you are weak and sickly, and not a few sleep.' Paul, then, goes so far as to say that the meal, if eaten worthily, wards off sickness and even death. This very bold idea clearly assumes that the Supper is never eaten in a wholly worthy manner so long as the present age lasts. The risen body of Christ is never fully realized, as it should be, by believers assembled for the meal.

It has rightly been pointed out that Paul does not wish to imply that those who partake of the Supper unworthily receive *any* kind of punishment, but punishment which affects their own bodies. Participation in Christ's resurrection-body in the meal could wrest them here and now from the power of death. They deprive themselves of the life-giving power of the Supper, and by their unworthiness they prevent life from repulsing death here and now; *they prevent the working of miracles of healing and resurrection which could otherwise be wrought.*

In the risen body of Christ composed of the Church and realized in the Eucharist there should be no room for the power of death. So understood, the Eucharist is indeed the supreme anticipation of the end. Paul elsewhere in the same chapter (I Cor. 11.26) has this idea in mind when he says that at the Supper we proclaim the Lord's death 'until he comes'. This is truly the miracle of life which must enter into our very bodies in order to expel disease and death, as Jesus expelled them in his earthly ministry, and thereby encroached upon the events of the end.

All this is confirmed by Paul's views of marriage. Dealing with the case of incest in the Corinthian Church, he shows that all sexual intercourse outside marriage is an injury to the risen body of Christ. Thus physical union with the πόρνη is incompatible with membership of this other body, the body of Christ. The whole discussion in I Corinthians 6 on the relation between the body of Christ and our bodies presupposes this idea. 'He who is joined to a harlot is one body (with her)' (verse 16). It is impossible at the same time to be one body with a harlot and with Christ. The two unions are mutually exclusive.

This is solely because Paul conceives membership of the Church as a physical relationship. Apart from this conception the whole argument would be unintelligible. As members of the Church we are members of Christ. 'Shall I then take away the members of Christ, and make them members of a harlot?' Paul asks, after having said that our bodies are members of Christ (verse 15). He regards the union between our bodies and the body of Christ as so intimate that it can only be compared with sexual union between two bodies which makes them one flesh (verse 16). Hence the incompatibility between the two unions. The body cannot be united both to the πόρνη and to the Lord, because the body is 'for the Lord, and the Lord for the body' (verse 13). That is why the unchaste person must be excluded from the Church (I Cor. 5.5). He can no longer belong to the body of Christ; he has excluded himself through his immoral union.

All Paul's teaching on sexual morality is bound up with his idea of the body of Christ. This idea explains his reason for upholding the sanctity of marriage. It is that marriage is *the only sexual union of two bodies which is compatible with union with the body of Christ*. It must be remembered that while Paul in I Corinthians 7, in the case of those who have the gift, prefers celibacy to marriage for reasons of expediency, yet he regards *marriage as perfectly compatible with the union of our bodies with the body of Christ*. After what he has said in chapter 6, he starts from this idea in chapter 7, which deals with marriage. While not explicit, it clearly forms the background of what he has to say. If the marriage union is the only one for which there is room within the union with the body of Christ, marriage, in Paul's view, although he chose celibacy for himself, assumes a special honour from the theological point of view. It is only for this reason that he can write: 'The unbelieving husband is consecrated through his wife, and the unbelieving wife is consecrated through her husband' (I Cor. 7.14).

There is, therefore, no reason to regard I Corinthians 7 as at variance with Ephesians 5.28 f., on the ground that marriage is disparaged in the former passage, while it is esteemed only in the latter. On the contrary, in Ephesians 5.28 f. ideas are developed without which I Corinthians 7, and especially its connection with the preceding chapter, cannot be understood. In Ephesians 5.30 we meet again the statement of I Corinthians 6.15 that we are members of the body of Christ. This is the basis of the positive evaluation of marriage. But in Ephesians 5 we learn also the reason *why* marriage is compatible with union with the body of Christ: the physical relations of husband and wife correspond (καθώς, Eph. 5.29) to the relation between Christ and his Church.

We arrive, then, at the conclusion that in the New Testament the resurrection of Christ has consequences for our bodies. Here and now the body can be subject to the life-giving activity of the Holy Spirit, although its transformation into a spiritual body is only possible when all things shall be created anew by the Spirit.

This being so, the human body, far from being despised in New Testament thought, to which dualism is foreign, receives special honour in the light of Christ's resurrection. Hence an ethical principle for the human body which is entirely based on the christological fact of the resurrection and on belief in the Holy Spirit. Because the body in the Church is already united with Christ's resurrection-body, it must be watched carefully so that it preserves its dignity as a temple of the Holy Spirit. That is why Paul introduces the ethical part of the epistle to the Romans (12.1) with the exhortation that they present their bodies to God as an acceptable sacrifice.

VIII

Ο ΟΠΙΣΩ ΜΟΥ ΕΡΧΟΜΕΝΟΣ

Translated from the French in
Coniectanea Neotestamentica, XI, 1947, p. 26–32, Lund.

Ὁ ὀπίσω μου ἐρχόμενος

IN CONTROVERSIES of antiquity an important part is played by chronological arguments to prove the priority of one writer or founder of a school of thought to another. Jewish apologetic was particularly concerned to prove that Moses preceded the Greek philosophers and poets, a theme which Christian apologists borrowed and made use of from time to time. The more convincing theory of the *logos spermatikos* does not seem to have been regarded as sufficient in itself, and is usually found in combination with the argument, Jewish in origin, that the best of the Greek philosophers owe what is true in their writings to the Old Testament. How the Old Testament could have been accessible to a man like Plato is a question which is not asked. Christian apologists, like their Jewish predecessors, are content to prove by chronological arguments the priority of the Old Testament prophets, and thereby to assert their superiority to the Greek philosophers and poets.

The New Testament preserves traces of a controversy in which, though on a very different level from that of the apologists, chronology plays an equally important part. This is the controversy in the very early days of the Church between the followers of Christ and the followers of John the Baptist. There is no need to repeat here the evidence that the fourth Gospel particularly is concerned to refute the claims of the sect which took the name of John the Baptist and which seems to have been the most dangerous rival of the early Church in certain areas.[1] The brilliant thesis of W. Baldensperger[2] is accepted today by the most recent commentators on the fourth Gospel,[3] and is confirmed by the Mandaean texts made accessible through their publication twenty years ago by M. Lidzbarski.

Baldensperger had already drawn attention to the importance of

[1] Cf. M. Dibelius, *Die urchristliche Überlieferung von Johannes dem Täufer*, 1911; M. Goguel, *Jean Baptiste*, 1928.

[2] W. Baldensperger, *Der Prolog des vierten Evangeliums. Sein polemisch-apologetischer Zweck*, 1898.

[3] W. Bauer, *Das Johannesevangelium*, 3rd edn., 1933; R. Bultmann, *Das Evangelium des Johannes*, 1941.

the appeal to chronology made by the followers of the Baptist in support of the messiahship of their teacher and against that of Jesus. Ephraem, who in his commentary testifies to the existence of the sect,[4] preserves the memory of this chronological argument when he says that John the Baptist knew that he must precede Jesus in dying because he had preceded him in being born *in hanc vitam.*[5] I shall show that the central part itself of the oldest source of the Clementines, of which to date only *Rec.* 1.54 and 60 [6] have been cited in this connection, is concerned with the chronological argument, and allows us to give it the central position in the dispute between the followers of the Baptist and those of Christ, and to stress still more its place in the fourth Gospel.

The Clementines, or at any rate the Jewish Christian source of the Κηρύγματα Πέτρου incorporated in them,[7] emanate from an environment in which the sect of the Baptist must have been a rival all the more dangerous as it seems to have held Gnostic ideas similar to those which were current in this part of Jewish Christianity. Just as a better understanding of the anti-docetic polemic of the Johannine writings demands a study of later documents of the beginning of the second century which openly oppose Docetism, i.e. the Epistles of Ignatius of Antioch, so an examination of the anti-Baptist polemic of the Κηρύγματα Πέτρου is necessary in order to account for the Johannine endeavour to refute the arguments offered by the Baptist sect.

The polemic of the Κηρύγματα Πέτρου is distinguished by excessive radicalism which results in quite heretical notions. John the Baptist is reduced to the position of a false prophet, whereas the fourth Gospel directs its polemic against those who regard the Baptist as the Messiah, and not against John himself. In the Gospel the Baptist, so far from being held responsible for false opinions about himself, is the μάρτυς who refutes in advance the devotees of the sect by defining his actual relationship to Jesus Christ. With emphatic insistence which can only be explained as aimed at an assertion to the contrary, the evangelist declares: 'John the Baptist said openly and did not deny it, he said openly, I am not the Christ'.

The whole dispute was bound to revolve round the irrefutable fact that John the Baptist came before Jesus, and that chronologically

---

[4] Ephraem, *Evangelii expositio,* ed. Moesinger, 1876, p. 288.
[5] *Op. cit.,* p. 99.
[6] Cf. also *Hom.,* 2.22 f.
[7] O. Cullmann, *Le problème littéraire et historique du roman pseudo-clémentin,* 1930.

Jesus was therefore only the ὀπίσω Ἰωάννου ἐρχόμενος. The radical solution of the problem suggested by the Clementines shows very clearly the need for Christians to find a reply which, without denying the fact of the historical priority of John the Baptist, would yet invalidate the argument readily drawn from it by their opponents.

The Jewish Christians in the Clementines were led by their polemic to deny the validity of the chronological argument generally admitted in antiquity, and go as far as to assert that, on the contrary, priority in time is an indication of inferiority, and even of diabolical origin! The result of this strange principle is that John the Baptist becomes the representative of evil.

This means that in the Κηρύγματα Πέτρου the whole Jewish Christian theory of pairs (συζυγίαι),[8] a favourite Gnostic idea, is made to serve the polemic against the Baptist sect. The aim is to show that of two complementary elements the one which is prior chronologically represents the principle of evil, while the second which follows represents the principle of good. God has always associated two elements, a good and a bad. But whereas up to the creation of Adam the good element precedes the bad (sky—earth, day—night, light—fire, sun—moon, life—death, Adam—Eve), the order is reversed in the case of subsequent pairs of human beings in which the evil principle proceeding from Eve comes first, and the good principle proceeding from Adam second. This theory of pairs provides the criterion for distinguishing the representatives of the good principle from those of the evil principle, and this criterion is their chronological relationship. Cain comes before Abel, Ishmael before Isaac, Esau before Jacob, Aaron before Moses. At the end antichrist will come before the return of Christ. The coming of John the Baptist before the Son of Man is to be understood in the same way.

John the Baptist, then, the πρόοδος (Hom., 2.23), belongs to the line of succession of Eve, Cain, Ishmael, Esau, Aaron and antichrist. His very priority in time to Jesus proves this. He comes as the first, πρῶτος (Hom., 2.17), before the Son of Man. Thus the Jewish Christian theory of pairs, inspired by polemic against the Baptist,[9] differs from the prologue of the fourth Gospel, which regards Jesus as the πρῶτος (John 1.15), in conceding to the other

---

8 Hom., 2.16–17; Rec., 3.61.

9 An anti-Pauline polemic is combined with that against John the Baptist. In fact, Paul appears also in the series of the evil principle. As a false apostle he forms a pair with Peter, the true apostle who went to the Gentiles after him. The priority given to Paul shows that he represents the evil principle.

side that the πρῶτος is really John the Baptist. But this theory makes this the actual proof of his inferiority.

While this radical and heretical solution of the problem set by the existence of a community which claimed John the Baptist as its founder is not the one of which traces can be seen in the evangelists, yet it urges us to discover implicit answers to the same chronological argument in the form assumed by the Gospel tradition about John the Baptist. Although much less clearly than in the fourth Gospel, this concern shows through also in the Synoptic tradition.[10] The prophetic passages from the Old Testament (Mal. 3.1 and Isa. 40.3) quoted at the beginning of Mark's Gospel are used to prove that it was the divine intention that John the Baptist should precede Christ. The saying in Matthew 11.11b was certainly preserved to serve as a reply to the chronological argument utilized by champions of the Baptist sect. It is unfortunate that the following translation of this saying, suggested by Franz Dibelius,[11] has not been generally adopted: 'He who is less [Jesus] is greater than he [John the Baptist] in the kingdom of heaven'. Dibelius rightly points out that the early Fathers quite naturally always took the saying in this way. But he is wrong in attributing their translation of μικρότερος by 'younger' solely to their desire to weaken any offensiveness which might be thought to attach to the application of the word to Jesus. Chrysostom, for example, uses the expression μικρότερος κατὰ τὴν ἡλικίαν, an interpretation which is confirmed by the fact that the rival sect, as already indicated, regarded Jesus as 'less' in the sense of 'younger' than John, and which becomes still more plausible when it is remembered that זְעֵיר, the Aramaic for μικρότερος, means both 'less' and 'younger'.[12]

The description of Jesus as ὁ ὀπίσω Ἰωάννου ἐρχόμενος was clearly the centre of the whole dispute. That is why the Synoptists (Mark 1.7; Matt. 3.11) report a saying of the Baptist in which he uses it himself, but in the form that he who comes after him will be the ἰσχυρότερος.

It is of much interest that in the parallel saying in the fourth Gospel (1.15), for which the polemic against the disciples of the Baptist was much more of a burning issue,[13] John the Baptist is not

---

10 R. Bultmann, *Geschichte der synoptischen Tradition*, 2nd edn., 1931, p. 22, 177 f., 261 f.

11 'Zwei Worte Jesu', *Z.N.T.W.*, 1910, p. 190 f.

12 I owe this information to my colleague W. Baumgartner.

13 Even the prologue states that John was not the light (John 1.8).

content with a mere affirmation of the superiority of the ὀπίσω ἐρχόμενος, but remains within the framework of the chronological dispute: 'He who comes after me ranks before me, for he was before me'. This is quite a different reply to the great argument of the other side from that in the Clementines, for the validity of the chronological argument is expressly recognized, while the priority of John the Baptist to Jesus is, of course, denied. There is no need to take the words ἔμπροσθέν μου in a local sense, and no tautology results from understanding them chronologically as the context demands. The chronological question is viewed first in quite a general way: he who comes later does not really do so. The proposition introduced by ὅτι, looking at the matter from the standpoint of absolute chronology, which is that of the prologue, explains this general statement: he is before me because, being at the beginning of all things, ἐν ἀρχῇ, the ὀπίσω μου ἐρχόμενος is πρῶτος in an absolute way, and therefore also in relation to me, John the Baptist.

In 1.26, 30, the fourth Gospel returns to the chronological argument when the Baptist himself emphasizes that he who, in virtue of his pre-existence, is actually prior to himself, was present among men before his baptism in the Jordan, although at the time he did not yet know him (verse 30). Before he was known by others, before he had even begun his public ministry, Jesus stood among them: μέσος ὑμῶν στήκει (verse 26). The manifest concern of the evangelist to show that, contrary to the Synoptic account, Jesus began his ministry independently before the imprisonment of the Baptist, while he was still baptizing (John 3.22 f.), is explained by a parallel interest. This is his endeavour to prove that even in the sphere of historical chronology, the priority of John the Baptist is not as absolute as the other side, depending on the Synoptic account, tried to make out.

It may even be asked whether the enigmatic saying in John 10.8: 'All who came before me are thieves and robbers' is not also directed against the claims of the Baptist sect. W. Bauer [14] thinks not, because if so we should have a saying aimed at John the Baptist himself, whereas the evangelist always seeks to depict him as a witness to Jesus. Against this it may be urged that the context suggests that the saying about thieves and robbers is but a way of saying that Christ, the shepherd and the door, can have no predecessors. The saying is not aimed at John the Baptist the witness and

[14] Op. cit., ad loc.

forerunner, but at a John who was claimed to be a Messiah, and therefore a predecessor. R. Bultmann [15] rightly allows that John the Baptist is not excluded from the πάντες in this passage; what applies to all those who came before Christ necessarily applies to John also, just as the πάντες in John 1.16 and 3.31 implies John the Baptist and has him particularly in view.

This examination of the chronological argument, I think, confirms and corrects the thesis proposed by Baldensperger. I differ from him in believing that in the fourth Gospel it is not theology which is made to serve the ends of polemic, but polemic which is borrowed in the interests of the writer's theological principles. The evangelist is interested in chronology as a theological problem. Throughout his Gospel his purpose is to show how the life of Jesus is linked with definite ὥραι.[16] While the καιρός for other men is always here (John 7.6), the καιροί of the life of Jesus are precisely fixed by God in accordance with his plan of salvation. This plan is, on the one hand, entirely christocentric, on the other, completely bound up with its unfolding in time from the ἀρχή when the *Logos* was with God taking part in creation until the ὥρα when the dead will come forth from their tombs. In this history of salvation, which extends from the beginnings to the end, no one can be prior to Christ in the absolute sense, neither Abraham (John 8.58) nor John the Baptist, because throughout it is the story of Christ, first pre-existent, then incarnate, and returning during the period of the Paraclete and finally at the end of time.

[15] *Op. cit., ad loc.*
[16] O. Cullmann, *Christ and Time*, E.T., 1951, p. 43 f.

IX

Samaria and the Origins of the Christian Mission

Who are the ΆΛΛΟΙ of John 4. 38?

Translated from 'La Samarie et les Origines de la Mission Chrétienne', *Annuaire 1953–54, École Pratique des Hautes Études* (Section des Sciences Religieuses), p. 3–12, Paris

Samaria and the Origins of the Christian Mission

I N ST. MATTHEW'S GOSPEL (10.5) Jesus says to his disciples: 'Enter not into any city of the Samaritans'. Does this mean that he shared the hatred of the Jews for Samaria, that land of religious syncretism with its truncated type of Judaism?[1] The Samaritans recognized only the Pentateuch, and that in a modified form of text,[2] they rejected the worship of the temple in Jerusalem, and practised their own worship on Mount Gerizim[3] even after John Hyrcanus in 128 B.C. had destroyed the sanctuary they had built there.[4]

The command in Matthew 10.5 is preceded by another: 'Go not into any way of the Gentiles'. It is certain that it was not national prejudice which prompted Jesus to forbid the disciples to extend their mission to the heathen, but respect for the purpose of God that salvation should begin among the Jews (John 4.22). Thus, despite the prohibition in Matthew 10.5, he can also foretell that 'many will come from the east and the west, and sit down with Abraham, and Isaac, and Jacob in the kingdom of heaven; but the sons of the kingdom will be cast forth into the outer darkness' (Matt. 8.11 f.; Luke 13.28 f.), and that 'the men of Nineveh will stand up in the judgment with this generation and condemn it' (Matt. 12.41; Luke 11.32).

It is exactly the same with the attitude of Jesus to Samaria. St. Luke's Gospel, which does not record the saying of Matthew 10.5,

---

[1] On Samaria see E. Schürer, *Geschichte des jüdischen Volkes im Zeitalter Jesu Christi*, 4th edn., 1907, p. 19 f.; J. A. Montgomery, *The Samaritans*, 1907; A. E. Cowley, *The Samaritan Liturgy*, 1909; J. E. H. Thomson, *The Samaritans*, 1919; E. Haefeli, *Geschichte der Landschaft Samarien von 722 v. Chr. bis 67 n. Chr.*, 1922; M. Gaster, *The Samaritans*, 1925; J. Jeremias, *Die Passahfeier der Samaritaner*, 1932.

[2] The first sacrifice in Canaan (Deut. 27.4) did not take place on Mount Ebal, but on Gerizim, the mount of blessing (Deut. 11.29; 27.12).

[3] Joseph., *Ant.*, xiii, 2. 3; xiii, 3. 4; xviii, 4. 1; John 4.20.

[4] *Ibid.*, xiii, 9. 1.

attributes to Jesus the intention of making at least one halt in Samaria on his way to Jerusalem. When the disciples, faced with the refusal of the Samaritans to receive him, ask that fire should come down upon them from heaven, Jesus rebukes them (Luke 9.51 f.). Also in Luke (10.30 f.) there is the parable of the good Samaritan, which is an implicit condemnation of race prejudice. It is in Luke again that we read of the ten lepers healed by Jesus, of whom only the Samaritan fell at his feet to give him thanks (17.11 f.). The third Gospel is particularly interested in the contacts of Jesus with Samaria.

We know that after the death of their Master the apostles inaugurated the Gentile mission. But the book of Acts informs us that it was preceded by the mission in Samaria. The latter prepared the way, we might say, for the preaching of the gospel to the Gentiles. We may even say, then, that it was Samaria which saw *the actual beginnings of the Christian mission*. For the first time the gospel entered a country which did not belong to the Jewish community. Clearly, then, this mission in Samaria is of first-rate importance.

The Christians who went to Samaria, like those who later inaugurated the Gentile mission, were certain that they were not acting contrary to the purpose of Jesus. Matthew 28.19 records the command of the risen Lord to the disciples to 'make disciples of all the nations', and in Acts 1.8 Jesus appears to them and tells them that they will be his 'witnesses in Jerusalem and in all Judaea and Samaria and to the end of the earth'. Moreover, the idea that the gospel must be preached to the Gentiles before the end forms part of the common stock of primitive Christian beliefs.[5] Samaria was the first step in the execution of the divine plan, and it was all the more important for the first Christians to be sure that they were acting in accordance with the will of Christ in going there.

This question, I think, is one of the many interests of the author of the fourth Gospel. His aim is to show that the Christ of the Church corresponds to the Jesus of history, and to trace the direct connection between the life of Jesus and the varied expressions of Church life. I have tried elsewhere to demonstrate this in the sphere of worship.[6] But worship is not the only expression of this life. Alongside it there is the mission. And in its manner of recording the life of Jesus the fourth Gospel betrays a special interest in the missionary task.

[5] Cf. O. Cullmann, *Christ and Time*, E.T., 1951, p. 158 f.

[6] O. Cullmann, *Les sacrements dans l'évangile johannique. La vie de Jésus et la culte de l'Église primitive*, 1951. [English readers may consult Cullmann's *Early Christian Worship*, E.T., 1953, Ed.].

In 12.20 f. we read of Greeks who wish to see Jesus, who, however, refuses their request and speaks of the need of his first dying and being glorified. In this way the evangelist wishes to emphasize the fact that it was the desire of Jesus himself that the Gentile mission ought only to be undertaken after his death.

But his chief interest is in the actual origin of the preaching of the gospel beyond the Jewish people in the mission in Samaria. His aim is to prove that it was begun by Jesus himself even though, during his life, he counselled his followers to avoid the Samaritan towns. The fourth chapter describes the encounter of Jesus with the woman of Samaria. Their conversation provides the opportunity of speaking of the true worship 'in spirit and in truth' as distinct both from Jewish worship in the temple at Jerusalem and from the Samaritan worship on Mount Gerizim (4.20 f.). But what interests him just as much is the actual foundation of the mission in Samaria by Jesus. He answers the question which was certainly asked by the first Christians: is the mission in this half-Jewish country, which was so unfaithful to the divine plan, in accordance with Christ's purpose?

I do not think that the evangelist regards the Samaritan woman as a mere imaginary figure symbolizing Samaria. It is more likely that, as throughout the Gospel, there is here a combination of tradition about the life of Jesus and its meaning for the Church.[7] Thus throughout this narrative the evangelist at the same time assigns a symbolic significance to the Samaritan woman. The five husbands she has had and her present husband who is not her husband correspond, whatever may be said, too closely to the position of Samaria described in II Kings 17.24–34 and Josephus, Ant., ix, 14. 3, for the comparison which suggests itself to have been unknown to the evangelist.[8] According to the passages mentioned, after the destruction

[7] Ibid., p. 9 f.

[8] This idea, perceived by a copyist of the thirteenth century (see E. Nestle, 'Die fünf Männer des samaritanischen Weibes', Z.N.T.W., 1904, p. 166 f.), is attributed to the evangelist by W. Bauer, Das Johannesevangelium, 3rd edn., 1933, p. 75; E. C. Hoskyns, The Fourth Gospel, 1947, p. 242; H. Strathmann, Das Evangelium nach Johannes (Das Neue Testament Deutsch, 1951), p. 84, and others. M. J. Lagrange, Évangile selon saint Jean, 1948, p. 110; J. H. Bernard, The Gospel according to St. John, 1928, vol. i, p. 143 f.; W. F. Howard, The Fourth Gospel in Recent Criticism and Interpretation, 1931, p. 184 f., and R. Bultmann, Das Evangelium des Johannes, 1941, p. 138, n. 4, stress the difficulties of this comparison (see next note). In Les sacrements dans l'évangile johannique, p. 54 [E.T. (see n. 6 supra), p. 83], I myself adopted a cautious attitude to this interpretation which I now think it is difficult to reject, while not denying the other meaning which the evangelist seems to attach to the incident.

of the northern kingdom five Babylonian tribes were transplanted to Samaria. They brought their own gods with them,[9] but afterwards worshipped Yahweh as well. The matrimonial relationships of the woman of Samaria, which, in the narrative as a whole, serve indeed a different purpose, illustrate very well the unlawful cult of Samaria whose inhabitants are described in Ecclesiasticus 50.25 f., after the manner of Hosea, as no people. The conversion of Samaria to Christianity is prefigured in this incident by Jacob's well in John 4. The Samaritans have a certain messianic belief: they await the coming of Taeb [10] who will manifest himself in a purely earthly setting. The woman of Samaria refers to this and Jesus says to her: 'I who speak to you am he' (4.25 f.).

But it is the epilogue of this story in verses 31 f., the conversation with the disciples on their return from the city, which is of the greatest importance. While the Samaritans of Sychar are approaching (verse 30) Jesus looks at the fields round Jacob's well. They make him think of the mission field. We find the same idea in the saying about the harvest and the labourers in Matthew 9.37 f. In considering the mission in Samaria the Johannine Christ thinks of the time of sowing and the time of harvest: 'Do you not say, there are yet four months, and then comes the harvest?' (verse 35). We know that in Palestine the sowing takes place in October or November and the harvest in April,[11] so that usually they are separated by a period of six months. The fields which Jesus and his disciples see before them four months before the harvest are therefore still green. We now see the meaning of the saying. When applied to the actual fields, a certain period must elapse between sowing and harvest, but when applied metaphorically to the mission field it is not so. When he says, 'Lift up your eyes' Jesus is supposed to point to the Samaritans coming out of Sychar who, on the information of the woman, come to see what all this was about him who had told her her past. He makes the disciples see a field where the time of sowing and the time of harvest coincide. In this field the time when the corn is ripe is already here; already the Samaritans are approaching. This is emphasized in verse 36b: ' . . . that he who sows and he who reaps may rejoice together'.

9 The point raised by, among others, W. F. Howard and R. Bultmann, that two of the five tribes brought two gods, so that the total is not five but seven, is not as important as they think. In their use of the Old Testament Christian writers were never troubled by details of that kind.

10 A. Merx, *Der Messias oder Ta'eb der Samaritaner*, 1910.

11 G. Dalman, *Arbeit und Sitte in Palästina*, i, 1928, p. 164 f., 413 f.

Yet the harvest Jesus reaps when the people of Sychar flock to him is but an anticipation of the real harvest in Samaria which will be kept for the apostles until after his death. Therefore, although in Jesus he who sows is identical with him who reaps, the old proverb [12] quoted in verse 37 is nevertheless also justified: 'One sows and another reaps'.[13] It is true if it is taken in conjunction with the preceding saying about the sower and the reaper rejoicing at one and the same time, for Jesus will still stand behind the apostles when they reap. Thus what takes place by Jacob's well where Jesus sows and reaps at the same time will be repeated during the mission which the disciples will undertake in Samaria after his death. Of course, it will then be the disciples who will be reaping, but Christ will still be at work: ἐγὼ ἀπέστειλα ὑμᾶς (verse 38).

In accordance with his usual practice the evangelist traces the connection between the life of the Jesus of history and the Church. The sowing (John 4) and the reaping (the future mission in Samaria) go back to Jesus. The evangelist wishes to break down prejudices concerning this missionary task, based, probably mistakenly, on the saying of Jesus in Matthew: 'Enter not into any city of the Samaritans'.

So far the text is comparatively easy to interpret, but a complication is introduced in verse 38b: '*Others* have laboured, and you have entered into their labour'. Between him who sows and those who reap a third category is introduced, 'others' who have laboured (in Samaria) before the apostles. Who are these ἄλλοι? They cannot be identical with the sower, Jesus, since the plural is used, nor with the apostles who reap. It must be remembered that here the Johannine Christ expresses the point of view of the Church in the time of . the evangelist, since, by using the perfect tense (εἰσεληλύθατε), he refers to the missionary task which is to be performed by the apostles alone. There is, therefore, no need to think, with some of the Fathers,[14] followed by M. J. Lagrange,[15] of the prophets or righteous men of the Old Testament, of whom there is no suggestion in the passage, and still less of John the Baptist, as E. Lohmeyer suggested.[16] Bultmann comes nearest to the explanation which I

---

[12] λόγος = proverb; see the references in W. Bauer, *op. cit.*, p. 74.

[13] The idea alone is attested; see the texts in R. Bultmann, *op. cit.*, p. 146, n. 6.

[14] Origen, xiii, 50, 325 f.; Chrys., p. 198a; Theod. Mops., p. 104 and others (see W. Bauer, *op. cit.*, p. 74).

[15] *Évangile selon saint Jean*, 1948, p. 120.

[16] *Das Urchristentum*, i, 1932, p. 26, n. 3, following a suggestion of W. Bacon, 'New and Old in Jesus' Relation to John', *J.B.L.*, 1929, p. 53 f.

favour, when he says that what is meant is all those who, with Jesus, are forerunners in the missionary work. Moreover, Harnack rightly pointed out that in Christian writings of the first century κοπιάω is a technical term for missionary activity.[17]

But the evangelist is alluding to a particular case, the mission in Samaria. Who, then, are these mysterious missionaries who paved the way for the apostles in Samaria?

The book of Acts supplies the answer. The third evangelist, as we saw, has a special interest in contacts between Jesus and the Samaritans. What information does Acts furnish about the origins of the mission in Samaria? According to Acts 8.1, 4 f. the mission in Samaria was begun by the Hellenists, especially Philip, one of the Seven, and only afterwards did the apostles Peter and John 'enter into their labour'—for that is, in fact, what they did. 'Now when the apostles at Jerusalem heard that Samaria had received the word of God, they sent to them Peter and John' (Acts 8.14).

These Hellenists deserve to be given a more important place in the history of the early Church. It is really only Stephen that we know much about. Of Philip we are told that he preached successfully in Samaria with others of the same group; we know only the names of the other five, and the rest are anonymous. It has been rightly recognized for some time that the duties of the Seven must have gone beyond the provision of material needs, and that they must have occupied among the Hellenists a position of authority corresponding to that of the Twelve.[18]

The characteristic theological ideas of the Hellenists appear in Stephen's speech (Acts 7.2 f.). They condemned the temple worship. Stephen finds the crowning act of the infidelity of the Jews in the building of the temple by Solomon, since 'the Most High does not dwell in houses made with hands'.[19] It was revolutionary ideas of this kind which led to Stephen's death by stoning at the hands of the Jews, and they were the cause of the first persecution of Christians. This first persecution did not affect the whole of the Jerusalem Church, but only the Hellenists, the followers of Stephen. It would be interesting to discover whether there is some connection

[17] A. von Harnack, 'Κόπος im frühchristlichen Sprachgebrauch', Z.N.T.W., 1928, p. 1 f.
[18] Cf. S. G. F. Brandon, The Fall of Jerusalem and the Christian Church, 1951, p. 89, 127 f.
[19] On the antecedents of the polemic against the temple, see H. J. Schoeps, Theologie und Geschichte des Judenchristentums, 1949, p. 233, and M. Simon, Verus Israel, 1948, p. 56.

between these Hellenists and the Essene sect known from the Qumran scrolls. The Twelve did not share the views of the Hellenists about the temple worship, and clearly were not at one with them when the persecution broke out. They were not molested, and were even able to remain in Jerusalem (Acts 8.1).

This first persecution led to the first Christian mission, the mission in Samaria. For the Hellenists, on being driven from Jerusalem, preached the gospel in the places where they took refuge, and Acts records their activity in Samaria. But why was it Samaria to which they turned? The explanation is perfectly simple when it is remembered that the Samaritans also rejected the temple worship, and so in this respect were akin to them. What was more natural than that those who had been persecuted because of their hostility to the temple at Jerusalem should take refuge among those who for the same reason had long been separated from the Jews?

This was of great importance in the expansion of Christianity. Although later, according to remarks of Justin Martyr [20] and some hints preserved in Acts (8.18 f.), the religion of Simon Magus appears to have been a dangerous rival to Christianity,[21] this first mission to people who, while not Jews, were nevertheless akin to them in holding certain common beliefs, formed the natural transition to the Gentile mission.

Peter and John had only to reap in Samaria where the real missionary work had already been done by these 'others', the mostly anonymous Hellenists. Yet this work must have been decisive for Peter also, because shortly after these events we find him, according to Acts, inaugurating the Gentile mission. At that time was not Peter, who always appears to have occupied a middle position between the two sides, nearer to the Hellenists than some of his colleagues, especially James? [22] And was he not a little later to share the lot of the Hellenists? Did not history repeat itself when he was imprisoned at Jerusalem, whereas nothing happened to James, just as previously the Hellenists had been persecuted when the Twelve were not disturbed? And is this not the reason why Peter leaves Jerusalem and James finally becomes the leader of the community there?

[20] *Apol. I*, 26.2 f.; *I, 56; Dial. with Trypho*, 120.
[21] Cf. L. Cerfaux, 'La gnose simonienne. Nos principales sources', *Recherches de science religieuse*, 1926, p. 5 f., 1929, p. 489 f.
[22] Cf. O. Cullmann, *Peter: Disciple—Apostle—Martyr*, E.T., 1953, p. 50, and W. Grundmann, 'Das Problem des hellenistischen Christentums innerhalb der Jerusalemer Urgemeinde', *Z.N.T.W.*, 1939, p. 45.

There is some special connection between St. Luke's Gospel and the fourth Gospel. It is, therefore, not surprising that the fourth Gospel also knows the tradition of the connection of the Hellenists with Samaria, of which Acts preserves traces but minimizes its importance. The fourth evangelist has a special interest in these first missionaries. He gives them the honour they deserve by emphasizing their part as pioneers of the proclamation of the gospel among these Samaritans who also rejected the worship in the temple at Jerusalem. It should also be borne in mind that the question of the temple arises quite early in the fourth Gospel (2.13 f.).

Is not the reproach addressed by the Jews to Jesus, 'You are a Samaritan' (John 8.48) something more than a vague insult? Is it not an allusion to the fact that Jesus himself, like the Samaritans and later the Hellenists, was criticized for his attitude to the temple worship?

However that may be, the evangelist (John 4.33 f.) is concerned to show that this mission was intended by Christ. He laid the foundations of it at Jacob's well. It is he who stands behind the ἄλλοι, the gallant Hellenist missionaries. It is he who directs the mission wherever the gospel is preached, even in the difficult land of Samaria.

X

Early Christianity and Civilization

Translated from 'Le Christianisme primitif et la civilisation', *Verbum Caro*, vol. V (nos. 17–20), 1951, p. 57–68, Neuchâtel

Early Christianity and Civilization[1]

THE BOOKS of the New Testament contain hardly any precise information on the relations which the disciples of Christ are to maintain towards the civilization, culture and institutions of the ancient world. The gospel is only interested explicitly in the contemporary Roman state which the early Christian writings enable us to set in relation to the Christian community. For the rest these writings contain merely sporadic and indirect references to the relations between Christianity and secular institutions. They presuppose rather than express directly the fact that the gospel arose in the midst of an ancient culture which, although it had already attained its zenith, was far from having lost all its vitality.[2] It is possible to read whole pages and chapters of the New Testament without being aware of this background. What the Romans regarded as the pleasures of this life is not mentioned either critically or approvingly. From the second century, however, the situation changes. Among Christian writers, some like Tatian and Tertullian were to fulminate against pagan civilization, whilst others, the apologists, and, above all, Clement of Alexandria, were to apply themselves to reconciling the achievements of pagan culture with the demands of the gospel. They were confronted with the whole range of the problem of the relationship between the gospel and the world. In the first century the problem had arisen only in connection with a few specific points such as the pagan state and, possibly, marriage.

The indifference of the first Christian century to pagan civilization in general, and literature and art in particular, is no doubt partly explained by the humble station of most of the members of the Apostolic Church. They were not interested in culture as such. After all, the only contact that any of them, including the humblest,

[1] The article here translated is the French version of a contribution by Professor Cullmann to the two-volume Dutch work *Het oudste Christendom en de antieke Cultuur* (Tjeenk Willink, Haarlem, 1951). [Ed.].
[2] Cf. W. Eltester, 'Die Krisis der Alten Welt und das Christentum', *Z.N.T.W.*, 1949, p. 1 f.

inevitably had with ancient civilization was with the state. In this regard, too, things were to change in the second century when Christians were recruited more and more from all ranks of society. In the first century it was comparatively rare for well-to-do citizens such as Philemon to belong to the Christian community. From the second century, however, and earlier, under Domitian, we find Christians even in the immediate entourage of the emperors. And with this infiltration of Christianity into all classes of society the problem became increasingly acute.

These social considerations, however, important though they are, do not explain everything. The attitude of the Christians of the first two centuries towards the world, sometimes indifferent, sometimes conciliatory, sometimes hostile, flows in the last resort from their theological convictions. And these convictions, however varied their consequences, all result from the judgment which the early Church passed on the world. This judgment is very complex. It is not one either of pure indifference, absolute approval or complete hostility.

We propose to study this Christian judgment on the world, then the inferences which the Christians of the first two centuries drew from it, and in a third section we shall study the deviations which took place in the very bosom of the Church from the outset of the second century.

(1) In the eyes of the early Christians, who believed in the imminent end of the world, neither the institutions nor the culture of this world could have any ultimate value. 'The form of this world is passing away', as the apostle says (I Cor. 7.31). Franz Overbeck and Albert Schweitzer have pointed out, quite rightly, that the thought and conduct of the Christians of the first century can only be understood in the light of this ardent waiting for the end. How could they possibly be interested in the spiritual values and institutions of a world whose early disappearance they were awaiting so fervently? To be sure, they were working in the midst of this world and even claimed to be serving its true interests. But they considered the best way they could serve the world was by preparing men for its disappearance, not by prolonging and perfecting the present 'form' of the world which merely represented the framework of their activities. They had no time to waste on the frivolities of society. All their efforts were concentrated on the preaching of the gospel within the given framework of their daily life.

When they realized that the Kingdom of God would not come

as quickly as they had at first imagined, they stuck to their convictions. Even after the apostle Paul had changed his opinion and conceded the possibility that he might die before the end of the world, the ardour of his expectation of the end remained unaltered and he never came to think of civilization and all it involved as an end in itself.

Are we, then, bound to conclude, with Overbeck and Schweitzer, that early Christianity was radically hostile to the values which the pagans of the time acknowledged as supreme? Such a deduction would be far too simple. To believe that the end was imminent meant recognizing, passively, it may be, but positively, the validity of the effective framework in which human life is set. To believe that God alone would cause the end and bring the fashion of this world to naught meant refusing to usurp his divine sovereignty, refusing to arrogate to themselves a task which it was not theirs to fulfil; it implied respecting the divine plan of salvation and God's will to allow the world to continue until the moment known to him alone. In fact, the Christians never made common cause with the zealots, those Jews who wanted to drive the Romans out of Palestine by violence in order to establish the messianic kingdom there, and whom Jesus very probably had in mind when he spoke of the violent who attempt to take the kingdom of heaven by force (Matt. 11.12).[3] To ask whether the Christians of the apostolic age adopted a positive or negative attitude to the ancient world is, therefore, a false question. In fact, they neither accepted it nor rejected it absolutely. Their conviction was that God had set them in the world, a world which, though destined to disappear, was still continuing by the divine will, although Christ had already overcome the world and the gospel had already been preached by them in this world. So, whilst not forgetting that in the famous passage in I Corinthians 7.30 the emphasis is on the negations:

'let those who have wives be as though they had none, and those who weep as though they wept not, and those who rejoice as though they rejoiced not, and those who buy as though they possessed not, and those who use the world as though they did not use it',

[3] It may be noted in passing that the Twelve included one who had belonged to the zealots, Simon, nicknamed the Cananaean (Κανανοῖος), according to Matthew (10.4) and Mark (3.18). The name has, however, no connection with Canaan and is merely the transcription of the Aramaic word for zealot, as correctly translated by Luke (6.15).

we must not overlook the affirmations that are implied, the 'acceptances', which, we may put it, subtend the 'denials'. Christians still make use of the world which is destined to disappear: they still marry, they weep, they rejoice, they buy.

But they do not accept the framework of their life unconditionally; they submit to it only in so far as they are able to do so without being disloyal to the demands of the gospel. An example, to which we shall return, is that the Christian will admit that the state is willed by God; he will submit to it and contribute to its existence so long as it does not require him to deny Christ and acknowledge the divine lordship of the emperor. He will not object to the existence of pagan law-courts, though he will refuse to have recourse to them himself (I Cor. 6.1 f.), since the Christian community must settle its disputes within its own fold. In principle, he will not shrink from consuming meat bought from pagan butchers who have sacrificed it to pagan gods, since he knows that these gods do not exist. But if there is a risk of this freedom scandalizing the 'weak', as St. Paul calls them, Christian love will require him to abstain (I Cor. 8–10). It is obvious that none of these problems can be solved on its own, in isolation from the context of the faith. They must be related to the demands of the faith and the moral principles of the gospel. Whether it is a question of marriage, the state, or meat sacrificed to idols, the Christian will always have to face the same question: how can I fulfil my duty to Christ most faithfully? And the answer will differ according to the particular case: sometimes he will eat meat sacrificed to idols, sometimes he will abstain for love of the brethren who are weak in the faith; sometimes he will submit to the state, at others he will resist it. Some Christians will marry, others will remain celibate, in obedience to the faith. Pagan culture and institutions are neither accepted nor rejected in a lump, a priori. It is always the gospel which determines the solution in each particular case.

It is, therefore, not correct to assert that the waiting for the end of the world in the apostolic age necessarily entailed the rejection of all culture. In fact, primitive Christianity advocated neither asceticism nor a complete surrender to the enjoyment of life.

To get as complete an idea as possible of the early Christians' attitude to the world and civilization, it should be noted that the faith in Christ, the Lord of the universe, which was theirs, contains a more positive germ of appreciation of pagan culture and its spiritual values. Far from referring merely to the members of the

Church, the lordship of Christ embraces the whole pagan world. 'All authority has been given to me in heaven and on earth' (Matt. 28.18; cf. Phil. 2.9). As far as the kingship of Christ is concerned the only difference between Christians and pagans is that the latter are unaware of his rule. Christ raised to the right hand of God is Lord both of the universe and of the Church. The Church, that is, the fellowship of those who know that Christ is already reigning, forms the centre of the Kingdom of Christ the Lord, the starting-point of the invisible rule which he exerts from now on over the whole universe and which he will make manifest at the end of the world.[4]

This contains the promise of further elaboration. The New Testament itself merely applied the results which flow from the lordship of Christ to the state (Rom. 13. 1f.),[5] indicating both the positive value of this institution and the limits of its power. The Christian writings of the first century do not mention other aspects of civilization, such as literature and art, explicitly. But one can infer from Romans 13 the apostle's attitude to civilization in general. Why should pagan literature and art not unwittingly serve the Kingdom of Christ like the pagan state? Why should they not come in the same category as the state—Nero's state—which the apostle regards with positive respect because he believes in the victory of Christ over the invisible powers and in his effective rule over the universe?

The example of the state indicates quite clearly, however, that culture and civilization can only be appreciated positively in the light of the rule of Christ if they are limited to their own sphere and remain neutral in religious affairs. If they give up their neutrality and ally themselves with pagan religion, they will fall away from the rule of Christ and become demonic. Thus the fact that they are non-Christian is not sufficient in itself to make them demonic. They will fall into this condition only if they make religious claims, just as the state, which is neutral in itself, usurps the majesty of God when the person of the emperor is made an object of worship. The pagan state which requires the Christian to acknowledge the divinity of the emperor is none other than the 'beast from the abyss' (Rev. 13). It is self-condemned. And the same applies to the other spheres of civilization and culture.

[4] Cf. O. Cullmann, 'The Kingship of Christ and the Church in the New Testament', no. 5 in this volume.

[5] On the interpretation of this passage and its relation to the kingship of Christ, cf. O. Cullmann, *Christ and Time*, E.T., 1951, p. 191 f.

Hence the apparently contradictory assertions of the early Christian writers. In fact, there is no contradiction, since everything they say is based on a single coherent conviction: the present world will pass away, nothing in it is of ultimate value, but the Christian is bound to accept it as the framework of his activities until God himself causes it to disappear. All the same, he will fight it and even reject it if he is forced to choose between the world and his faith. But since the world, even the pagan world, is from now on subject to the rule of Christ, it can produce values rooted in Christ, who is the foundation of all things, whom the world still does not know but who already reigns over it.

(2) How did the principles laid down in the New Testament condition the practical approach of the Church to the world in the second century? We may note right away that they were sometimes respected and sometimes abandoned. At times Christians accepted civilization to the extent that it was neutral, at others they rejected it in so far as it was bound up with idolatry; and, possibly without intending to, they created new forms of civilization. Sometimes they allowed themselves to be influenced by the elements of the pagan world which were incompatible with the Christian faith, or, falling into the opposite error, they embraced asceticism.

We have already mentioned the apostle Paul's completely loyal attitude to the state (Rom. 13.1 f.). In spite of persecutions, we find the same loyalty in the Church from the end of the first century. According to Polycarp, who was himself condemned to death by the state in the end, the Christian must give loyal obedience to the authorities so long as they do not attack his faith and do not force him to say: 'The emperor is God'.[6] We find the same loyalty in the apologists, from Justin Martyr to Tertullian. They vie with one another in denying that they are anarchists or revolutionaries, they remind their readers that they pray for the emperors and acknowledge their authority.[7] Likewise, they accept the framework of life in the world. The pagans accused the Christians of 'hating the human race'.[8] Tertullian retorts: 'We are not Brahmins or Hindu fakirs; we do not live away from ordinary life in the forests'.[9] 'We live', he continues, 'in this world, with you; we often visit the forum, the market, the baths, the shops, the workshops, the

---

6 *Martyrdom of Polycarp*, 10.
7 Cf., for example, Justin, *Apol.* I, 17.
8 Tacitus, *Annals*, 15.44.
9 *Apol.*, 42.

stables, the fairs. We bear arms, we till the soil, we trade, we culti-
vate the same arts as you.' Addressing Christians themselves,
however, Tertullian spoke quite a different language; he put them
on their guard against pagan culture and civilization. But here, in
the Apology addressed to the pagans, he describes the situation as it
is: Christians live in the world, they accept its framework, and
nothing of this is contrary to the gospel so long as it is a matter of a
passive acceptance always ready to criticize, which was characteristic
of the apostolic age.

Following Paul's example the Christians of the second century
commend the value of labour, though labour and business are not
considered the purpose of life and its end and justification. In the
Sermon on the Mount Jesus himself already preaches a certain
indifference to worldly gain, since God will not allow his children
to starve to death. Nevertheless, the apostle Paul never fails to
commend the virtue of labour to members of the Christian Churches;
he condemns idleness and refuses to admit that waiting for the end
of the world is a valid excuse for not working, as the Thessalonians
seem to have believed at one time.[10] He himself sets them an example
by never giving up his craft as a tent-maker.[11] But he never attributes an intrinsic value to labour. It is valuable only in relation to
the gospel and the life of the Church.[12] If it is necessary to earn one's
living, it is for the gospel's sake, for love of one's neighbour. The
Christian must not steal, but work with his hands 'that he may be able
to give to him who is in need' (Eph. 4.28). Later on the *Didache* laid
down (chap. 12): 'Let there be no idlers among you'. Hermas, the
author of the *Shepherd* (*Sim.* V), and Aristides, the apologist (chap.
15), recommend fasting and the saving which results from it as a
means of helping the poor.

Here, too, we find the same attitude to the world: the framework
of human life is not rejected, but it is only accepted in order to fulfil
a life consistent with the requirements of the gospel.

At first sight it is more difficult to understand how Christians
were able to accept with the same passivity the fundamentally unjust social institution of slavery. Should not passive acceptance have
yielded here at any rate to violent protest and a declaration of war
against an essentially inhuman institution? The apostle Paul recommends Christian slaves (I Cor. 7.21) to remain in the condition in

[10] I Thess. 4.11; II Thess. 3.6, 10.
[11] I Cor. 9.6; Acts 18.3; 20.34.
[12] Eph. 4.20 and I Tim. 5.17.

which they were called and to live, as Christians, in that condition.
At the same time, however, he lays down that masters should
behave as Christians towards the brothers who are their
slaves. In the Christian community there is no longer slave or
master. As members of the Church, slaves cease to be slaves
and masters cease to be masters: all are disciples of Christ.
Nevertheless, since the members of the Church continue to live in
the world, slavery, which is an institution of this world, continues
to exist.

This example is typical of the Christian approach. It shows that
the gospel does not begin by formulating a social policy. The first
change must take place in individual men and women: social
changes will then result. 'Seek first the Kingdom of God'. The early
Christians did not start by attacking the outer framework of in-
justice. They began not by suppressing or reforming the existing
social framework but by observing the fulness of love towards all
their brethren, inside the existing framework. In this way they
created a new community, the Church, alongside the social institutions of the world. They believed that when Christian brethren
really attained this love one toward the other, slavery would collapse
automatically, even outside the Church.

It is clear from this extreme example in what sense Christians
accepted the institutions of the world. They did not in the least
approve of slavery; they did not recommend its preservation. But
they did not want to destroy the social framework before changing
men's hearts, just as they did not approve of the zealots and their
religious war against the Roman state.

Is it not necessary to change institutions first in order to change
the human heart? One might think so. But such was certainly not
the conviction of Paul and most Christians in the apostolic age.
One has only to recall the apostle's attitude to pagan law-courts
(I Cor. 6): he does not in the least invite the Church to fight to
suppress them, but he does ask Christians to settle their differences
within the Christian community, as between brothers, as Jesus
himself laid down. With the same attitude in mind he does not
preach the suppression of slavery, but requires the abolition of all
differences between slaves and masters within the Christian community, which must be extended ever more widely.

It should be remembered, however, that he does not concede
that the institution of slavery, as it exists in the world, necessarily
forces Christians to deny their faith. This is proved by I Corinthians

7.21 and the precepts which he gives to masters and servants.[13] We find the same attitude in the Christians of the second century who did not attack the institution itself.[14] This has caused some surprise. But it was in accordance with the general attitude of primitive Christianity to the world.

Nevertheless, certain pagan institutions, certain manifestations of pagan culture, cannot serve as a framework for the Christian life, not because they are not Christian (we have seen that they do not have to be Christian to be acceptable) but because they have religious pretentions. Here and here alone, the Christian must reject the world. Acceptance, even passive, would entail the surrender of faith in Christ. In the ancient world, pagan civilization was closely bound up with pagan religion. In our own time, too, the secularized world often depends on atheistic mystics of a religious or pseudo-religious nature. Yet in wide sectors of modern civilization the religious or pseudo-religious element plays no part at all, and the Christian is therefore the more easily able to accept the world.

In the ancient world, on the other hand, many human activities were impregnated with religion: literature, the theatre, the market (the meat market in particular), military service. Contact with civilization was, therefore, far more often a defiling influence, and it is easy to understand the wildly uncompromising attitude of a man like Tertullian. The numerous professions of which he disapproves did, in fact, force Christians to deny their faith. Administrative and military offices,[15] although they depended on a state whose legitimacy was acknowledged, entailed participation in the worship of the emperor. When Christian civil servants objected that they had to earn their living somehow, Tertullian replied that they were wrong to fear hunger. Furthermore, he protests above all against Christian participation in pagan festivals with a religious character, and in this he is faithful to apostolic precepts. On the other hand, he is willing to make certain concessions: he allows participation in a pagan festival provided it does not involve the worship of an idol but merely doing honour in a simple, human way to a non-deified mortal.[16]

As for the state itself, Christians must refuse to obey it once it

---

13 Col. 4.1; Eph. 6.5; I Tim. 6.2.
14 Cf. Justin, *Apol.* II, 12; *Barnabas*, 19; Clement of Alexandria, *Paed.*, 3.11 *passim*.
15 Tertullian condemns military service for another reason too: the Christian must not bear arms. He quotes Jesus's words to Peter. *De idololatria*, 19.
16 *De idololatria*, 13 f.

requires worship of the emperor. From the earliest times and in spite of their loyalty they proved unyielding on this point. If worship of the emperor had not existed it is highly probable that there would have been no persecutions or martyrdoms. But once the state ceased to be neutral, resistance was inevitable. Acknowledging but one Lord, the Christian could not possibly confess, *Kyrios Kaisar*, Caesar is Lord. According to the account of the *Martyrdom of Polycarp*, the officer who arrested this bishop of the Church asked him: 'What is there so terrible in saying: *Kyrios Kaisar?*' If the Roman state had taken the trouble to study Christian principles, it would have realized that the members of the Church were, in fact, its most loyal subjects and that their resistance would come to an end once they were excused from participating in worship of the emperor. But the Romans were determined to interpret the Christian attitude as one of revolt and anarchy, a gross mistake, which led to the martyrdoms of two centuries, until the coming of Constantine.

Thus the astonishing indifference of Christians to civilization was far from absolute: it ended the moment the state abandoned its religious neutrality.

It was also limited in another sense. If the early Christians never sought, as a Church, to destroy the old framework of society, it has to be remembered that, to the extent that the Holy Spirit was at work among them, it tended to create new forms, specifically Christian forms of civilization, spontaneous creations which took their place alongside the ancient institutions of society. The new sociological pattern of the Church, with a discipline of its own, distinct from the jurisdiction of the state, is one example. Nevertheless, the early Christians were careful not to take the initiative in replacing the state by the Church prematurely. Unlike certain Popes of a later age, they did not seek to establish a theocracy. 'Render to Caesar the things that are Caesar's' so long as God has not destroyed Caesar and all political states. All the same, the Christian community is a reality, a spontaneous creation of the Holy Spirit, with its own specific and irreducible existence.

The sharing of possessions, to which the Acts of the Apostles refers, is a typical example of Christian community. It is not the deliberate creation of a new social framework. It does not involve any social organization or general obligations. That is quite clear from the account given in Acts 4 and 5. It is a spontaneous creation of the Holy Spirit within the Church.

In the same order of ideas but on a different plane the Gospels are another example of a new creation. Despite certain resemblances to the minor literature of the time, they represent a unique departure without parallel in secular literature. Unintentionally, the early Christians, who had no literary pretensions of any kind, created a new *genre*, a specifically Christian work of art, which had nothing in common with the art of the ancient world, despite certain similarities of form. Unwittingly, therefore, the evangelists overcame the old antithesis between 'Greeks' and 'barbarians'.

The new creations of the Holy Spirit took place above all in the realm of thought, in the very specific science which we call Christian theology. Let us recall what St. Paul says of the wisdom of the Spirit in the first two chapters of I Corinthians. It would be wrong to concentrate exclusively on his condemnation of human wisdom. The apostle is, in fact, not alluding to the religiously neutral secular knowledge which stays within its own borders. What he does condemn is the wisdom which claims to fathom the divine mysteries by purely human means, without recourse to the revelation of God. There is, however, a wisdom created by the Holy Spirit 'which searches everything, even the depths of God'. This wisdom is not to be condemned and, rightly understood, it is the basis of Christian theology. In the course of the centuries and right down to the present day there has been a tendency in the Christian Church to think of theology as a kind of fall, as a useless, even reprehensible occupation. St. Paul protests emphatically against a contempt for theology; man of action though he was, in his soul he was a theologian, in the sense of the word implied in his own reference to the wisdom created by the Holy Spirit.

A theology thus understood, based on revelation, shows that Christianity, though making use of human reason, has been able to produce something absolutely unique. There is nothing to compare with this Christian theology of the first two centuries which laid the foundations of all theology. Among the attainments of the early Church let us not forget this magnificent piece of work, produced in the midst of some of the most violent persecutions in the Church's history, when numerous martyrs were fighting the good fight to secure its very life. This bloodstained history of the early Church gives the lie to the facile catch-phrase which opposes theology to Christian life. Never has Christianity been more active; never, on the other hand, has it made such an intense effort in the intellectual sphere.

Admittedly, once the Holy Spirit is absent, once theology becomes a science like any other, or claims to replace the secular sciences, it ceases to be an original creation and degenerates into a mere pseudo-wisdom. That has often happened, as we shall see. In all pheres Christianity continually runs the risk of being distorted. Alongside the Gospels of the New Testament there are apocryphal Gospels, Gospels merely in name and, for the most part, a tissue of secular fables. Similarly, alongside the genuine and legitimate theology we find Gnosticism, a pseudo-theology and a disease of the Christian mind.

We come, then, to the Christian errors concerning the relationship between the gospel and the world. They appeared from the first century onwards. Heresy is as old as authentic Christianity.

(3) In the domain of thought the second century is not merely the century of theology: it is also the century of heresy. Never has Christianity been in such danger of foundering in syncretism, that mixture of oriental religions and philosophies, that false universalism which, in order to integrate Christianity into one vast synthesis, sacrifices the very heart of the gospel. The danger was at any rate partially averted. But it was a grave menace to the new-born Church, and we can measure it even better now that we are more familiar with the details of the Gnostic heresy from the numerous papyri discovered in Egypt six years ago. The adherents of the sect abandoned the sanely critical attitude to ancient culture of the Christians of the apostolic age. They forgot the provisional value of the world; above all, they forgot that the Christian must examine the elements of pagan culture with the utmost vigilance before using and assimilating them.

The Gnostics, as they are called, tried to establish a kind of universal synthesis of wisdom and religion. What this implied was an attempt to fuse the gospel with the whole of pagan culture, including its religious pretensions. It meant abandoning the fundamental Christian position without which Christianity ceases to be Christian. Ever since the first two centuries most Christians have, with a sure instinct, recognized the danger. The triumph of this movement would have meant the end of Christianity.

This spurious attempt to secularize the Christian faith was on a par with a general tendency to expose the Christian way of life too freely to the influences of pagan civilization. Tertullian's polemics on this subject are not merely inspired by his personal asceticism but by a legitimate concern to remind Christians of their duty to uphold the purity of the gospel. The extremely assured ability to discriminate between the permissible and the forbidden, to which St. Paul's letters bear witness, was beginning to lose its edge. To the horror of Tertullian, Christians were illuminating their houses on pagan festivals, and adorning them with garlands even more than the pagans themselves, a sure sign that the Christian hope was becoming blurred.

In the *Pedagogue* Clement of Alexandria gives the Christians of the second century some general instructions on how they are to conduct themselves in the world. How different his advice is from the recommendations of St. Paul! He employs a casuistry borrowed from the Stoic moralists. To decide what is right in a particular case he does not seek the inspiration of a total view of the attitude which the Christian must adopt in relation to the pagan world. He decides *a priori*, drawing his inspiration more from Stoic moderation than the Holy Spirit. He often reduces the whole thing to a matter of mere etiquette: how a Christian is to behave at table, how he is to eat and drink, how he is to sleep, dress, and so on. And he always chooses the Stoic way of moderation: not too much and not too little. Primitive Christianity also recommended the virtue of moderation, but a completely different sort of moderation, one that flowed from eschatology: the end of the world is near; we are living in an intermediary period; the new era has already been inaugurated, but in accordance with God's will, our life is still unfolding within the old framework of society.

At the other extreme we find, from the second century onwards, the ascetic reaction. In the middle of the century a Christian called Montanus tried to root out all the influences of ancient civilization from the Church, which was now already all too comfortably established in the world. This attempt was no more in accordance with St. Paul's wholesome directives than the opposite extreme of Gnosticism. The intention of reviving the Christian hope, the decay of which was responsible for all the concessions made to paganism, was perfectly justified but, in the Jewish manner, the hope was conceived as belonging entirely to the future. For the Christian, on the other hand, the Christian era has already begun, we have to continue living within the framework of the world so long as God wills, with our eyes set on a future world which God himself will establish. The Montanists wrongly advocated an escape from the world. They imagined, moreover, that the action of the Holy Spirit would be catastrophic. According to the Bible, however, the Holy Spirit is already permeating the world; it has already begun its work of revival and redemption.

As we know, Tertullian ended by foundering in Montanism. He had always had a tendency to asceticism. In his treatise *De idololatria* he forbade Christians to be merchants, since commerce proceeds from avarice. He condemns almost all the artisan trades (chap. 8): carpentry, joinery, tilery, carving, sculpture, because they are all associated with idolatry. Judging from his attitude to the problem of meat sacrificed to idols, St. Paul would very likely have been more prepared to compromise. Again, Tertullian certainly exceeds the thought of the New Testament when he demands that Christians should not be school-teachers because mythology formed part of the curriculum. By recommending a flight from the world Tertullian desires to protect the Christian from all conflicts. According to the New Testament, however, the Christian should not evade necessary conflicts but endeavour to resolve them on the basis of the gospel.

Tertullian's hatred of pagan civilization blazes most violently of all in regard to the public shows to which he devoted a whole treatise. He is absolutely uncompromising on this point. It would have been useless to retort, following the opponents of rigorism mentioned a little later by Novatian, that David had danced before the ark and that Paul had not shrunk from comparing the Christian life to a race (I Cor. 9.24). Tertullian would not have been convinced by such arguments. For him, one spectacle alone was legitimate: the Last Judgment.

His attitude to marriage is equally stern. Whereas Paul did not prescribe celibacy or marriage, but exhorted every Christian to be faithful to his own calling, Tertullian regarded marriage as inferior to celibacy and expressly condemned the remarriage of the surviving partner.

Tatian shows a similar intransigence of thought about the year 180. Whereas the other apologists, above all Justin, sought to prove that the pre-existent Christ was manifest in all the truths propounded by pagan philosophers, Tatian attacks the whole of Greek literature with great violence and churlishness. According to him it was one mass of impurities, with nothing good in it at all. Plato was a drunkard, Diogenes a bluffer, Aristippus a rake and a hypocrite, Aristotle a flatterer, and so on. Hardly a point of view that would find support in the Bible.

To sum up: from the second century we find two kinds of divergence from apostolic teaching: a compromise with paganism, and asceticism. In neither case is the attitude to the world that enjoined by the apostolic faith. For the latter, the end of the world is imminent, but God desires the present framework to continue as long as the present age. Moreover, Christ is already reigning and the Holy Spirit is already creating new forms of civilization of its own accord, without changing the face of the world. Of all the writings of the second century the Epistle to Diognetus seems to me to be most in accordance with the apostolic faith: live in the world, but as strangers; live as strangers, but in the world.

Index of Authors

Aetheria, 27
Alfaric, P., 61
Allmen, J. J. von, 64n.
Allo, E. B., 61, 64
Ambrose, 29n., 30, 36
Aristides, 201
Aristotle, 208
Assemani, 32n., 34n.
Augustine, 29n., 32, 113n.

Bacon, W., 189n.
Bakhuizen van der Brink, J. N., 59n., 84n.
Baldensperger, W., 177, 182
Bar Salibi, 34n.
Barth, K., 3, 15, 16, 90n., 92n., 114n., 121n., 135
Basilides, 24, 47, 50
Bauer, W., 39, 45n., 177n., 181, 187n., 189n.
Baumgartner, W., 180n.
Baur, C. F., 68, 151n.
Bavaud, G., 80n., 85n., 88n.
Bengel, 60
Bernard, J. H., 187n.
Bernoulli, C. A., 44n.
Bickell, G., 25n.
Botte, B., 20
Bousset, 6
Brandon, S. G. F., 190n.
Brunner, E., 3n.
Brunner, G., 20, 29n.
Bultmann, R., 3n., 8, 11n., 61, 64, 73, 144, 177n., 180n., 182, 187n., 188n., 189
Burkitt, F. C., 49n.

Calvin, 66
Campenhausen, H. von, 74n., 94n.
Carrington, P., 65n.
Celsus, 49, 53

Cerfaux, L., 191n.
Chronography of Philocalus of the year 354, 29n.
Chrysostom, 33, 62, 180, 189n.
I Clement, 96, 105n.
II Clement, 96
Clement of Alexandria, 22n., 23, 24, 45n., 47n., 195, 203n., 207
Clementines, 22, 178, 179, 181
Couchoud, P. L., 61
Courvoisier, J., 84n.
Cowley, A. E., 185n.
Cullmann, O., 75n., 78n., 95n., 134n., 146n., 149n., 159n., 178n., 182n., 186n., 191n., 195n., 199n.
Cyprian, 22n.

Dalman, G., 188n.
Daniélou, J., 57, 58, 62n., 75n., 80n., 81n., 82n., 83n., 85n., 91, 93n., 95n.
Davies, W. D., 70
Dehn, G., 135
Delling, 114n.
Dibelius, F., 180
Dibelius, M., 60, 134, 177n.
Didache, 201
Diem, H., 90n.
Dobschütz, E. von, 3n.
Dodd, C. H., 71n.
Duchesne, L., 19, 29n.

Eck, O., 127n., 135
Eltester, W., 195n.
Ephraem Syrus, 27, 178
Epiphanius, 42n.
Epistle of Barnabas, 96, 105n., 130n., 203n.
Epistle to Diognetus, 209
Epistle of Polycarp, 96, 106, 131n.
Eusebius, 43n., 46n.

211

Index of Biblical Passages

214

1.8   180n.
1.15   179, 180
1.16   182
1.26, 30   181
1.46   10
1.49   109n.
2.13 f.   192
2.19 f.   169
3.22 f.   181
3.31   182
4.20   185n.
4.20 f.   187
4.22   185
4.25 f., 30, 31 f., 35, 36, 188
4.33 f.   192
4.37   189
4.38   183, 189
7.6   182
7.39   117, 167
7.41   10
8.48   192
8.58   182
9.2 f.   167
10.8   181
12.13   109n.
12.20 f.   187
14.26   71, 72
16.13   71, 72
17   79
17.20   79, 80
18.33, 37, 39   109n.
18.36   120n.
19.3, 14, 19, 21   109n.
20.22   83
20.30   44
21.20 f.   44n.

Acts
1.6 f.   150, 159
1.7   155
1.8   186
1.11   112
1.21   72
1.22   72, 77
1.23 f.   89
2.14 f.   117
2.16 f.   93
2.17   117, 156

2.24   165
2.34   105n.
4–5   204
5.31   105n., 132
7.2 f.   190
7.55   105n.
8.1   190, 191
8.4 f., 14   190
8.18 f.   191
9.4   124
9.10 f.   66
17.7   110
18.3   201n.
20.34   201n.
22.7   124
26.14   124

Romans
2.16   48
5.12 f.   130
6.3   117
6.3 f.   125
6.17   63, 64
7.24   166
8.6 f.   166
8.10   167
8.11   122, 148, 155, 166
8.17   125
8.19   147
8.19 f.   36
8.20   108, 128
8.21 f.   108
8.23   117, 119, 122, 156, 166, 171
8.23 f.   119, 171
8.29   169
8.34   105 n.
10.9   106
11.25   151
12.1   173
12.4   127
12.5   169
13   127n.
13.1   121n., 135, 136, 137
13.1 f.   121, 122, 134, 199, 200
13.4   136

13.6   127
15.19   69

I Corinthians
1–2   205
1.18 f.   14
2.7 f.   121, 137
2.8   132, 135
3.16   169
4.8   131
5.5   172
6   169, 172, 173, 202
6.1 f.   198
6.2 f.   119
6. 3   121, 131, 137
6.13, 16   172
6.15   169, 172, 173
6.19, 20   169
7   65, 172, 173
7.10   60, 65, 68, 69, 74
7.14   173
7.21   201, 203
7.25   60, 65, 74
7.30   159, 197
7.31   196
8–10   198
8.6   107, 146
9.1   72
9.6   201n.
9.14   60, 65, 68
9.24   208
10.16 f.   125, 171
11.2   63, 64
11.20 f.   125
11.23   60, 61, 62, 63, 64, 65, 67, 68, 73, 74
11.23 f.   66n.
11.26   172
11.27 f., 30   126
11.29 f.   171
12.13   117, 125, 170
12.27   124, 169
13.1   171
13.13   143
15.1   63, 64
15.2   63
15.3   63, 64, 65, 66, 73
15.3 f.   64, 66, 67, 72, 73